The
Center for
Adoptive Families

HOW
TO RAISE
AN ADOPTED
CHILD

The
Center for
Adoptive Families

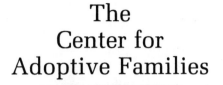

HOW
TO RAISE
AN ADOPTED
CHILD

A Guide to
*Help Your Child Flourish
from Infancy Through
Adolescence*

Judith Schaffer
and Christina Lindstrom

A Copestone Press Inc. Book
Crown Publishers, Inc., New York

Copyright © 1989 by Copestone Press, Inc.

Published by Crown Publishers, Inc.,
201 East 50th Street,
New York, New York 10022
CROWN is a trademark of Crown Publishers, Inc.
Manufactured in the U.S.A.

Library of Congress Cataloging-in-Publication Data

Schaffer, Judith.
    How to raise an adopted child/by
Judith Schaffer and Christina Lindstrom.
        p. cm.
    Includes index.
    1. Children, Adopted—United States.
2. Child rearing—United States.
3. Parenting—United States.
I. Lindstrom, Christina.
II. Title.
HV875.55.S33 1989   89-1243
649'.145—dc19   CIP
ISBN 0-517-57303-2

Book Design: Shari deMiskey

10 9 8 7 6 5 4 3 2 1

FIRST EDITION

Contents

Acknowledgments

First, our thanks to Gene Brown, who made this
book a reality by helping us turn our clinical experience,
research, and knowledge into written words.

A special thanks goes to the original partners in the
Center for Adoptive Families, Sherry Bunin, Yvette
Obadia, M.D., and Mary Walker. Also to Mary Talen, who
helped make those early days at the Center exciting and
rewarding. We owe, as well, a special debt of gratitude to
Arnold Frucht, M.D., whose ongoing belief in us and
support of the Center made many things possible. To
those who participated in our Extern Programs, which are
the source of many of the treatment strategies and ideas
about adoptive family functioning, we are also indebted,
as we are to the hundreds of adoptive families who
inspired us, with their commitment and openness, to
write this book.

It is difficult to adequately thank Ron Kral,
coordinator of the Adoptive Family Project at the Brief
Family Therapy Center in Milwaukee. We have
collaborated with him so often over the past five years
that we can no longer separate our thinking on adoption
from his. His suggestions, support, and comments on the
final manuscript were, as usual, wise and helpful. Ellen
Oler, Joyce Pavao, and Mark Schulman read parts of this

manuscript and made helpful suggestions. Insoo Kim Berg, David Brodzinsky, Jo Cobb, Betsy Cole, Steve deShazer, Kay Donely, Mary Ellen Eisenberg, Patti Feureissen, Steve Goldstein, Sharon Kaplan, Bob Lewis, and Eve Lipchick have helped us to broaden our thinking and kept us on our toes.

We also want to express our admiration and appreciation to the Board of Directors of the North American Council on Adoptable Children and all the other advocates who have fought for the right of permanence for foster children over the past nearly two decades, as well as the Family Builder's Agencies, who have advocated for national standards of excellence in adoption.

Estelle Rubenstein and Inga Sethness gave encouragement and financial support to get the Center for Adoptive Families going in the first place. The First Women's Bank of New York, the American Women's Economic Development Council, and Malcolm Chaifitz advised us in the early stages.

Finally, and most important, we want to thank Robert and Stacey Schaffer, who reminded us about what it is to be adopted.

Preface

This book comes out of our experiences at the Center for Adoptive Families, an independent treatment, research, and training facility in New York City, which specialized in working with adoptees and their families. Founded by five women, three of whom are also adoptive parents, the Center focused on the special nature of the adoptive relationship.

Our premise is that adoptive families are in some ways different from birth families. Although this may sound obvious, some adoptive parents and adoptees believe that if they can just pretend that they are exactly like birth families, they will be. But when the unexpected happens and their experience diverges from what they take to be normal for all families, they worry that they have done something wrong.

Parents and staff members of agencies we have dealt with through our work at the Center have often remarked on the lack of good models for raising adopted children. They say, "Where in the flood of books about child rearing is the one that speaks to us? Where is our Dr. Spock?" We hope that our book will begin to fill this important gap.

In this book we discuss the various stages of growth and behavior that all children go through, concentrating on complications that adopted children (and their parents) sometimes experience. We begin with infancy and proceed stage by stage to late adolescence. You'll find special topics, such as transracial adoptions, single-parent adoptions, and the adoption of children from foreign countries and of older children treated in separate sections.

For each stage of childhood we offer a model of the broad range of what you can expect from your child. This includes norms for motor development, language acquisition and learning milestones, social and personality development, relationships with peers and family members, and family life-cycle issues that may have some connection to the fact of adoption. We also suggest what you can do if things don't seem to be going quite right.

Since these are models, we emphasize that there are many variations from the norm. Your child may pass through a given stage when he's somewhat younger or older. No child follows the script precisely. We are talking about tendencies and averages, not rigid scientific categories of right and wrong. Some variation from the model is, in itself, no reason for concern.

At the end of each chapter you will find a sample of questions that typify what parents often ask about the subjects covered in that chapter. We trust that the answers will prove helpful and make your own job of parenting easier.

Judith Schaffer

Christina Lindstrom

Cofounders, the Center for Adoptive Families

1

An Introduction to Adoption Issues

What does it mean to be a parent? How do you raise a child? A family about to experience childbirth would already have many of the answers. They learned the basics of parenthood from their own mothers and fathers. As they grew up they also saw other parents caring for their children. Many of these parents-to-be assumed all along that some day they would do the same thing.

When most new mothers and fathers confront a situation for which they have no precedent, they can consult experts. Their pediatrician will tell them what it means and what they should do; if things get a little rough they can ask a therapist. They can read magazine advice columns on how to parent. If they want to read a book about it, they can start with Dr. Spock and go on to hundreds of other volumes on the subject. They can ask friends and neighbors how they did it. If they live in a big city, they can harvest practical advice from the park mothers' grapevine. And, of course, there is always the ultimate help line: the phone call to Mother.

But for adoptive parents, useful information is harder to acquire. Adoption is both the same as *and* different from raising a birth child. While you know as much as other parents do about child rearing, there are likely to be some aspects of adoptive parenthood you never encountered or thought about. When your experience differs from what most other people go through, the standard guideposts drop away. Your own upbringing—unless you were adopted—no longer offers a precedent. Other parents' experience may not always be relevant. You may lack readily available examples that you can copy.

Unfortunately, the mass media, when it deals with adoption, often focuses on the exceptional rather than the norm, leaving people with the negative image of the ill-adjusted adopted child. Though many studies show that adoptees fare well, maybe even better in some ways than their nonadopted peers, this cultural stereotype remains.

Professional expertise in the field is still hard to come by. There is not that much useful literature on adoption, and many social workers, psychologists, and psychiatrists who offer advice on the subject were not adequately trained in the area—or had no adoption-related training at all. They may still cling to classical Freudian attitudes that see adoption as portending possible psychological disaster for your child.

That's the bad news. The good news is that the basic requirements for raising adopted children, for the most part, are the same as for parenting a birth child—love, empathy, patience, trust, and understanding. You will also need a substantial amount of information about what to expect at each stage of your child's development and some advice on how to handle the occasional extra complications involved in raising adopted children.

In a sense you might compare adoptive parenting to an interfaith marriage. In each, the family confronts issues that other families don't. For example, as an adoptive parent you will have to deal with matters besides the usual child-rearing ones, including what others think about your family and how your child reacts to their remarks. But that's nothing you can't overcome.

ADOPTION:
THE BACKGROUND

One of the reasons there is so little easily accessible folk wisdom about how to bring up an adopted child is that adoption as we know it—and as you're now experiencing it—is a recent phenomenon. We simply haven't been doing it long enough to become comfortable with it.

Yet adoption is as old as written history. Families in ancient Babylon adopted children. But in ancient and traditional societies, adoption served primarily the function of providing a male heir for religious obligations or inheriting property where a male child had not been born to a family. There was no pretending that it was just as if the child had been born to the family, no thought of keeping the fact of the adoption a secret. For the most part, only males were adopted. Other children who did not have parents either fended for themselves or were informally taken in by neighbors or relatives. The focus was on the family's needs, not the child's. In fact, the present American idea of adoption with the interests of the child paramount is almost revolutionary.

Nineteenth-century methods of caring for orphans form the backdrop for our present adoption practices. Children who had no parents often stayed in orphanages until they came of age. Sometimes they were put to work in factories— there were no child-labor laws—or sent to work on farms in the Midwest and West, actually "farmed out." These children arrived on "orphan trains" from eastern cities and lived with the farm families who came down to the train station and picked them out. The children worked on the farms in return for room and board.

People commonly took in children who were not related to them. American adoption laws became a method of formalizing these relationships. The first state to pass an adoption statute was Massachusetts in 1851. By 1929 all states had adoption statutes. Originally all adoptions were done by private agreements which the courts formalized. Lawyers and physicians often acted as intermediaries. Licensed agencies for placing children were a later development. In many cases, groups of concerned women, often those who did charitable work, set up agencies to search for and screen prospective adoptive parents for their fitness to raise a child.

This adoption system focused on finding babies for white infertile couples. Destitute children were cared for by the state, either by placing them in orphanages or in foster-care families until they grew up. It was not until the late 1960s that public agencies began to place these children in adoptive families.

The laws regulating adoption and their revisions sometimes have negative consequences for adoptive parents and their children. For example, they may create trouble for you or your child if either of you wishes to find more extensive information about your child's birth parents. Most state laws require the sealing of all identifying records about your child's origins. While you might convince a judge to open the file on your child, it is rare that this will occur. Judges usually open files only for serious medical reasons.

In recent years, some changes have occurred, and adopted children have entered their new families in several ways. The first method is the oldest: private agreements formalized by the courts. The private agency method that evolved in the 1920s continues. If you are now engaged in this process or have already adopted your child through it, you know that most child-welfare agencies have strict limitations about who can adopt healthy infants. For example, if you're over forty, it is especially difficult to adopt an infant through the agency channel.

Public child-welfare agencies are mandated by law and public policy to be concerned primarily with the adoption of current foster children who cannot return to their birth families and have had their legal ties with them severed in the courts, or who have been surrendered for adoption. The agency process is, necessarily, somewhat invasive. The social workers who look into virtually every aspect of your life have a duty to protect the best interests of the child; indeed, the law specifies that they do so. They are responsible for making the best possible placement for each child.

Some children have been traditionally considered more adoptable than others. Most in demand are healthy white babies. In the past, children who didn't fit into this category and were considered unadoptable grew up in foster care. Black, Hispanic, and Native American children were among them, as were sibling groups who could present a financial burden to many families if adopted together, and children with health problems or disabilities.

By the early 1970s, some states began to subsidize the adoption of children by the foster families in which they had been placed, making it possible for families of lesser means to join the ranks of adoptive parents. In 1979, the federal government began to take over part of the cost of these subsidies.

Under the subsidy system, federal and state governments pay a stipend to these families until the child comes of age. Besides making the adoption process less dependent on a family's income, the new laws are also intended to encourage minority families to adopt children from similar backgrounds—black families, for example, who might have lower average incomes can now more easily adopt black children. This system also makes it possible for families to adopt children with disabilities involving substantial medical expenses. Previously, such families could have gone bankrupt—and some did—because their medical insurance did not cover children with preexisting conditions requiring care.

The new government policy was not entirely idealistic. Adoption has always had a connection to economics. Not only is it better for the child to be living in a family; it is also cheaper. At present, it can cost as much as $44,000 a year to support a child in a specialized institution in New York—$810,000 over the course of 18 years.

After the Korean War, the adoption of foreign-born children became increasingly common. Today, South Korea, South America, and India are significant sources of children available for adoption.

However, although we do not have statistics to prove it, there are indications that most nonrelative adoptions are now accomplished via the private route. Private adoptions may take place because adoptive parents have heard of someone who must give up her baby. In some states, prospective adoptive parents can advertise their desire to meet a pregnant woman who must place her child for adoption.

Sometimes physicians and lawyers serve as intermediaries. For example, a doctor treating a woman who is about to give birth and wants to relinquish her child might contact a lawyer to find out whether he or she knows of a couple who wishes to adopt a child. The adoptive family often agrees to pay for the birth mother's prenatal and childbirth expenses. Since this can get expensive, such an arrangement is limited to families with sufficient resources to enter such an agreement. These intermediaries are not allowed to profit beyond the fees they earn for providing either medical services or the legal advice and work necessary for formalizing the adoption.

YOU ARE NOT ALONE

Adoption has become a common, everyday phenomenon in our society. According to sociologist David Kirk, one out of every five people in this country has some kind of close connection to adoption. They either have a relative or good friend who was adopted, or they have adopted children or were adopted themselves. Although no accurate data exist, estimates are that there is a pool in this country of about eight hundred thousand adoptees under the age of eighteen.

For several reasons, adoption is increasing. Couples now wait longer to have children, and they often find it more difficult to conceive and to carry a healthy baby to term when they reach the age at which they feel ready to be parents. Many researchers believe that long-term use of the IUD and the pill have contributed to this increasing incidence of infertility.

Because many parents adopt privately and states have not kept systematic records, we don't have accurate national statistics about adoption. (The 1990 census will contain a question about whether you have any adopted children. Your answer will be voluntary.) Most estimates put the number of adoptees in the United States at 2 to 4 percent of the population. That's five to ten million people!

THE STIGMA REMAINS

If adoption has become so widespread, and there are so many other parents who could share their experiences with you, why is it so hard to get accurate information and empathetic support? There are several reasons. We have already mentioned the comparative newness of the process as we know it, and the gap in the knowledge of many professional mental health workers about the dynamics of adoption.

In addition, some people still focus on the stigma surrounding an unmarried birth mother, associating adoption with illegitimacy. Others persist in regarding adopted children as somehow less than "real." They may actually refer to your birth children as your "real (or natural) children," if you have birth as well as adopted children.

One of the most chilling examples of this attitude we have heard was sociologist David Kirk's report of the comment made to a parent whose adopted child had died.

"At least she wasn't your real child," said the consoler, with all good intentions.

GET BY WITH A LITTLE HELP FROM YOUR FRIENDS

Fortunately, there are many organizations of adoptive parents who share your experiences and can offer information and support. Adoptive parents' support groups are a common source of help. You may have joined one while looking for a child to adopt. Many parents remain active with these groups after they get their children. Some drop out after the first few years but sometimes get reinvolved when the children are older and run into what appear to be—or actually are—difficulties.

To find a group that meets near you, contact the North American Council on Adoptable Children (NACAC), 1821 University Avenue, Suite S-275, St. Paul, Minnesota 55104, (612) 644-3036. Their newsletter reviews books on adoption and contains articles by adoptive parents about their experiences. There is also a group devoted to the needs of parents who have adopted foreign children: OURS, 3307 Highway 100 North, Minneapolis, Minnesota 55422, (612) 535-4829. If you write to either group, include a self-addressed stamped envelope for a reply.

Adoptive parents' groups can be very useful. One caution, however: their meetings can turn into sessions in which parents merely exchange "war stories," commiserating over "problems" they might be having, rather than focusing on constructive suggestions on how to handle snags in parent-child relationships. Since group meetings are often arranged to bring together parents with children of approximately the same age, you might suggest that the group bring in adoptive parents with older kids, who may already have experienced and overcome the problems you're having. If that doesn't work, a professional skilled in dealing with parent-child issues might help your group focus discussions on solutions.

Just as parents of any child may occasionally require the services of mental health professionals to deal with particularly troublesome behavior or conflicts, so too do adoptive parents. They also need to know where to go to find trained professionals for guidance and, if necessary, therapy, if things seem to be getting out of hand.

Who would you turn to? The professionals most parents call may not fully understand your family complications. In fact, they may be totally unaware of how adoption may or may not relate to your family. Parents often bring in their adopted children with what they assume are adoption-related problems. A therapist may confirm their fears and agree to treat the child with the aim of dealing with the problem of the child's adoptive status.

Yet, in a majority of such cases, in our experience, the whole adoptive family is feeling the effects of the difficulty. The situation may be only partially related to adoption, or not related at all. Adoption may have been a handy peg on which to hang the difficulty. We find it useful to refrain from pointing to one family member who has a "problem"; rather, in our view, it's more effective to encourage members of the family to work together to resolve the issue. After all, they are the *real* experts about their own family. Experience shows that when everybody works together, they can clear up the difficulty, usually within a brief time.

Fortunately, attitudes have been changing in the past ten or fifteen years, and many therapists—particularly family therapists—have begun to treat the occasional difficulties accompanying adoption within the context of family interaction, rather than as simply the inner psychological problem of the adopted child. Should you ever encounter such difficulties, you can get empathetic, knowledgeable help by getting in touch either with the organizations we list in the appendix of this book or by sending a self-addressed, stamped envelope to the American Association for Marriage and Family Therapy, 1717 K Street, N.W., Suite 407, Washington, D.C. 20006. The AAMFT will send you a list of therapists in your area.

While we list these resources so you will know that there is a growing number of trained professionals to turn to, we by no means suggest that you will need to do this; only a very small percentage of families who adopt babies do. Those adopting older children with special needs are more likely to need such services. But you may experience a few more bumps than a birth parent would on the road to your child's adulthood, because adoptive family life is somewhat more complicated.

You may have noticed our use of the word "complication." These are the things in life that you can't do anything about. They are facts—like your child's adoption. However, if you view complications as "problems"—to be solved— you could be creating trouble for your family. You might blow out of proportion something you just need to accept and work around.

What's an example of one of these complications? A family we counseled had a sixteen-year-old adopted daughter. Sarah,* an only child, had always been bright and cooperative, but now she was having trouble in school. When asked to do her share of the chores around the house, she screamed: "You're not my *real* parents and you can't make me!"

Sarah's parents took her to a psychiatrist, who told them that their daughter had poor self-esteem, a natural result of having been given up for adoption in infancy, and thus suffered from trauma and loss. The parents interpreted this to mean that to assure her that they loved her they should be less strict and demanding with Sarah and not "gang up" on her. Afterward, whenever one parent scolded Sarah for not doing her chores or homework or not coming

* All names used in case descriptions are fictitious.

home before her curfew, the other took her side so she would not experience the criticism as traumatic.

The strategy did not work. Now even more worried, her parents began to wonder if some basic flaw in her character, perhaps something genetic, was surfacing. By the time they got to us, Sarah was acting out in very serious ways and her parents were panic-stricken.

We helped them to see that what Sarah was going through was typical adolescent turmoil, combined with a few extra twists added by her efforts to deal with her identity as an adopted child. Her ploy when asked to do something she didn't want to do—saying they were not her real parents—was something that most adopted kids will try once or twice to see how their parents will react. It is nothing to worry about, though it is not easy for parents to hear. Many adoptive parents we have spoken to over the years have taught us that the way to respond is to address the issue at hand. We suggested to Sarah's parent's that they could say something like: "Yes, it's true that we adopted you [the complication], and we can talk about that later. But the issue right now is that your job is to take out the garbage. So take it out."

If anything, it seemed to us that, like many adolescents, Sarah needed clearer, not fewer, limits and rules; she needed better defined boundaries between herself and her parents so she could realistically determine where she stood in relationship to them. Of one thing we were certain: having parents play good cop/bad cop is a sure way to confuse any kid—adopted or not.

The point of the story is that when you try to "solve" a complication as if it were a problem, your "solution" may actually create a problem that was not there before. A little knowledge of what Sarah was experiencing would have put the "problem" in its proper perspective. At issue was her behavior, at that point. She was being unpleasant and giving her parents a hard time. Not exactly revolutionary behavior for a teenager. Knowing exactly what was happening and how to deal with it meant that for her parents, this too would soon pass. And it did.

THE BIG PICTURE

Starting with the next chapter we will accompany you, step by step, through each stage of your child's growing-up process. We will systematically cover infancy through late adolescence, pointing out what to look for, telling you how to handle the trials and tribulations of adoption (while also pointing out the pleasures to come), explaining the sources of behavior that may seem a little puzzling to you, and suggesting various ways to deal with problems that sometimes come up.

We will also show you how the progress of your family through the cycles of family development affects the way you handle adoption issues. All families change as couples decide to have children, start raising them, send them off to school, and then finally launch them into the adult world while they begin to cope with the empty nest. The transition from one stage of your family life to another is where difficulties are likely to occur—particularly in preparing adolescents for independent adulthood.

Families that do not successfully negotiate these transitions may get stuck in old and inappropriate ways of interacting with their children. For example, parents may rigidly insist that they still know what's best for their teenager at all times, when they need to be letting their son or daughter make more decisions for him- or herself. The result could be a child who misbehaves and parents who mistakenly think that they are seeing acting out related to their child's adoption.

Right now an overview of general issues necessarily involved—but not always acknowledged—in adoption is in order. Let's take a look at the big picture.

ACCEPTING THEM FOR THEMSELVES

Mr. Jordan is a black college teacher in New England; his wife is a white therapist. The Jordans have two adopted children: a sixteen-year-old girl and a fourteen-year-old boy of mixed racial background. If you ask the Jordans what's special about being adoptive parents, they'll tell you that if Mrs. Jordan had given birth to their children, they would be watching for the kids' talents to evolve, on the assumption that they would recognize elements of themselves in what they saw. But because they knew little about the children's birth parents, not even where they came from, the Jordans cherished every new talent and characteristic that appeared, especially the ones that were *not* like theirs. For example, when their children are athletic, unlike either adoptive parent, or when they show the artistic talent that their adoptive parents lack, the Jordans delight in those differences.

This illustrates a key element in the successful parenting of adopted children: being open and excited about the innate talents that they display. Such parents don't expect their children to mirror their own endowments, but take pleasure in watching their children's talents emerge and develop.

TEMPERAMENT

All children are born with psychological tendencies. Each child has what developmental psychologists call a temperament. So your child already has inherent characteristics, even if you bring her home within days of her birth. For example, some babies are simply more active than others. One may walk and talk sooner than another her age. However, early or late achievement of these milestones, within normal limits, has no direct connection to intelligence.

Psychologists accept an interrelationship between environment and heredity, although which has primacy for any given trait is never totally clear. For example, the experts generally hold that both influence intelligence as measured by I.Q. tests, although here they accord somewhat more weight to environment than to heredity. You will certainly influence your child's values and personality, but you should not expect to transmit to her your exact values or shape her personality to your specifications any more than you would that of a birth child. Set the best model you can and then hope your child will make sound choices for herself when she is old enough.

What about the worst case? Could there be a "bad seed" waiting to germinate? What if you discover that either of your adopted child's birth parents had some problem—perhaps emotional—that might possibly have been genetically passed on to their offspring?

While children inherit tendencies for all sorts of things, they are just that: tendencies. Environment affects whether those tendencies ever develop. You are not helpless in steering your child away from trouble. In fact, your influence is great. By providing a warm, nurturing family environment, you can minimize the risk.

GHOSTS

Most infants, if adopted before the age of nine months—but possibly even later according to some studies—will take to their new parents as if they were born to them, developing an attachment to them as they would have done to their birth parents.

Children who are a bit older at placement have a history of relationships. Those connections may be to the birth mother, foster parents, foster siblings, or anyone else who cared for them and was important to them. Such ties do not present a barrier to the establishment and strengthening of your own bonds with your child, but it is useful to take them into account. As your child grows up, they may become part of his or her fantasies and may influence some behavior. Even children adopted at birth will have thoughts about their birth parents. This is not only perfectly normal but necessary in developing a clear and strong identity.

Open adoption, in which birth parents remain in touch with their child and his or her adoptive parents, avoids these ghosts entirely. We will have more to say about this burgeoning phenomenon in a later chapter.

UNRESOLVED PARENTAL CONFLICTS

No one approaches adoption with a blank slate. Aside from the anxieties about competence that most parents, birth or adoptive, have, adoptive parents sometimes have unresolved conflicts about their relationship to the adoption process.

If you've chosen adoption because you weren't able to give birth to a baby—the most traditional reason for adopting a child—you might have a lingering sense that adoption is something that's "second best." Perhaps infertility left you with doubts about your ability to parent. Some parents feel insecure about their roles because they actually had to go to somebody and ask for a child. Being judged by an agency may have been especially upsetting.

Others have not yet resolved conflicts with their own parents over the adoption issue. Adult children whose parents oppose adoption may feel great ambivalence over the decision to become parents. Sometimes, if they do adopt, they may have lingering doubts that they are fully entitled to raise their child as his or her parent.

None of these are inevitable, but if you should sense any of these feelings in yourself, discuss them with your spouse and close friends; if you feel they are affecting your relationship with your child, consider getting some professional counseling from a therapist trained to deal with family problems. It is likely that you will need to continue to resolve certain feelings related to infertility from time to time. As our colleague Ron Kral says, "It is like having a small pebble in your shoe. Mostly you are unaware of it, but then you feel it."

SIBLINGS

The Lindner family has two adopted children and a birth child. Over the years, the little girl who was born to the Lindners has talked longingly and with envy about her brother and sister having two sets of parents while she has only one. That's not the reaction most people would expect her to have. Kids often shatter your assumptions about how members of a family with both adopted and birth children will react to each other.

An adoptive family is, first, a family. Where there are siblings, you should expect some rivalry. But you're not likely to encounter anything more serious than that.

"WHERE DID I COME FROM?"

A colleague of ours related a too-familiar story. Joan was adopted in infancy but as a child was never told about it. Being adopted had never occurred to her. But every time she went to a new doctor with her mother there was a discernible tension when the doctor asked about her medical history and her mother sent her out of the room. Finally, Joan asked her mother, "Could it be that you adopted me?" Still unwilling to tell the truth, the mother answered, "No."

There is still too much secrecy and pretending in adoption. If you've had your child since she or he was an infant, look at your daughter or son's birth certificate. Do you see the word "adoption"? In most states, you see what appears to be a document that records an actual birth, with you as a birth parent. This exercise in mythology can be humorous when the certificate implies that two white American parents have somehow (by coincidence?) produced a Korean baby—in Korea, no less.

There is no "correct" level of openness about the subject of adoption. Some families do best by discussing it freely—with their children and with those outside their immediate family. For others, minimizing the differences between birth and adoptive parenting works better.

The extremes, however, don't work. Dwelling on the subject obsessively is not openness as much as it is a way of isolating and hurting an adopted child, however unintentionally. On the other hand, absolute denial can confuse and possibly stigmatize a child, who at some point will inevitably learn that there is a family secret concerning him.

How about telling? When? How? The parents of three-year-old Heather were anxious to be open with her and so they often tried to talk to her about adoption, but every time they brought up the subject she put her hands over her ears and ran from the room. Heather's parents didn't realize that children of this age are too young to handle the subject and all its complexities. At three, a simple account is enough—that she grew in the tummy of another mommy who couldn't take care of her, and that you wanted a baby so you adopted her and took her home and loved her very much.

No matter how you look at it, telling remains, for most adoptive families, a big issue. We suggest that you treat it as you would the question of where do babies come from—frankly, openly, straightforwardly. Give your children the information they want or can handle at their age (more about this later). It's better not to confuse them and give them what they haven't asked for. They simply do not have the ability to understand all the complexities until they are much older. The key is to be responsive without leading your child into those complexities. And when you do discuss the subject with your child, always use "adoption" as a loving word, meaning that she belongs to you.

Believe it or not, some children will want to talk about adoption over and over. The parents of an eleven-year-old brought this situation to us, thinking they had a grave problem. Their daughter asked about her origins every day. Each time the parents responded as openly and honestly as they could. But after six months of this, they began to worry about this confusing behavior.

We assured these parents that they had been open and loving; that was why their daughter could inquire so freely. Despite this, she simply had not settled the issue in her mind and was going about the task of integrating this information into her view of herself in her own way. Eventually, we predicted, she would be satisfied; and before long, she was.

Discussing adoption with a child is a delicate process. You first need to be comfortable with the subject yourself so that your child doesn't sense that the topic makes you nervous. If she does detect that you feel uneasy about adoption—perhaps through your body language or tone of voice—she may not want to bring it up for fear that you can't handle it.

·What if your child never asks? Then bring it up yourself every few months. Buy some books about adoption and read them together. You could begin by saying something casual about your memory of getting her from the agency, talking about her adoption social worker, or reading to her a story or book about adoption. If this doesn't start a conversation, don't worry. Some children don't talk about it. But occasionally continue to confirm, in a loving way, that you adopted her.

OUTSIDERS

Almost 30 percent of adoptive parents in one study reported hearing disparaging remarks about adoption from people outside their immediate family. Such sentiments, bad enough coming from total strangers, are worse when they issue from your own relatives. Sad to say, when it comes to adoption, sometimes friends are more supportive than family.

Lack of understanding can be annoying when people who should know better don't. If an adopted child has difficulty in school, her parents may get a call from the teacher or guidance counselor explaining their child's slow progress or misbehavior solely in terms of her adoption. It may have a bearing, but it's not likely to be *the* reason.

Should you let the school know you adopted your child? In a famous study, psychologists told teachers at the beginning of the year that half their pupils were very smart and the other half were at best of average intelligence. In fact, the children were randomly selected for each group. Not surprisingly, over time, the "smart" ones did better, probably because the teacher treated them as if they were smart. If your child's teacher views adoption as a negative, you might do better to avoid the subject unless you're willing to try to educate her. Before you tell her, attempt to get a sense of how broad-minded she is—perhaps through a conversation during open school week. If you find that she's willing to learn more about adoption, supply her with articles about the subject.

If your family looks atypical, people may come up to you on the street and say odd things. Strangers often feel free to be intrusive when it comes to children. We've all heard stories of people who walk up to a pregnant woman, uninvited, and touch her belly. The same kind of intrusiveness can prompt all sorts of comments.

One white woman was walking with her husband, also white, and their dark-skinned Colombian adopted daughter when a stranger walked over and said: "Your child is dark, but you aren't and neither is your husband." They told her that they had adopted their child. She replied:

"Well, what are you going to do if she wants to marry a black man?"

You can feel insulted or invaded by such incidents or you can see them as something you can deal with by educating others as the situation calls for it (although sometimes, in truth, it can be tiresome). You can also treat them with humor or ignore them.

Don't be surprised if you get a lot of unsolicited and useless advice from people you don't know when they discover that you have an adopted child. There are all kinds of misinformation floating around out there. Here are some samples of myths from our colleague Ron Kral about adoption:

Adopted children are less well-adjusted than those born to their parents. There is some evidence that adoptees are referred for mental health intervention more often than children raised by their birth parents. But many middle-class families adopt children and, clearly, they are more likely in any case to use professionals when child-related difficulties arise. The fact that they have adopted means the family has already gone to a lawyer or an agency to get a child in the first place and so may be more willing than birth parents to return to their agency or turn to other professionals outside the family for help.

Since adoptive parents are sometimes more attuned to any little nuance in their child's behavior—especially during the trials of the teenage years—they may be more likely to consult a therapist for the same behavior that other parents would chalk up to the unsettled state of adolescence. Parents who have already had birth children sometimes have an easier time because they are more likely to recognize such behavior for what it is: normal "growing pains."

Adoptees seem more often involved in sensational crimes than nonadoptees. Unfortunately, this kind of sen-

sationalism does sell newspapers. Adoption is not a factor in crime—a poor environment is most likely to blame. True, all adoptive families are not supportive and loving, just as all birth children are not raised in good families. However, the vast majority of adoptive parents are caring and responsive and their children are no more likely to have criminal thoughts or commit crimes than any other normal children.

Only ill-adjusted adoptees want to find their birth parents. If you had been a good parent, your child would never pursue the matter. Why so? Wouldn't you want to know more about where you came from? Girls are perhaps more likely to have an interest in this because they are brought up to be more family-oriented in our society. But it is normal and healthy for any adoptee to be curious about his origins, and you should respect it. This is not a threat to you—your child will remember who cared for him in crucial moments.

QUESTIONS AND ANSWERS

I've been thinking about adopting for a while and have finally decided to go ahead with it. But everybody I speak to tries to discourage me and instead urges that I keep trying to have a child "of my own." What should I tell them?

Tell them: "I'm ready to be a parent." Remind them that you've had plenty of time to consider the adoption alternative. Explain that if you adopt you're either foreclosing the possibility of having a birth child in the future or not, according to which is true in your case.

☐

I want to adopt a child but my husband is quite hesitant. Family blood lines are very important to his relatives. I think he'll come around once we have the child, but I'm a little worried. How do I handle this?

If you are counting on your husband to be supportive and join in rearing the child, you and he need to resolve his ambivalence *before* the adoption. Don't assume that he will get over it spontaneously. Some counseling is in order from either your adoption agency or a family therapist.

☐

My father-in-law is dead-set against our adopting a child. He says he wants no part of such a "grandchild." What do I do?

Try to reason with him. After the child is yours, encourage him to at least have some contact with his grandchild. Ask at your adoptive parents' group if the organization has an adoptive grandparents' section. Your father-in-law might find it easier to talk to them about adoption. If this doesn't work, for your child's sake you and your husband may have to limit your own contact with your husband's father. Only very occasionally does this lead to the breaking off of a relationship, and you should consider doing this only in exceptional circumstances.

☐

I would like to try to conceive even after I adopt a child. What do you think of this?

Sure, go ahead. Lots of families have both adoptive and birth children and thrive on the richness and variety that such child rearing brings.

☐

I've considered adopting through an agency. The child they've shown me appears healthy now but her mother was an intravenous drug user. What are the risks?

Discuss this with your agency and your pediatrician. An AIDS test should be performed on babies of intravenous drug users. Even if the child was not born drug addicted there may be a drug-related problem from the mother's use early in the pregnancy and her prenatal care may have been deficient. You should get an indication of this by her birth weight, her Apgar scores, and an evaluation of her scores on the Brazelton Neonatal Behavioral Scales.

☐

I have decided to adopt. What kind of information do I need about my child's medical condition and birth parents?

You need to know, at minimum, if possible, the birth mother's history during pregnancy. Was there bleeding during the first trimester, did she suffer from toxemia, diabetes, or have a thyroid problem? What medications did she take? Did she use alcohol or drugs? You will also want to know the baby's birth weight, head circumference, and length, Apgar scores, due date, when he or she was actually born, and any complications connected to delivery such as premature rupture of the membranes, excessive bleeding, or whether it was a cesarean birth. In addition, it would be helpful to know if the infant needed resuscitation or suffered from jaundice, an infection, a breathing problem, or other trouble at birth. You should also find out about congenital impairments including physical defects, if any, and the medical past history of the birth mother and father as well as the present health or cause of death of mother, father, and siblings.

☐

How do I prepare my children, birth or adopted, for a new adopted child in the family?

If you have only children to whom you gave birth, speak to them a little bit about the adoption process. Tell them why Mommy and Daddy are adopting this child—"We want another child because we love you so much." Then just concentrate on reassuring them that the new child will not displace them—the same thing you would do if you were about to give birth. If your other children are also adopted, this could be a wonderful opportunity to educate them further about adoption and their own origins. If it's an agency adoption, all your children, birth or adopted, will take part in the home-study interviews; again, an education for everyone.

□

My child is five and we haven't yet told him that we adopted him. What should I do?

Start now. He won't understand it fully, but begin. You might want to show him some books that treat the subject on a level that he can now deal with: *Why Was I Adopted?* by Carole Livingston (Lyle Stuart), *Is That Your Sister?* by Sherry Bunin (Knopf), *Our Baby: A Birth and Adoption Story* by Janice Koch (Perspective Press), and *The Chosen Baby* by Valentina P. Wasson (Lippincott). And join an adoptive parents' group and get a sampling of other parents' experience with this issue. Make an effort to take your child to their parties and get-togethers so that he sees other adopted children and begins to understand adoption as a different but normal phenomenon.

□

My child's birth mother was hospitalized for a mental disturbance. What do I tell him about her?

Telling him about his mother's condition depends on his level of maturity and how badly he might want the information. You would be the best judge of that for your child. Short of that, though, you could insist that the agency find out some positive things about her, what she looked like or songs she liked, what hobbies she pursued. Did any other members of his birth family care for him for a while? If they did, try to get similar information about them and relate it to your child.

□

She's finally asked the question I dreaded: "Why was I given up for adoption?" What should I say?

In the old days, they told children that their parents had died. Unless that's the truth, it's not a good idea to fall back on this old solution. Tell her, for example, "Your mommy was only fourteen or fifteen and, while she loved you, she was not able to take care of you." If she answers that her baby sitter is that age, explain that the sitter still has a mommy to take care of *her* and wouldn't be able to take on the job of a parent at that age. Remind her that when something comes up, the sitter has to call *you*, the parent. If you don't have a reasonable explanation, tell the child you don't know and when she gets older you and she will try to find out.

Learn as much as you can about the child's father as well. Sometimes agencies are unable to obtain much information from birth mothers, but try to get as much as you can. If you haven't adopted yet, tell the agency that you want to know about both the father and the mother of your child. The more information you have, the better. You can always use your discretion about how much to tell your child in the early years. *The Art of Adoption* by Linda Cannon Burgess (W. W. Norton) describes how one adoption agency worker is able to get information about birth fathers and why this is important.

☐

My child asked me recently why I adopted her. Do I say it was because I couldn't have a baby, or should I just say that it was because I loved her?

Tell her it's because you wanted to be a parent and wanted a child to love and take care of. Later, if you want to introduce the idea of infertility, that's fine. If you feel comfortable with your response, your child will too.

☐

How will I deal with comments from other people about my child being adopted?

Read up on adoption so that you can educate people. If you're not comfortable responding to a particular question, you might develop one or more stock replies. Find a style of responding that becomes second nature to you.

□

A story just came out in the newspaper about an adopted child who was convicted of a heinous murder. How do I respond to my child's and neighbors' questions and comments about this story?

Hardly any murderers are adopted and hardly any commit heinous murders. We just seem to hear about every one of these cases. This is what we mean when we say there is a stigma about adoption. Somehow it is newsworthy when criminals are adoptees. Perhaps it goes back to the idea of the "bad seed." Few of the mass murderers we have all read about were adopted as healthy infants into good and loving families. It could just as easily have been a person with diabetes or short hair who did this. In other words, there's no connection.

□

I know that Ronald Reagan is an adoptive father. Do you know of other adoptive parents whose names I would recognize?

Adoptive parents come from all walks of life. Among the more well known are Mia Farrow, Woody Allen, Barbara Walters, Gail Sheehy, and Elizabeth Taylor. Each of the four candidates in the 1988 presidential election has a member of his family who is adopted. Governor Dukakis adopted his wife's son, Senator Bentsen has adopted children, President Bush has an adopted grandchild, and Vice-President Quayle has adopted siblings.

□

My mother tells me that I shouldn't tell my son that he's adopted because he's "illegitimate." What should I say to my mother?

In your mother's day, having a child without being married was more of a stigma. It was also a good excuse for not telling a child she was adopted. Explain to your mother how times have changed.

□

Should I refer to my child's "real" mother? Is birth child a term that makes sense?

We prefer birth child, birth mother, and birth father; or first mother and second mother, etc. We would also like to point out that most adoptees beyond their mid-teenage years do not like being referred to as adopted children. Adoptee or adult adoptee would certainly be more descriptive.

□

My husband and I are both high intellectual achievers. How can we ensure that our child measures up to our standards?

You will have a substantial influence on your child's intellectual development but your child may not ever achieve as you do. It's generally thought that a good environment can raise a child's I.Q. by as much as 15 points. That means lots of praise and encouragement from you. But no child will be able to exceed his own genetic potential. That means that if both of his birth parents scored in the average range on an I.Q. test (about 100), your family environment could make it possible, on average, for his score to be 15 or so points higher than his siblings who remain with his birth parents. If your I.Q. scores are in the 130 or above range, that might not seem like very much since his score would more likely range from 115 to 120 or so. Part of the job of being a parent is coming to terms with that—taking pleasure in helping him achieve whatever he can. But bear in mind that even if you give birth to a child, there is a phenomenon that statisticians call "regression to the mean" to contend with. If you're both extremely bright, chances are that even a birth child would not quite reach your level although he would be very bright compared to other children.

□

I am white and I have a three-year-old daughter from Mexico who has a dark skin tone. Recently, a neighbor said:

"Isn't it wonderful that you've taken in this child." My daughter heard this. What should I tell her?

Tell her that this lady is just curious "because we look different and she doesn't understand why." Later you will be able to explain to her about how difficult life is for poor children who live in orphanages and never do get adopted. And, if you wish, tell the neighbor that you are the lucky one to have such a wonderful child.

☐

My husband and I have not been getting along for some time and we are considering a divorce. We have two adopted children and we are worried that a divorce would be far more traumatic for them than it would be for birth children. Is this true? What special steps should we take to minimize the trauma for them?

Because your children have already lost one set of parents, another such loss could be particularly difficult for them—unless you both work to minimize the stress to which they are subjected. We have found that divorcing parents with adopted children get through their separation with fewer problems for their kids when they plan in advance to cooperate on the issue of child rearing, if nothing else. These people agree on clear and definite boundaries when dealing with anything involving their children. For instance, when they speak on the phone to discuss the children, it's the only subject they allow to come up. Some form of coparenting, at least for the first—and almost always the most difficult—year is also helpful. Having the kids alternate between living in one parent's home for a week and then the other's is one way of handling this, but you can probably come up with many other creative solutions, depending on your situation.

☐

I have just heard that AIDS among infants is increasing. We want to adopt a baby, but aren't willing to adopt one with AIDS. We just don't want to take care of a chronically ill baby who will die in a short period of time. How can we be certain that the baby who is placed with us does not have AIDS?

You have identified a very serious issue, which is only just now beginning to receive public attention. It is likely that you will know whether or not the baby has AIDS if the birth mother and the infant have both been tested. A major complication for adoptive parents who choose not to adopt an AIDS baby is that the birth mother may not, in fact, know that she has AIDS and has, therefore, exposed her fetus to the virus. She herself may not belong to one of the high-risk groups. She may have been infected by a partner who has AIDS or ARC and who also may not have known that he was infected. The baby who has AIDS may appear healthy for the first six months and then begins to deteriorate, usually developing pulmonary symptoms first. Many birth mothers first learn that they have AIDS themselves when their babies become symptomatic and then are positively diagnosed, at which point they are tested. Some attorneys who do independent adoptions, as well as private adoption agencies, are now requiring a series of AIDS tests for pregnant birth mothers who come to them desiring to surrender their babies for adoption. AIDS is a growing concern in many major metropolitan areas and a consideration for families who choose to adopt a healthy infant.

2

The First Year

—Was Marsha Harrington doing something wrong? Why didn't her adopted baby cry more? Isn't that what infants are supposed to do? Even on the long ride home from the agency the day she and her husband, Ralph, had claimed her, the baby just lay there quietly while her new mother struggled ineffectively to secure the infant's Pampers with masking tape. Since then Marsha had experienced several moments of panic after rereading Dr. Spock and realizing that she had mishandled diaper rash, among other things. Would she ever make a good parent? Would she have been better at it if she had given birth?

If this sounds at all familiar, remember that child rearing is a process in which all mothers and fathers constantly learn to be more effective parents. *Nobody* begins as an expert. Children are enormously resilient; they are not likely to be hurt by one or even several mistakes.

Child behavior is always a little unpredictable, no matter how much you've read about the subject. Should you ever feel that you are not handling a situation correctly, you can always develop new strategies. Even when your child grows older and realizes that you have erred, you can apologize. In fact, it's important for children to learn that their parents, too, can make mistakes.

We emphasize that no parent is perfect because adoptive parents often strive for flawlessness. They may have undergone painful scrutiny about their qualifications to parent before being given their child. They know that, depending on the law in their state, for the first few months they have their child he or she can, theoretically, be taken back. They realize that their child has no blood ties to them, and thus could lack the automatic loyalty birth parents might assume. And what if she finds her birth mother one day? Will she love her more? One can understand why adoptive parents might feel constantly judged and would believe that they had to be exemplary mothers and fathers.

Unfortunately, in this age of statistics and quantification, it's easy to find "scientific" standards against which to measure your parental competence. Examples of this are the stages of child development, the things that many parents feel that children should do at specific chronological points in their growth—unless, of course, there's something wrong with them. These guidelines are useful when seen as general outlines of what to expect from a child, but they can cause unnecessary parental anxiety when interpreted too exactly. Some parents see them as reflecting on their own skills as parents.

Adoptive parents should exercise even more caution than other mothers and fathers when interpreting their child's "progress" in the developmental process. An adoptee's development will not differ from that of his or her nonadopted peers. But your interaction with your child could vary just enough from the birth parent–child relationship to make you more insecure about any developmental discrepancies you do notice.

THE BEGINNING

Robin Stanton always envisioned herself as an earth mother, her infant strapped to her chest while she shopped, cleaned, and did all the other things that make for a glowing hearth and home. That's why it came as a shock when she discovered that the 2½-month-old baby she had worked so hard to adopt was too heavy for her to carry in that way.

We don't know if pregnancy and the increasing weight she would need to bear would have prepared her physically for that task. However, those nine months would have given her certain emotional advantages. While the entry of a child into a family can briefly overwhelm any parent, the period of gestation does permit birth parents-to-be to gradually prepare for the many impending changes in their lives and absorb what it will mean to be responsible for another human life.

After all, you can read about child rearing, discuss it with your mate and friends, go to classes at the Y, and do all the other things that prospective parents do to get ready for the big day. But if, as it was with Robin and her husband, Allen, and many other adoptive parents, you have two weeks or fewer between hearing that a baby is available and having that wonderful bundle handed to you as *your child,* the feelings can be positively disorienting.

Robin had been on the phone having a long conversation with a friend that Friday, so the woman at the agency had called her husband at his office to tell him that she was putting in the mail some pictures of a child who they thought would be just right for them. The child had been born to a fourteen-year-old girl; the father was a high school senior. The photos and the biographical and medical information came on Monday, and Robin and Allen knew right away that this child was *the one.*

Little Molly might have graced the Stanton household within a few days, but the foster family caring for the infant had become attached to her and asked if they could keep the child for an extra week. That gave the Stantons a chance to rush to prepare a room for their daughter. They spent the better part of an afternoon in a children's furniture store, directing a lot of nervous energy into the choice of a crib, a chest of drawers, and accessories.

The First Year

A day in advance the Stantons drove to the town in the next state where they would pick up their child, so they would not be tired at the big moment. But they were so excited that they couldn't sleep and instead stayed up all night talking and playing cards. The next morning they arrived at the welfare center an hour early, but when the social worker came out to chat, Robin and Allen couldn't focus on what she was saying. When the agency worker finally come out and handed Robin her blanket-wrapped baby, Robin all but melted. First she sat holding the baby, new mother and daughter staring into each other's eyes, then Allen got his chance to hold the infant and make eye contact. The Stantons can document almost everything that happened that morning with their photo album; they also kept the clothes both they and she wore to give to their daughter as a memento of her arrival.

Robin and Allen didn't realize how much help they would get from friends and relatives. Most of the couple's friends did not have children, but the one woman with whom Robin was close who was a mother (of a two-year-old) brought over clothes, toys, and books on child care. Neighbors dug into old chests to recycle items their kids had used. Robin's in-laws, without being asked, took care of every minor bit of necessary shopping that the harried about-to-be-parents might have overlooked. By the time Molly made her grand entrance, a spontaneous support network had considerably eased the transition to parenthood for the Stantons.

In truth, the only difficulty they had in the first few weeks was a little jealousy from Robin's cousin, Barbara, who drove up to Robin and Allen's country house to spend a summer weekend, bringing along her baby, a birth child, for her first "vacation." Barbara's daughter, Samantha, was colicky, putting everyone's nerves a bit on edge that weekend, while Molly was quiet and peaceful.

It's not unusual for the arrival of an adopted child to turn into a communal affair. One way you can encourage the formation of this helpful network, if it doesn't make you uncomfortable, is to discuss your pending adoption with your neighbors before your child arrives. Answer their questions about the adoption process, and answer their children's questions if they're curious. They may ask you, "How do you adopt a child? Do you know about her parents? How did you choose this child? Were the parents married?"

However, also prepare for some odd responses. At work, one of his colleagues actually came up to Allen Stanton and asked, "Don't you *do* it?" Friends of Robin's, both college teachers, came over to the house and while chatting about the baby awkwardly posed several random questions concerning the birth mother and father. It took a while before Robin realized what they were getting at. They were uncomfortable with the child's "illegitimacy"!

If you already have children, you will have to deal with questions of a different sort. For example, your children might want to know if you could give *them* away, just as the birth parents of your new child did. This calls for some factual reassurance. As a rule, it's better not to tell them that the baby is coming until you get the call. First, you won't experience till then the full emotional awareness that you are about to receive the child, and you might communicate to your kids a little of the "unreality" that the event may hold for you. Also, holding off this information blunts the effect on your children of any last-minute delays or hitches in the adoption.

Many adoptive parents overlook the potentially "communal" aspect of their own relationship to their child. In an age when men have increasingly taken on the role of co-nurturer in their families, adoptive parents have a unique opportunity to foster more equality in parenting, beginning with the time they first bring their child into their home.

Because of the lack of a physical connection to the mother for nine months in adoptive parenthood, an adopted child can "belong" as much to the father as to the mother;

there is less of a proprietary relationship built into the connection between the mother and the child. Feeding is the crucial element, since it is during feeding—ordinarily the mother's sphere—that a baby is most conscious of his relationship to his care-giver. Robin Stanton chose to give Molly a bottle, making it equally possible for Allen to feed the child. (Should you prefer to breast-feed, you might want to discuss it with the local chapter of La Leche. It is a difficult and complicated process, however, unless you have given birth to a child already.)

In our experience, adoptive fathers generally do get more involved in the rearing of their children. Feeding the child is an opportunity to begin raising her so that she grows up with positive images of, and feelings about, men, and we urge you to consider taking advantage of it.

START OFF RIGHT

In preparing for parenthood, one of your first tasks is to choose a pediatrician. Any parent should choose this doctor with much care. Since you will have to establish a relationship with this professional, depending on her for advice about your child's health as well as treatment for specific conditions, the doctor's attitude and personality are as critical as her medical skills. The way she makes you feel about your parental competence and the degree to which you can feel confident in her ability to keep your child healthy will go a long way toward giving you peace of mind.

As an adoptive parent, you will want to be even more selective than birth parents in choosing a pediatrician. This is the last person you can allow to have prejudices about adoption. A woman we know was shocked when her eight-year-old adopted daughter related this to her about her pediatrician. The doctor was examining the child one day and the girl asked this previously sensitive and gentle man if he knew anything about her birth mother. "You're a very ungrateful person," he replied sharply. "How can you do that to your parents?" Whatever *that* was, it had thrown him into a tizzy. Fortunately, the exchange had no traumatic effect on the girl because her mother quickly reassured her that it was okay to ask such questions. The mother also began searching for a new pediatrician.

You also don't want to stay with a pediatrician who will not acknowledge that your child *is* your child. For example, if the adoption has not yet been made final and the doctor, noticing your child twitching, says, "Look, I think this kid is going to be hyperactive. Why don't you return her to the agency before it's too late?" you should reconsider your choice of doctors.

Many adoptive parents have already had difficult experiences with doctors through the drawn-out process of dealing with infertility. If you underwent this ordeal, you may have had the feeling that you were being acted upon, repeatedly pushed toward trying "one more" procedure in an attempt to repair you as if you were a defective automobile. Therefore it is important that you find a pediatrician who is not just one more person in a white coat about to take charge of your life. She certainly should not be sending out signals that you are less than adequate because you adopted rather than gave birth to your child.

How do you select this important person? You could begin with a referral from a friend, relative, or neighbor. Also ask any other adoptive parents you know for a recommendation. Inquire at your adoptive parents' support group for the names of physicians they have found to be both medically competent and sympathetic to the needs of adoptive parents. When you interview a prospective doctor for your child, bring up the subject of adoption. Ask her about her experiences with other adoptive families and what, if anything, in particular she's noticed about their children. Would she feel uncomfortable not having a full medical history for the child? Watch for any prejudice or discomfort she exhibits during the conversation. In general, does she make you feel comfortable when discussing adoption?

Your pediatrician can also advise you about the later medical problems for children whose histories may include poor prenatal care or drug and alcohol use by the birth mother, as well as low birth weight and low Apgar scores. Then you will be better able to make an informed decision about whether or not a particular child would be right for your family.

Once you've selected a pediatrician, talk to her about how you plan to discuss adoption with your child, when you'll first bring it up, and how much you plan to tell him. This is important because the doctor might later say something to your child about adoption and you want to make sure that you and she are saying the same thing.

Make sure you give the pediatrician every bit of information you have about your child that might be relevant to caring for him. The agency or lawyer should have given you a full report which you should share with the pediatrician, but supplement it with anything else you know or have already observed.

Bring your child in for an examination as soon as possible after he is placed with you. This enables your pediatrician to advise you on any condition that needs immediate treatment and it establishes a baseline of information for how your child should be when his health is "normal." This will prove useful anytime something seems amiss. For example, the doctor can check his reflexes to see how he responds to stimulation under average circumstances.

THE TIES THAT BIND

Ed and Marge have two children: Roberta, adopted at age six weeks, and Philip, adopted when he was seven months old. Roberta was pure pleasure to raise, but Philip had more than his share of problems in his first few years, and whenever they arose his parents blamed them on a lack of sufficient bonding between mother and son. Marge had been seriously ill at several crucial points in Philip's young life, but they did not consider that fact, since adoption seemed to be a more convenient explanation for the child's difficulties.

"We weren't with our child from the beginning, and that's why we're having this problem now," goes an occasionally heard explanation from adoptive parents for any problem that arises in their child's development. The image of the newborn infant in his mother's arms, bonding to her in one of the most intimate ways one human being can create ties to another, is an attractive one. But inspiring as it is, it can evoke some mistaken conclusions about the relationship between parents and infants.

The literature about the ties between a child and her first nurturer concentrates on the way the adult has bonded to the child, more than how the child has developed ties to the care-giver. In our experience, and in some of the recent writing on the subject, such as that by psychologist Jerome Kagan, the quality of care-giving more than the identity of that care-giver has greater significance for roughly the first nine months of the baby's life. To be sure, a baby needs consistent physical and emotional nurturing from one set of care-givers during that time and will suffer if she doesn't get it. But whether that sustenance comes from one person or several, as happens in a large family, from a birth mother or a sister or an adoptive mother or father, may not be crucial to healthy development.

People who adopt infants may thus develop emotional ties with a child similar to those the child might have developed with her birth parents. This doesn't mean that people who adopt older children can't form deep and enduring ties with their child, but the quality of that relationship may differ at least somewhat from one created near the beginning of the child's life. We will have more to say about that later when we discuss the adoption of children with special needs.

How about the bonding process from your end? It comes naturally for birth parents, who are raising a child to whom they have a biological connection. By taking care of your adopted child you will also establish some deep, enduring ties to her without thinking much about it.

However, we also know that sometimes adoptive parents may have doubts about whether they are fully entitled to raise as their own a child not born to them. Psychologists say that such parents have not fully "claimed" their baby. When that happens, the parent-child relationship may not take hold as strongly as it should, possibly producing difficulties for the family when the child gets older. It doesn't happen often, and you can take some steps to ensure that it does not arise in your family.

Periodically remind yourself that this is your child and that you will do your best to raise her, that you *are* her parent. Don't second-guess yourself if you make a mistake in your child-rearing work. You are entitled to your quota of mistakes, a quota most parents easily fulfill.

New parents often feel trapped and burdened by their awesome responsibilities. You and your spouse are bound to at least occasionally have ambivalent feelings about your child. That's normal and not a sign that you are not bonding with the child.

"Is there an adoption equivalent of postpartum depression?" we are sometimes asked. In a word, yes. Becoming a parent has to be a little anticlimactic after all you've gone through to get a child. Now you notice how much laundry you have to do. If you were a working woman who quit or took a leave of absence from her job, you may suddenly find yourself home alone with an infant who is all feelings and no intellectual stimulation at all. What's more, there are times when nothing you do can comfort your baby.

While ordinarily none of this threatens the bonding process, you should talk it out with your spouse and friends to vent your feelings. It's important for you to see that you're not alone in experiencing these emotions; any mother, birth or adoptive, can confirm that. One important way you can counter the effect of this letdown is to find ways of being out in the world without your baby from time to time.

TEMPERAMENT

Mike Wagner was worried. He and his wife, Lena, had two children: five-year-old George, who was born to them, and seven-month-old Debbie, who they adopted when she was three months old. Mike's relationship with his son was not always smooth, yet he still derived much enjoyment and satisfaction from his interaction with the youngster. But where Mike had always felt a closeness to George, his ties to Debbie were somewhat problematic. Sure, he loved her, but from a bit of a distance. The chemistry between the two seemed slightly off, and Mike was concerned that he and his daughter were missing a one-time chance to establish a close familial bond. Mike was also beginning to wonder if there wasn't a simple explanation for this problem: Debbie wasn't his "real" daughter.

He needn't have worried so much; and it wasn't helpful to look for an answer in the adoptive relationship. The chemistry between parent and child can be a little off at any time in the child's development, starting with infancy, and it can happen in any family. It involves people with different temperaments coming together in an intense relationship. In families with more than one child, a parent will always feel a different kind of kinship with each. He or she develops different levels of attachment and "like" with each child. That doesn't mean that the parent doesn't love the others. Nor does the favorite always remain the same, since children often change as they grow, especially after infancy. Clashing chemistries only call for professional intervention when they prevent a mother or father from effectively parenting.

It used to be fashionable to blame the mother (and sometimes the father) for children's difficulties. Current research by child development psychologists and especially by Drs. Alexander Thomas and Stella Chess indicates that while most babies are what they call "easy to handle," a small number appear to be born somewhat fussy or overactive and are, as a result, more difficult to handle. Others, fearful or oversensitive, are somewhat slow to warm up to people. Although babies are born with these characteristics, they are not static, however.

It is important to remember that a child's personality develops through interaction between her own inborn tendencies and her environment, so that certain qualities can change as a result of experience. Just as the easy-to-handle baby can, if reared in particular ways, develop as a difficult child, the opposite can be true as well. Some psychiatrists and psychologists have hypothesized that adopted babies may be more likely than other babies to be more difficult to handle, or slow to warm up to others. As a possible explanation, they suggest that because the birth mother is considering surrender of her baby to adoption, she is likely to be under greater stress during her pregnancy. Because this stress can affect the prenatal environment of the developing fetus, the result may be a greater risk for certain temperamental difficulties. While this is interesting and certainly should be studied by researchers, at this time there is no evidence to confirm this hypothesis.

DEVELOPMENT: INITIAL STAGES

Ruth Roland could have worried when her adopted daughter approached the age of two without ever having said a word. Many mothers would have worried about that. But Ruth already had three birth children—all sons—and she knew how much each child could vary, reaching developmental milestones at different times. Since the brothers adored their little sister and seemed to anticipate whatever she wanted, the child did not yet have a need to speak—at least, that's what their mother reasoned. Besides, the pediatrician had said there was nothing wrong with the bright-eyed girl.

Ruth had deftly avoided a potential trap for any parent: the temptation to take a model of child development too literally and to overlook the peculiarities of a particular child. When parents interpret the stages of development too precisely, as tests that their child must pass on the road to normality, they undermine their ability to respond to the specific, idiosyncratic human being in front of them. If they are adoptive parents and yield to the temptation to see a missed or late stage of development as connected to adoption, they could truly be creating something out of nothing.

Of course, parents should never ignore anything that seems out of the ordinary about their child's development. But there is no clear connection between when your child reaches a developmental landmark and the nature of his future development. A missed milestone is no cause for alarm, although a pattern of veering far from the norm would be reason to consult your doctor.

Unfortunately, friends, neighbors, and relatives can sometimes add to the pressure on you to produce a "normal" child, with their constant questions: "Has she talked (rolled over, sat up) yet?" "Has she taken her first step yet?" "Since she's taking so long, don't you think you should have her tested for some possible problems?" If you're hearing this, just tell them that your pediatrician has checked her and she's fine.

"Normal" development covers a lot of territory— witness the descriptions of these babies, all normal:

Jimmy. This child never seemed to sleep. He expressed a constant need to be held and cried a lot, and his mother felt that she could do nothing to comfort him. Within weeks of getting him she was feeling drained and had to go back to work, hiring a baby-sitter to help with the child care. Jimmy was always a vigilant baby, alert to everything going on around him. He didn't like toys—only adults. He rolled over at the age of one month, pushed himself up and tried to crawl at five months, walked at seven months, and taught himself to read at age two.

Bill. This was a much more self-sufficient child. He needed considerably less contact with people than did Jimmy and did not reach out to be held. He was content to entertain himself, sitting in his crib playing with stuffed animals or listening to music. He was also happy when his parents put him in front of the TV. Bill's parents feared he would never roll over and he didn't sit up by himself until the age of ten months; he was sixteen months old before he took his first step alone.

Alice. She shared some traits with the other children, but the combination of characteristics made her an entirely different kind of child to be with than either Jimmy or Bill. Alice was responsive to attention and affection from adults, but also liked quiet time by herself. She rolled over at three months and began to walk unaided at thirteen months. Alice liked to play with toys and be around adults, but she was shy with noisy children. Overall, Alice was not a child you would think of as adventurous.

These traits in your child's early stages tell you nothing about his intelligence. Some kids, for example, are just more inwardly oriented; they may become avid readers. Shyness and inhibition are the temperamental characteristics that tend to remain most constant from infancy into adulthood— but the way you bring him up will diminish or strengthen even them. So how your infant appears to you now will not give you the full picture of what he'll be like when he's twenty-one.

By all means read the fine guidebooks to early child development by experts such as Benjamin Spock and T. Berry Brazelton. They are good "ages and stages" guides to early childhood, but don't try to use them like Bibles. There are also videotapes available at your local video store with information about child development: *Baby Comes Home* (Karl/Lorimar), *Creative Parenting* (A&M), and *What Every Baby Knows* with Dr. T. Berry Brazelton (FHE).

Ultimately, the only person qualified to write the book on *your* child is *you*. Unfortunately, you won't have the full and accurate picture of any particular stage for your child until he or she has passed through it, making its predictive value worthless.

That you adopted your child also makes her first few years an open book when it comes to her physical development, since you may have little or no genetic information upon which to make an educated guess about how she'll look. For example, your pediatrician should be able to give you some idea of whether your child will be tall or short, but her skin tone will take a few months to develop and so will her eye and hair color, and the doctor will not be able to predict them.

If you can, cultivate an attitude of "benign curiosity" toward your child's development. Sit back and watch the patterns emerge; experience the mystery of it. But if you're among the many people who feel anxious doing this and yearn for more control, we have a suggestion. Give yourself observation tasks. Note (perhaps literally, in a notebook or baby book) how your child responds to other people, when she rolls over, what she does if you put your finger or other object near her. Record all the milestones: when she first drinks from a cup, takes her first step, says her first word. Watch how she reacts to people in the supermarket who go "kitchy-koo." In effect, you will be training yourself to respect the essence of your child—and to appreciate her for who she is.

A FAMILY AFFAIR

Those first few months with your child will be hectic, and at times you may feel that you have a little less control over your life than you'd like. It would be nice if you could just concentrate all your energies on developing a relationship with your child and giving her the nurturing she needs. But there is a social component in any kind of parenthood, and adoptive parents often have to devote more energies to this side of raising their child than do birth parents.

If you adopted through an agency, you were probably required to discuss your relationship to your parents and in-laws and their attitude toward your intention to adopt. Those relatives, and your own and your mate's brothers and sisters, can be a source of support in your efforts, or they can become one of the complications of adoption with which you will have to deal; or perhaps they will be some combination of the two.

Even if your parents or in-laws expressed strong reservations about adoption, they may sing a different tune—perhaps a lullaby—once they're holding their grandchild. It's much easier to resist an idea than to remain cold toward a child. But if they still don't warm up to your youngster, or if they observe what they consider to be a hitch in her development, you may have some work to do to either win them over or to at least make sure that they don't let your son or daughter know about their prejudices.

If you think that your child is beginning to sense his grandparents' ambivalence about him, structure his time with them so that the family is involved in some activity, such as going to the zoo, rather than just having dinner together. You might also confine visits to Grandma and Grandpa's house to those times when other people will be around, thus diffusing any negative feelings the grandparents have.

Even if you and your mate have more or less resolved your infertility dilemma, your relatives could still be hung up on this issue. This is particularly true for potential grandparents who have a strong desire to pass on their genes. If this is bothering your parents, you could see if your adoptive parents' group has a program to help adoptive grandparents adjust to their new status, and check with your adoption agency because they may also have such a program.

In its extreme form, your parents' ire might even sound something like, "How can you bring a stranger into the family? I'll be damned if I'll have my name on some—some *bastard*. Why don't you keep on trying to have a child? I've heard about another fertility doctor." You may also hear talk of "bad seeds," or sense an active scrutiny for flaws in your child even when the grandparents have seemingly given you their blessings.

What can you say to your parents if they feel this strongly about it? Here's a possibility: "I know that you have some strong views about this, but I'd appreciate it if you would think it over. Johnny can't change his background, but you can modify your objections. This is our decision, mine and my husband's. I hope you can come to terms with our decision, but it's final. Johnny is our son and, we hope, the grandchild you will come to love."

In some families, resistance to accepting an adopted child as a grandchild may emerge at holidays, such as Christmas and Thanksgiving, or at other occasions for family gatherings. The prejudice may come out in the form of showing favoritism to birth grandchildren over your adopted youngster. If that happens, you could say: "Look, I understand how you feel, but I don't want to expose my child to discrimination, so please try, at least consciously, to treat them equally."

Perhaps you would be more comfortable responding differently. Think about a time when you wanted something from your parents and you had to convince them to change their minds. Couch your argument in the way you did then; adapt it to your style.

Adoptive parents we have spoken to have also found it helpful to introduce reluctant adoptive grandparents to other people who have adopted and are enthusiastic about the process and can tell them of the satisfactions that come with it. Perhaps your spouse's parents as well could speak to your mother and father. They may be more willing to listen to somebody their own age. A clergyman's voice on your side might also help.

Some people have such deep-seated feelings about illegitimacy and the background of the child who will carry on their name that they will stubbornly cling to their antiadoption prejudices no matter what. If this describes your parents' or in-laws' sentiments, you may have to put some emotional distance between them and yourself. Should this become a constant irritant, you might even consider moving away from them to diffuse a perpetually tense relationship. In rare cases, adoptive parents have decided to break off their relationship with these relatives rather than subject their child to their hurtful remarks and behavior and possible emotional abuse. But we stress that this is a last resort, used only after you've tried everything else.

FRIENDS, NEIGHBORS, AND STRANGERS

Many adoptive parents discover that their friends are their greatest resource—often more helpful than their own parents. As for friends who are not supportive of your adoptive parenthood, it would be hard to imagine how your friendship with them could survive, since for many years parenting will consume so much of your time, energy, and attention. Could you feel comfortable with people who devalued this activity?

Neighbors could be very helpful during your child-rearing years. They are repositories of advice and folk wisdom if they have kids, and they're close by should you ever have to deal with an emergency. When your child gets a little older, you may find yourself exchanging baby-sitting chores with other parents on the block or in your building to your mutual advantage.

These are good reasons to bring the neighbors in on this new part of your life, if you're comfortable doing it. As we previously pointed out, it can help to invite them over before you get your child to share your feelings and information with them. Talk to their children, who probably have many questions to ask if they've never known an adoptive family. Talking to kids about adoption may also give you some good practice before you have to respond to the questions of people who have more hardened attitudes on the subject.

Adoptive mothers often find themselves bombarded by questions from birth mothers—"park mothers" in big cities or over-the-fence, neighboring parents in more rural areas—about what adoptive parenting is like. Remember that they're still sorting out their feelings about their birth children, so it may be difficult for them to assimilate what your parenthood is all about. For example, they might be thinking that if you can love a child as your own even though she's not related to you by blood, what does that say about love? They will want to compare their experience to yours, and their questions are likely to be neither malicious nor critical, but rather philosophical and affectionate. They could ask you questions like:

"Can you love her as much as a child to whom you might have given birth?"

"What's it like not to carry her for nine months and then have her handed to you?"

"Do you ever think about your child's birth parents?"

"Do you ever think about what your birth child would have been like?"

"How does your husband (wife) feel about the baby?"

"Who wanted most to adopt?"

"Do you feel like you missed something not going through a pregnancy?"

Perhaps at first you will feel a little uncomfortable responding to these questions. But even if you do, try to see them also as an opportunity to give some thought to how you feel about the issues they raise, which you might not have had time to deal with in the work and excitement of getting and caring for your child. Most often, such questions come from a benign, neutral perspective, so they offer you an opportunity for introspection without the need to defend yourself.

Strangers, unfortunately, are often another matter. Their questions, at their worst, can be intrusive, hurtful, totally insensitive. An adoptive father we know who was in the supermarket with his eleven-month-old adopted Korean child actually had a stranger walk up to him and say, "Gee, you must have adopted her. How much did she cost?" Or you may hear people say dumb things about adoption right in front of you when they don't know that you are an adoptive parent. If they know that you adopted your child, they may ask you about the adoption in her presence, even if she is old enough to understand the question, as if she were invisible. A stranger's remarks can create awkward situations. For instance, you might be introduced to somebody as a new mother, only to hear, "You sure got your figure back fast."

This won't happen constantly, but it's worth preparing yourself to deal with even occasional thoughtless remarks or comments. There is no single correct way of handling these reactions to adoption. You could change the subject or ignore a comment, give a short response and then go on to something else, or, if you're up to it, educate people with straight, comprehensive answers and explanations. It depends on your temperament or how you're feeling at the moment when it happens.

One strategy we learned about from a client could prove useful to you. It offers you the chance to take the initiative and thus diffuse awkward or painful situations before they get a chance to develop. He always waits for a stranger to say something complimentary about his son—most people will do that with a child—at which point he tells him that he adopted the child, catching the stranger on the upbeat.

QUESTIONS AND ANSWERS

My husband and I went through so many infertility tests and had to look so hard for an agency that had the right available child that finally getting our baby has seemed almost anticlimactic. How can we put all the negative memories aside so that we can parent our child?

It's understandable that you feel that way. Achieving any long-sought goal often leaves people with such feelings. It will take time for you to adjust to this new part of your life. Try not to pressure yourself to feel any particular way. You might also want to remind yourself that getting your baby and raising your child are two separate processes. After a few months of parenthood the travails of getting your baby will start to seem like memories that do not impinge on your present status: parents of a child.

☐

We adopted privately. Next week the court probation officer is coming for an inspection and we are nervous wrecks. Our child is colicky and we're afraid that if she cries incessantly during the visit the officer will think that we've been abusing her. Are we overreacting?

Every adoptive parent gets nervous before the visit of a probation officer or social worker. We can reassure you that the aim of such visits is not to see if you are being perfect parents; rather, it's to root out the occasional abusive parents. It's rare that such visits result in a child's removal from a home. To feel more in control of the situation, get a note from your pediatrician to the effect that your child has some digestive problems and that her crying does not reflect mistreatment on your part. You're very unlikely to need the note, but having it will probably make you feel better. You could take control of the way your house looks—perhaps even put out some fresh flowers. Try to view the visit as a collegial experience in which you will exchange thoughts about being parents with the court officer, rather than as a confrontation.

☐

When we brought our baby home there was a great outpouring of interest, warmth, and empathy from our friends, neighbors, and relatives. In fact, so many people have been trying to participate in caring for him that I'm starting to feel crowded out. Our child's positive response to everyone who has come over strengthens that feeling. There are times when I feel as if I do not have a special place in his life. It's all getting to be too much. How can I get all these well-wishers to back off a little?

Parents often find it necessary to consciously develop boundaries at this time. One solution is to make yourself and your child unavailable for at least several hours each day. Other new mothers take the phone off the hook or find some other way to control contact. Try it.

☐

I know that babies in carriages often draw the interest of, and comments from, strangers. But I think that my child is getting more than his share because my husband and I are dark-complexioned and our adopted son has blond hair and blue eyes. I'm not ashamed of being an adoptive parent, but I am getting very tired of answering the same old questions about how we got him. How can I get people to stop bothering me?

It's okay not to discuss your child's adoption at all with strangers. You don't owe them an explanation of anything and if they press the issue you can tell them that you would like to discuss it but that you don't have the time at the moment. With neighbors, though, you might want to try to be patient and answer their questions, since you're likely to interact with them socially and your child might eventually play with their children. You could also view the questions of neighbors you don't know too well as an opportunity to make new friends.

□

While talking about my new adopted baby with my best friend and her six-year-old son, the boy remarked, "What did he do wrong? Why did his mother give him up?" That made me feel sad and I don't know how I'm going to respond to other comments like that, especially from my son as he gets older.

You can respond to this and similar remarks by saying that "his mother couldn't take care of him and she loved him enough to make sure he was raised by a family who could care for him." Add that you feel lucky to be his parent.

□

Lately I've had the feeling that our pediatrician is uncomfortable with our adoption. She doesn't say anything outright, but the gaps in our child's medical record appear to bother her. Besides constantly referring to the incomplete records, she puts our child through what I regard as an inordinately large number of painful medical tests. No other adoptive mother I speak to has a similar story about her child. Is it time to switch doctors?

Tell the doctor why you're feeling uneasy about the way she's treating your child. Ask her if there is a special medical condition which she is trying to isolate. Make it clear that you prefer less testing and ask her straightforwardly if she can come to terms with the lack of complete medical records. Remember that physicians depend a great deal on precise medical histories. More and more inherited tendencies for illness and chronic conditions are being uncovered. For example, a physician can, if she knows there is diabetes in your child's family, insist that he stay slender as a preventive measure. Suggest that she consult with the adoption subcommittee of the American Academy of Pediatrics if she would like to have more information about the

general subject of caring for an adopted child. If this conversation leaves you with any doubts about her attitude, look for another physician. Some adoptive parents have told us that older doctors seem to be more comfortable working with skimpier records and don't seem to feel the need to subject children to an excessive amount of testing in order to fill in the blanks.

☐

When I look at my adopted child in her crib at night I can't help thinking that I don't deserve to have such a beautiful, sweet, wonderful baby. Why would I feel this way?

It might take you a while to feel that you fully deserve to have your child, perhaps because you did not experience the nine months of pregnancy or childbirth. In time, as she responds positively to you, you'll know that you made the right decision and that your daughter is lucky to have you as a parent.

3
Ages One to Six

These are years of amazing growth for your child. She will get bigger, walk, talk, explore her world, and formulate increasingly complex ideas about her experiences. Your growth is also important during this stage. It is vital to your family that you successfully make the transition from being part of a couple to being a parent. This is a formidable job for any new parent, and sometimes considerably harder for adoptive parents, who have to overcome an additional obstacle.

The excitement and work of caring for a baby can take most of your energy and time. However, as your child becomes old enough not to need your constant attention, you may surprisingly find yourself thinking of something you probably thought you had put behind you: infertility, if this was the reason you turned to adoption. It's not unusual for this issue to reappear for adoptive parents in their child's early years. If it doesn't come up spontaneously, questions from other mothers about the relative difficulty of your labor, how soon you got your figure back, or the hospital in which you gave birth could bring it to mind again.

Coming to terms with infertility is a major developmental task for adoptive mothers and fathers at this time.

To grow into the role of parents, you may have to acknowledge the probability that you will not give birth to a child. Unfortunately, doing this requires you to buck a strong social stereotype, since giving birth to children is seen by many in our society as a mark of adulthood.

Perhaps you sense that your own parents don't fully view you as an adult, even though you are raising a child, because you didn't become a "natural" parent. If it was your spouse who had the fertility problem, they may subtly suggest that you might have done better to have married someone else. If you encounter this, you can ask them to speak to members of the grandparents' division of your adoptive parents' group, who may be able to put your parents at ease about having an adopted grandchild. Sympathize with your parents' distress over not having a biological grandchild, but make it clear to them that you've resolved this issue for yourself.

Dashed expectations of procreation can also strain marriage ties. Wives sometimes wonder if their husband's love will survive the disappointment of not having their own biological child, even though they have, in fact, become parents.

If you still have substantial doubts about whether you are a "real" parent—an adult—you might also be uncertain of your right to exercise full parental authority in raising your child. Your child will need your firm guidance through the early years, so it's very important that you deal with any reservations you still have by discussing them with your spouse, other adoptive parents, friends, or if necessary, a therapist.

It's worth repeating: If infertility still bothers you, you're not alone. Many adoptive parents struggle to deal with it. It will probably always be in the back of your mind. To keep infertility from growing into a major problem that interferes with your becoming an effective parent, talk it out whenever you realize that it's troubling you.

YOUR PARENTAL STYLE

In your child's second year, she begins to shed her baby fat and her size, weight, and body type start to become clearly defined. Her physical appearance is now a more dramatic reminder that she was born to another couple. Yet she has probably already begun to reflect many of your family's shared characteristics. You may recognize familiar hand gestures, facial expressions, and smiles in her mannerisms. Perhaps she's already picked up some of your family code words. If you're beginning to think that she even resembles you or your spouse, you're not unusual. Adoptive parents—and others—often make this observation about their adopted children.

While you began to interact with her the first time you and she made eye contact, that interaction has gradually taken on a different quality. Now your child will be walking and talking and in every way possible making her presence known throughout your home. A force to be reckoned with, she will fully take her place in your family as an individual with tastes, sensibilities, needs, quirks—and opinions. A relationship, in the fullest sense of the word, is evolving between you and her.

As this relationship develops, you will establish a style of child rearing and start to define your family's characteristic way of interacting. Along with psychiatrist W. Robert Beavers, former president of the American Association for Marriage and Family Therapy, we believe that there is no single standard of family interaction against which all families should measure themselves. There is a wide spectrum of possibilities between strict and traditional and progressive and democratic. Your formula for success in child rearing and family interaction will depend much on the combination of your own and your spouse's upbringing with the goals you have set for yourselves.

However, we think there are some procedural rules worth keeping in mind to ensure that your family continues to work well. Since you are just now putting your own rules into place, this would probably be a good time to look at them and fine-tune them if necessary before they become too solidified. From researchers in the field and from our own practice, we can suggest that the following tips help promote the functioning of any kind of family:

- Try to remain open to disagreements and make sure family members always feel accepted despite differences of opinion.

- Let there be no doubt about who is running the family. Parents should act like parents.

- Make sure your children know what's expected of them. When you talk to them, do it on their level. For example, instead of telling your child that "Mommy likes a neat house and we all need to cooperate to keep it that way so I would like you to pick up your toys," say to your child, "Please pick up your toys." And then get down on the floor and help him.

- Teach respect for individual boundaries, both physical and psychological. Children should realize that they can't barge into your bedroom any time they want to; and you should be aware that by about the time your youngster is six, it's appropriate for you to knock before entering his bedroom. Similarly, family members should also avoid being invasive by telling others in the family how they should be thinking or feeling. For instance, if your child falls and starts to cry, don't run over and tell him, "Don't cry, it doesn't hurt."

- All family members should be able to make mistakes without being humiliated.

- Accept the changes that must come with your child's development and be ready to adapt your family to those changes. For example, when your child has gained the competence and maturity required to do something appropriate to his age level—and his peers are allowed to do it—let him do it. That could range from permitting a nine-year-old to play with friends without close supervision, to allowing a sixteen-year-old to date.

PREPARING YOUR CHILD FOR THE WORLD

Parents today, adoptive and nonadoptive, can consult experts on child care and development through widely available and inexpensive books such as the Boston Women's Health Book Collective's *Ourselves and Our Children* (Random House), Stella Chess, Alexander Thomas, and Herbert G. Birch's *Your Child Is a Person* (Penguin), T. Berry Brazelton's *Toddlers and Parents* (Delta), Benjamin Spock and Michael B. Rothenberg's *Baby and Child Care* (Pocket Books), and Burton White's *The First Three Years of Life* (Prentice Hall). We will not attempt to offer a comprehensive view of the early years of childhood, already covered so well in these volumes. However, we will focus on certain areas that are sometimes difficult for adoptive parents.

One negative interactive style for which adoptive parents are particularly at risk is the overly child-centered family. They share this with parents of first-borns and only children, and indeed, adopted youngsters often fit into these categories as well.

As an adoptive parent you worked hard to get your child, and the temptation is to hover over him. It's not unusual for adoptive parents to be overprotective. Of course, at the age of one, your child will try to climb into, or on, or reach out for just about everything that's accessible to him. You will have to childproof your house to keep your explorer from hurting himself. (*Keeping Your Kids Safe: A Handbook for Caring Parents*, by Gene Brown, is a good guide to this aspect of child rearing.) Also you might rent the videotape *Baby-Safe Home* (Embassy) with David

Horowitz for information on this subject. Two other tapes—
Too Smart for Strangers (Disney) and *Strong Kids, Safe Kids*
(Paramount) would be best utilized by watching them with
your child so that you could answer any questions that
arise. But falls are a part of life, and they will happen no
matter what you do. An occasional scraped elbow or knee is
not too high a price to pay for some important learning
experiences, and they're nothing to worry about.

Emotional overprotectiveness is an equally important
issue. Your child needs a balance of attention and distance
from you; otherwise, he will grow up thinking he's the
center of the universe and will experience difficulty in
developing satisfying relationships with others. If you overreact to his misbehavior, he will learn that breaking the
rules is the way to get your undivided attention. If you pay
too much attention to him when he's sick, you will be
teaching him that he can get people to care for him by being
helpless.

Balance is also the key to launching your child on the
road that will eventually take him to a state of healthy
autonomy. At about the age of one, he may cry when you
leave the room. The awareness of how dependent he is
could have frightened him, causing the tears. But he's also
curious and wants to be on his own. This ambivalence about
dependence and independence is a central theme in the
second year and will recur through much of your youngster's early childhood years. Your job is to help your
youngster develop a healthy combination of connectedness
and self-reliance.

Behavior resulting from this ambivalence could give
you some tough moments—as it does for many adoptive
parents. For example, you may have noticed that your child
occasionally likes to get away from you but does not want
you to leave him. When scared by the prospects of separation from you, a parting he can't control, your two-year-old
may run to you and cling. If it's a necessary separation—say,
leaving him with a baby sitter while you are out—you may

have to resist some heartrending sobbing and possible hysteria aimed at reversing your decision.

Temper tantrums are normal behavior for many children in the one-to-four age range. They have nothing to do with adoption and will usually play themselves out after a while. But if you are ambivalent about your right to stand firm and let his temper tantrum run its course, vacillating about a decision that causes him such visible distress, he will learn an effective method of getting his way at any time. If he can work that on you, how will he interact with others—people who do not see his wants and needs as their highest priority? So you will just have to remind yourself that you know best about what is good for him and the family of which he is an integral part.

DISCIPLINE

Your child must realize that the world does not revolve around him and that he can't always get what he wants, when he wants it. To help him learn this, you will have to develop techniques that will enable you to make him hear and heed a particularly important word whenever you say it. Unfortunately, he has his own uses for that word.

No! In truth, one-year-olds already know the concept and, if they talk, are likely to favor this word. But when you start to hear it often from your two-year-old, you know you have your work cut out for you. It is comforting, though, to realize that so many other parents are also experiencing this negativity and that it even has a name: "the terrible twos." Do you think you might be having a bit more anxiety over this phenomenon than does your neighbor, who is a birth parent? Many adoptive parents do. Some adoptive mothers and fathers interpret this rebellion as a sign that their child doesn't like them. Could they be doing something wrong? Does their child act this way because she senses that they are not her "real" parents? Will their child still love them if they stand firm?

This is your child's first major manifestation of independence—a moving away from you. While it might be natural for you to respond by questioning your parental competence, you're not likely to be doing anything wrong to elicit this obstinacy and you would be mistaken to let your anxieties influence the firmness with which you respond to your child's refusal to cooperate. Action is required rather than long lectures. Kids have short attention spans. Letting them have their way could cause trouble and give you real reasons to doubt your ability to parent. They not only need limits at this point, they are also beginning to ask for them and it's your job to supply them.

You will be setting many limits for your child now—presenting him with your own "nos." He needs to learn where he can't walk, what he can't touch, when he shouldn't interrupt. Your child will have to learn not only rules for safety, but also that he must consider the needs and rights of others. Remember, two-year-olds have small vocabularies and very little judgment or common sense.

Adoptive parents sometimes feel guilty about disciplining "another person's child." While we can understand that you might have doubts about your entitlement to impose discipline on your child, you need to realize that you not only have the right and obligation to do this, it is also an expression of your love for your child.

Believe it or not, we've had adoptive parents come into our office, towering over the four-year-old they have in tow, and complain that they can't "control" their child. We find it hard to believe that these adults are so helpless that they can't deal with a small child.

Usually, you can effectively control a one-year-old's behavior through direct physical action. If he's doing something that could endanger him, lift him and carry him away from the source of the danger; or distract him by taking away the object he should not play with and exchange it for something else that interests him. When you tell him "No" or "Don't do that," say it in a steady, firm tone of voice. Let him hear the seriousness with which you view his misconduct; you should not confuse him by saying no with a chuckle or bemused expression. He needs to get the message straight.

As your child gets older and you become aware of just how much and what kind of misbehavior you and your spouse will tolerate, stick to the limits you set. If your youngster is carrying on, don't try to be too patient and understanding. Remind her that "this is the way we do it," without a long and involved explanation and defense of why that's the case. If she still doesn't do it your way, correct her immediately. Then, if necessary, some consequence or punishment for the misbehavior may be in order. We feel that small and brief but sure punishments work best—ten minutes in her room, for example. And don't allow any back talk when you're correcting her.

If this all sounds a bit stern, remember that disciplining only accounts for a small part of the time you spend with your child. Take a "firm but friendly" approach to correcting him, as Dr. Benjamin Spock suggests, and he'll accept it in that spirit. Your child wants you to set limits for him; he knows when he's getting away with too much. Don't worry, he will love you just as much after you impose discipline, though he may like you less at the moment.

While we will not cover every kind of misbehavior you are likely to see, we think it's important that you stay alert to types of misconduct that can easily be blown out of proportion. The way that adoptive parents interpret their young child's behavior is perhaps even more crucial than the comparable perceptions of birth parents. In some instances you might be tempted to resort to a handy explanation for misbehavior: your child's adoption. Unfortunately, that pushes into the realm of pathology actions that probably have their roots in something much more mundane.

For instance, many children of three or four will be

fascinated by and use bathroom language. This sometimes shocks parents and gains attention for the child. If you are surprised by such words coming from your adopted child, and possibly vulnerable to someone making a silly observation like, "This language reflects the child's lower-class roots," you could create an adoption problem where none exists. You might start doubting that you can truly affect your child's character and behavior. Children outgrow this. It is just a phase.

It can really upset some people to hear a little child spouting such words. Ideally, you will be able to understand his fascination at this point in his development and be reassured that it is likely to stop when he outgrows this stage. It has nothing to do with class or adoption. But if you can't let it go, try not to express shock. That gives your youngster a message that he can use words to get to you. Just correct your child, tell him why you don't like it and make up new funny words with him; if he persists, you may wish to have a consequence for such behavior to remind him of your disapproval.

Another type of behavior that many parents, including adoptive mothers and fathers, are prone to mistakenly regard as serious misconduct, is what they perceive as "lying" from their three- or four-year-old. Adoptive parents sometimes think this is related to their child's origins. Children of this age have vivid, active imaginations. They love to make up stories and, because of their cognitive development at this stage, may sometimes blur the boundary between reality and fantasy. They are not willfully distorting the truth, trying to put something over on you; they have no bad intent. They're just acting their age and they shouldn't be punished—or regarded as sick—for it.

Don't be hard on yourself if you realize that you've occasionally given in a little to fears that such behavior is adoption-related. Take it as an opportunity to prepare yourself to recognize these incidents for what they are in the future. So much of this is uncharted territory; you simply need to try to do your best knowing that all parents make mistakes and kids survive quite well despite that fact.

One way you can avoid making too much of a minor incident is to try to train yourself to be open to more than one explanation of why your child has acted in a particular way. If you have no reason to believe otherwise, assume that the most benign explanation is the correct one. What if you find this difficult to do? You could practice on the little mishaps and mischief that arise with any child of this age.

Dr. W. Robert Beavers, former president of the American Association for Marriage and Family Therapy, offers the following as an example of the many ways parents could interpret the simple act of their three-year-old spilling a glass of milk at the table:

1. It was an accident, involving no motive.
2. The child was trying to get back at her mother for something.
3. The child was expressing hostility not connected to the parent.
4. The child was tired and anxious and likely to make a mistake at the time.
5. The glass was too large for the child's fingers.

Depending on the context, any of these explanations could have been correct. The point is not to immediately seize on the same explanation every time to the exclusion of others. Parents who do that may be seeing a "symptom," which suggests that a diagnosis and treatment will logically follow, possibly turning a trivial event with a simple explanation into a major crisis. Child rearing is a tough enough job without making it unnecessarily tougher.

TELLING YOUR CHILD
ABOUT ADOPTION

An adopted child, four years old, went up to his mother one day and asked, "Where did I come from?" His mother, who was relieved to be asked such a direct question, finally had an opportunity to use the response she had carefully prepared when the youngster was two. She told him how he had grown in another mommy's tummy, and how that mommy had brought him to the agency, which gave him to his adoptive mother and father, who brought him home and loved him very much. "Is there anything else you would like to know?" his mother added, partly looking forward to and partly dreading the dialogue she thought would follow. The child looked quizzical. "Yeah," he replied. "Johnny next door said he came from Ohio. Where did I come from?"

Understandably, when, how, and what to tell an adopted child about the way he joined their family is one of the prime concerns of adoptive parents. They sometimes get very anxious about "doing it right." Fortunately, fewer and fewer people think that the answer is keeping adoption a secret from their child. Unfortunately, there's still a lot of confusion about how to go about telling a youngster the truth.

There are only two things surrounding the issue of telling that could harm your child: keeping it a secret, or using the information as a weapon in a moment of anger. Your family's style will determine the mechanics of telling. For example, some parents begin when their child is in the cradle, calling their infant their "beautiful adopted baby." Others wait until their child asks about childbirth, usually when asking about a pregnant woman he had observed, or a friend's mother.

Some parents pick an arbitrary age at which they think their child should hear the story. While that's not likely to do any harm, you should realize that no matter what you tell your child, she will not fully understand the concept of adoption until she is considerably older. In fact, kids are usually at least fourteen or so before the impact of their adoption can completely sink in.

Until about the age of five, your child's cognitive abilities will not really be up to the task of making sense of what she hears about adoption. That might surprise some parents, who tell their child the whole story and then hear her relate it accurately to someone else. The catch is that the child is largely parroting words, not grasping their meaning, although she may have begun to understand some of the simplest aspects of the process.

Psychologist David M. Brodzinsky, an authority on adoption, illustrates this by relating his attempt to see how much a four-year-old understood about adoption and child-birth. He asked the child, an adoptee, to describe the adoption process. The girl related how "the baby grows in one mommy's tummy and then comes out at the hospital and a new mommy and daddy come and adopt the baby and love it forever." Not bad for a child her age. And where, Brodzinsky asked her, do babies come from? "The baby grows in one mommy's tummy and then comes out at the hospital and a new mommy and daddy come and adopt the baby and love it forever," the child replied, indicating that the child was too young to understand fully the conceptual difference between birth and adoption.

It's helpful for even your young child to start to become comfortable with the vocabulary of adoption and to have at least a simple explanation of the process to supply if anybody asks him about it. When he does begin to understand it in greater depth, it will be not because of the passing of time and the gaining of experience, but rather because he has reached a new stage of cognitive development. Simply put, his mind will be capable of handling more complex ideas.

We think that the most useful approach to telling a child about her adoption is to let the child set the agenda, rather than delivering a lecture when you think she should be ready to hear it. If you've been using the word *adoption* all along, your two- or three-year-old may one day say, "My cousin says he wasn't adopted; why am I adopted?" There's your opening.

When you reply, give her a simple answer. "We wanted

to have a baby and we couldn't," you could say. Then tell her in as uncomplicated a way as you can how she came to be in your family, but nothing more unless she asks. If you exhaust her with a long story, she may hesitate to ask you about adoption again. Read to her from books for children about adoption, such as *The Chosen Baby* by Valentina P. Wasson (Lippincott), one of the classic books children seem to love. You could also follow up by reading bedtime stories to her from books that have an adoption theme. The stories of Thumbelina and Heidi are fine for this purpose. If you notice that an upcoming TV show will treat the adoption theme on a kid's level, watch it with her so you can answer any questions she raises.

Tell your child as much as she seems to be able to deal with. Make sure she's satisfied with your answers. And always balance your description of how you got her with a statement about how much you wanted her and how much you love her. Her experience in your family will reinforce her perception that you love and care for her regardless of how she came to be with you.

The inevitable questions about childbirth offer a good way of bringing up adoption. If your child asks you about a pregnant woman he's seen, tell him where babies come from and then explain that another person carried him in her womb and that you adopted him. If he asks why, explain that the other woman couldn't take care of him and that you got him because you wanted him. Make sure you convey the idea that putting him up for adoption was an act of love by his birth mother—that everyone concerned had his best interests at heart. By the time he's older he may begin to question this, but then gradually he will be able to see the situation in a broader context.

Of course, the reality of it is never quite so neat and tidy. No matter how carefully you frame your answers, you'll probably hear "But why?" over and over. Or she may come back to you with different questions that you might think you sufficiently answered in your response to her initial questions. For example: "If this child [in the pregnant woman's womb] can stay with her mommy, why couldn't I?" Don't let it discourage you. It's natural for your child to ask you again about material you know you went over thoroughly. In young children this stems partly from their enjoyment of having the power of getting you to respond. But it derives even more from the nature of the process of taking in and assimilating this information. That will last for years.

What if your child seems unconcerned about adoption and never asks, or after hearing about it once, does not bring up the topic again? Generally, this is not a cause for concern. Every adoptee wonders why he was given up. But some kids are less prone to talk about it. Bring it up yourself, from time to time and every time he reaches a new stage of development—certainly when he starts school—perhaps by referring to a movie you saw or book you read that had a story that reminded you about how you got him through adoption.

Always be careful not to use anything relating to your child's adoption in a flippant, teasing, or angry way. For example, don't tell your child, "We got you from under the cabbage patch." Nor should you ever connect your child's misbehavior to adoption. There's a difference between hurtful remarks from a stranger and similar comments from you. Your child assumes that you know her better than anyone and your words would have an immensely greater impact.

While it's difficult, sometimes impossible, for a parent to apologize for angry remarks tied to their child's adoption, kids are resilient. Some children can shrug it off; others will take it as a challenge and try to prove their parent was wrong. But even those energized by this kind of abuse pay a price. One adoptee we know was goaded to achieve a Ph.D. in psychology by such treatment, partly to prove her mother wrong. But it also causes her great pain to this day.

SIBLINGS

On the day that Al and Sue Brookens took home Julie, their adopted daughter, the social worker handling the adoption made sure that five-year-old Carl, the Brookenses' adopted son, was in the middle of the ceremony. In fact, as soon as the parents got to exchange loving looks with their new daughter, the social worker handed the baby to Carl and said: "This is your baby."

Agencies know that when a new adopted infant enters a family, it's important that children already in the home begin immediately to form an attachment to the baby. The older child should not be made to feel external to the process. The phenomenon of sibling rivalry is present here as much as in any other family, so it's important to get the new sibling relationship off to a good start.

If you become parents for a second time, the adopted child you already have might react negatively to the addition to your family before the new child even arrives. "Can we send her back if we don't like her? Can't we get two cats instead?" and the like are normal reactions. Acting babyish is another common reaction to a new sibling. Unless such behavior is constant, it will do no harm to give in to it. But if it continues for three months or more, you might want to consult your pediatrician.

You can help ease the transition to becoming a two-child family by acknowledging your older child's frustration at having to share your attention with a sibling. It often helps to enlist the first child as a "helper" in taking care of his sibling, but of course you should supervise any help he gives you with the baby. You can also point out the privileges he has because he is older—going to the zoo with you, for example, while his little sister can't.

If you took pictures of your first adopted child, it would be nice if you did the same for your second. But the reality of it is that most parents don't make as complete a photographic record of their second child as they did of their first, so it's not worth the guilt feelings it can provoke. However, if you adopted your second child but gave birth to your first, you might want to be more self-conscious about taking those pictures of your adoptee. She could be a bit more sensitive to any family pattern that might suggest that she is any less your child than is her sibling.

Talk as much to the new child as you did to your first adoptee about adoption. We note this because it's only natural to slack off a bit after you've already gone through the process once. Remember that your second child has not experienced any of this and the attention is as important to him as it was to his older brother or sister.

If you've given birth to your second child and are nursing him, your adoptee may ask: "Did you do that to me?" If you didn't, explain that Mommy and Daddy held her close and smiled and sang to her while feeding her from a bottle. You could also use the question as another opportunity to discuss adoption with her.

Sibling rivalry can be unpleasant and disruptive. Your older child may express hostility by holding the baby too tightly or pinching her too hard, all the while saying how cute the new child looks. One mother we know became worried when it was too quiet in the next room where her three-year-old and her newly adopted baby were. She got up to look and found the older child holding the baby near the back door of the house. "I told you not to pick her up and carry her," she admonished her son. "I didn't," he replied in all innocence. "I rolled her."

That can happen in any family. But in an adoptive family, certain additional problems can result from sibling rivalry. Adopted kids are vulnerable to teasing from birth children that takes adoption as its theme. Remarks like "You're adopted and I'm not" hurt. So make it a rule in your home that nobody can use adoption to taunt or tease. And, naturally, avoid ever adding to possible tensions yourself by making comparisons between your children.

Don't overlook your birth child's possibly ambivalent

relationship to adoption. It would be normal for him to have fantasies about adoption and his own origins. If he does raise questions about the subject, answer them as carefully and clearly as you would similar queries from your adoptee. And make sure your birth child knows that it's okay for him to ask.

SEXUALITY

Marjorie Parsons and her husband had adopted a boy and a girl. While giving the children a bath one day when the boy was four and the girl was three, Marjorie noticed that her children were starting to touch each other all over. Marjorie was a sophisticated parent who had read extensively about child development and knew that her kids were just being naturally curious about each other's bodies. But the incident nevertheless unnerved her a bit. She had heard just enough scare stories about adoption—"bad seeds," incest, and the like—to have at least a few fears in the back of her mind.

These fears prey on the minds of many adoptive parents—it's one of the most frequent difficulties that they have when trying to square normal child behavior with the distorted ideas and misinformation about adoption that we all hear at one time or another. In our experience, adopted children are no different from other kids when it comes to expressing sexuality. They are curious and they explore their own bodies and sometimes those of their playmates— playing doctor, for example, is normal for four-year-olds. Parents who may not realize that most kids do this could be shocked by such behavior and incorrectly ascribe it to adoption.

Just as some kids are more curious than others, children vary in how physically affectionate they are with their parents and siblings. If you can, return your child's affection for you in kind. Should she unknowingly cross the boundary of propriety, straightforwardly tell her that there are some parts of your (and her or his) body that are private.

If your child seems to be extraordinarily affectionate, it could be from some insecurity for which he wants reassurance. Any kid can feel that way, adopted or nonadopted. Don't be afraid to respond to it. Most likely it's a stage he will soon get over. By the age of five or six it's also normal for kids to express something akin to a romantic attachment to their opposite-sex parent (more about this in the next chapter).

Children between the ages of three and six who show great curiosity about where babies come from are behaving well within the normal range. When your child asks such questions, use them to talk about adoption and her origins. This might be a good occasion to once again take out your favorite adoption book for kids, such as *The Chosen Baby*, and read to her from it.

There are many books that are useful for answering your child's questions about sexuality. Among them are Margaret Sheffield's *Where Do Babies Come From: A Book for Children and Their Parents* (Knopf) and Sara Bonnett's *Making Babies: An Open Family Book for Parents and Children Together* (Walker). Also useful is the videotape *Where Did I Come From?* (LCA). The latter should be viewed together with your child.

PLAYMATES AND NURSERY SCHOOL

By the age of two, kids are old enough to sit next to each other and play separately—a phenomenon called "parallel play." Don't worry if your child does not interact at all with the child busily moving blocks around right at her elbow. Kids this age have little empathy for others and do not share; they're just not yet developmentally ready to socialize fully.

Nevertheless, it's beneficial for your child to spend time

in this activity because it helps her get used to being with other children. A two-year-old may be timid and need all the practice she can get being in the presence of other kids. In fact, it's a good idea to encourage even this limited socializing by taking her to the park or playground and bringing her over to visit your friend or a neighbor who has kids her age.

Most children begin to play with others at about age two-and-a-half or three. (If your child is still completely a loner by four, you might want to consult your pediatrician about it.) Inevitably, as she gets older and begins to actually play with other children, the issue of her adoption may come up at some point. In these early years, the tone of anything other kids say to her is likely to be benign. For example, the parent of one of her playmates may tell her child that your youngster was adopted. That child then might ask your child a straight question about the subject.

If your child seems a little thrown by having to respond to such a question, reassure her that all kids are curious about any way they differ from others. Before you suggest how she should handle it, ask her what she would like to say. In her childhood interaction with others, it will often be a good idea to help her to work out and rehearse a response to anything requiring a reaction, rather than intervening and helping her directly. This will help build her confidence in her ability to handle her relationships with others.

Now that your youngster is taking her first tentative steps outside the safe confines of your family, you may start to encounter some situations in which you will have to decide whether to bring up the fact of her adoption. For instance, it might be appropriate to mention it if you become friends with the parents of your child's playmates. If you do tell them, don't be surprised to discover that there are a lot more adoptive families around than you had realized.

If you send your adopted child to nursery school, you may want to tell her teacher and the school's administrator that your child was adopted. Talk to them and try to get a sense of how they feel about adoption. You might ask if there are other adopted kids in the school. If there are, request that the school put your child in their class, if possible. Also make it clear that you will serve as a resource of information about adoption should the teacher need facts to answer a question raised by another child in the school.

QUESTIONS AND ANSWERS

My two-and-a-half-year-old adoptee is becoming willful and has begun to have temper tantrums. I'm very worried that he's inherited some kind of emotional problem that we knew nothing about when we adopted him. My husband says I'm overreacting. Is he right?

Unpleasant as this phase may be, that's all it is—a phase, common to all children. You might find it reassuring to read some child development books to see just how normal it is. However, you may also be observing the result of a rather fragile disposition, inherited by your child from his birth family. That would still not be a cause for alarm. A recent study by Finnish psychiatrists and psychologists indicates that even adopted children born to mothers hospitalized for schizophrenia can grow up healthy in healthy adoptive families.

Try to observe what happens just before he has these tantrums. It could be some sort of stimulus, such as too much noise, the presence of too many people, or the need to choose between one thing or another that is setting him off. You could avoid placing him in the kinds of situations that create the tantrums.

□

I'm wondering how much longer I can continue to take my four-year-old to her grandparents'—my husband's parents'—house. They have never been comfortable with

*her adoption and they continue to favor their birth grand-
children. Now my daughter is becoming aware of their
favoritism. We have tried to discuss this with them, but we
don't seem to be able to get them to reexamine their
attitude.*

If your spouse, who knows his parents best, can't
come up with a way to overcome their resistance to
accepting your child, you may have to limit contact with
them. They are, after all, the grownups, and they will have
to do the changing. There's nothing your daughter can do
to change her adoptive status. And if you don't protect
her from this cruel treatment, she could grow to resent you
for it.

Perhaps you could just see them for dinner occasionally, without your child. You may also have to leave them
out when you invite your other relatives to your home. Let
them know why you feel you need to do this and perhaps
that will start to bring them around.

□

*My four-year-old says that she wishes that she came from
my womb. I wish it too, and thinking about it makes me cry.
Is this a serious problem?*

If it's still that much of an issue for you, it would
probably be a good idea for you to talk to other adoptive
mothers, friends, perhaps even a therapist about it. It's okay
to tell your child that you wish you had given birth to her,
although stress that the most important thing for you was to
become a parent. At the same time, emphasize that you love
more than anything that she's your daughter. Also remind
her that giving birth is a brief experience and that the long
period of time that you have had her and will continue to
raise her is more important to you.

□

*My two-and-a-half-year-old insists on playing by himself.
Somebody told me this might be a sign of antisocial
behavior. Is there anything to that?*

Your child should be encouraged to play with his peers. Yet some children, often only children, genuinely enjoy playing alone. Your child needs to be given a chance to play with or near other children. Help your child by bringing one child to your home and gently assist in getting your child to play with her for a short time. Each time they play together, gradually lengthen the time that they play, judging by how your child appears able to tolerate it. Then introduce more children gradually. Behavior is a matter of temperament. If you would like to find out more about the subject of temperament, read *Your Child Is a Person: A Psychological Approach to Parenting Without Guilt* by Stella Chess, Alexander Thomas, and Herbert G. Birch.

☐

My adopted child, age two-and-a-half, has begun to call every woman he sees "Mommy" and every man "Daddy." Does this have anything to do with adoption?

Any child of this age might use these terms generically for a while. It's nothing to worry about.

☐

My neighbor walked into her daughter's bedroom the other day and found her playing doctor with my four-year-old adopted son. Now she won't let her daughter associate with my child. She also says that this happened because my child was adopted. What should I tell her?

Playing doctor at this age has nothing to do with sexual promiscuity—and certainly nothing to do with adoption. It's simply a child's healthy curiosity about his and others' bodies. Try to explain to your neighbor the facts of the matter. If she just won't hear it, you'll have to limit your child's contact with her child, certainly until things cool down. Children of this age do need to be supervised, however, when they play together.

☐

My three-year-old has been taking her older sister's favorite toy. I know she's young, but my husband and I worry that this stealing could be setting a pattern for the future. We're also wondering if this could be the beginning of some kind of complex related to adoption.

The problem here is in how you're framing your dilemma. Your child isn't "stealing." Kids don't have a fully developed sense of what is theirs and what belongs to others until somewhere between the ages of five and seven. Until then, honesty is an abstraction. At the age of three, your child's conscience is in the process of developing. You could help it along by offering her guidance and correction every time she takes something that doesn't belong to her so she will eventually learn to respect the rights of others, but don't expect her to really grasp it until she is older. This has nothing to do with adoption.

☐

We are considering adopting a second child now that our first adopted child is four years old. Our daughter is easygoing and bright. Both my spouse and I work at demanding professions and the time that we have to spend together as a family must, of necessity, be quality rather than quantity time. We, therefore, want our second child to be as healthy and enjoyable as our first. We have recently learned that infants born to mothers who have used cocaine even once during their pregnancy are likely to be quite handicapped. What are the facts about this and how can we ensure that the baby we adopt has not been exposed to cocaine as a fetus?

You are correct in being concerned about cocaine's effects on the fetus even when used occasionally during pregnancy. It appears, from recent research, that cocaine use during pregnancy almost certainly damages the central nervous system of the growing fetus and may damage other organs, as well. Cocaine or "crack" appears to be far more damaging to the developing fetus than other narcotics or alcohol. It is unlikely that you will be able to know absolutely whether or not a baby has been exposed to cocaine prenatally unless the birth mother has lived in an entirely restricted facility during the entire nine months of pregnancy. Sometimes cocaine was used in the first trimester, before the mother knew she was pregnant. Unfortunately, this is also when cocaine does the most damage to the fetus. Usually the characteristics of a "cocaine baby" are the following: low birth weight, small head circumference, small size, prematurity, a piercing cry, and muscular rigidity. These infants are difficult to comfort, feed, and interact with and require a great deal of parental time and attention. They will be likely to require intensive parenting to ensure that they can develop to capacity. These infants suffer from permanent damage to the central nervous system rather than withdrawal from narcotics. Researchers at the present time believe that the central nervous system damage will manifest itself, as the child grows, in attention-deficit disorders, hyperactivity, and school difficulties. High birth weight, normal head circumference, high Apgar scores, and high scores on all of the scales of the Brazelton Neonatal Behavioral Assessment Scales (BNBAS) should be useful in helping you to determine whether you should adopt a particular newborn.

4

The School Years, Ages Six to Nine

From age six on, the outside world increasingly affects your child's thoughts and behavior. Now she begins her formal school career. Where once you and you alone stipulated rules, limits, and moral tenets, you must now vie for influence with teachers and your son or daughter's school friends.

Going to school is the beginning of separation from the family—completed in late adolescence—and it can be a little trying for parents. If this is your first child, your family has never experienced this break; if your last child is starting school, his or her departure is the first intimation of the empty nest.

Some adoptive parents seem to have a particularly hard time with this process. They experienced less control than other parents over the way their child entered their family; now, just a few years later, they find themselves required to graciously begin to relinquish their parental omnipotence. If these parents still harbor doubts about their right and ability to effectively parent, they may wonder if they have adequately prepared their child to cope with the outside world.

This separation drama is played out against a backdrop of the child's dawning realization—as the result of comparing herself to her classmates—that it's different to be adopted. While a full understanding of her origins is still probably about seven or eight years away, she can now put into words the sometimes confused notions she may have about her relationship to you and her birth parents.

If no major problems have hindered her development, you should be confident that you've given your child enough resources to respond appropriately to the people and situations she will encounter. However, you should stay alert to the difficulties that her adoption may present to her in these years. For example, while it's not likely to happen, an occasional teacher or school guidance professional may misinterpret your child's minor classroom difficulties as problems stemming from his or her adoptive status. The parents of one of your child's friends might show prejudice toward your youngster—making things rough for her with her peers—under mistaken impressions about adoption. Or thoughtless adults could congratulate your child: "Weren't you lucky to be adopted!" These or similar events would require you to do a little educating. It is an adult responsibility which requires adult intervention. Your child is too young to handle it herself.

FEARS AND FANTASIES

The questions that some children this age ask about their background become more pointed—and more challenging than the ones they previously asked. When Jimmy was seven, he asked his adoptive mother if his "first mother" knew her, and if she didn't, how could she just give her her child? Wasn't he sufficiently valuable for his birth mother to want to know his adoptive mother before handing him over to her? His mother responded in a way that you could when faced with a similar question.

His mother first asked Jimmy if he could think of any reasons why a girl might do this. Among other reasons Jimmy said, "If she didn't know anybody who could take care of a baby." She then explained to Jimmy that in some kinds of adoption, when a mommy didn't know anybody who could take care of her baby, she goes to a place called an adoption agency. Here there are people called social workers who ask the mommy how she wants her baby taken care of and who then try to find a family that will give the baby just that kind of care and love. That's what they did for his birth mother. Jimmy's mother also told him that she wished that she had been able to meet his first mommy and that she had been able to decide if she liked his adoptive mother. But the social worker did that for them.

What if Jimmy had entered the family through private adoption and had asked the same question? Then his mother could have told him that some birth mothers get to choose from descriptions of several possible adoptive families, and that his birth mother chose the ones she liked best. When responding to any question from your child about his birth mother's motives, it is helpful to stress the positive, even if you do not have all the facts.

Jimmy's question falls within the typical range of thoughts, observations, and remarks about adoption that you may hear from a child of this age. As he moves out into the world, he will come into closer and more frequent contact with other families, which can be a constant reminder that his background differs from that of most kids in an important way. He may respond by questioning how that came about, and what that should mean to him. No matter how often, openly, and rationally you may have discussed this with him, his burgeoning imagination may well come up with creative, and possibly disconcerting, embellishments.

On the bleaker side, adopted kids at the age of nine may wonder, with fear, if their birth mother might return to take them away. At this stage, they consider such a turn of events as a real possibility. If that should happen, they wonder, to whom would they belong? Your child is still too young to understand the legal aspects of adoption that would reassure him that he belongs legally with you.

At age seven, Adam began waking up in the middle of

the night, crying out as the result of nightmares. When his parents went in to comfort him, they discovered that he had dreamt that his "real" mother had returned and wanted him back.

After some time, Adam's parents calmed him by reassuring him that "you are our son now, a real part of our family. No one will ever take you away."

Adam's parents reminded him that someday he would move away, probably first to go to college and maybe later to have a family of his own. But they reassured him that this would happen only when he was ready, not before. "And even then," they added, "we won't stop being your parents. You won't need us so much then, but you'll still be our son." Comforted, Adam went back to sleep.

Misunderstandings can also occur during this period as a consequence of punishment for bad behavior. Since, if she misbehaves, your child knows that you will discipline her, she may "reason" that she was given up for adoption because she was bad, perhaps for crying too much. (Similarly, children caught up in the middle of their parents' divorce may think that they could have prevented the split if only they had behaved better.)

If your child expresses such thoughts, tell her: "Parents don't give up children for adoption because they are bad. Sometimes, though, if a parent knows she can't take care of her child in the way that she should, she may decide to let another family, who *can* raise a child, bring her up. It's hard for a parent to give up a baby and making that decision means she loved you very much and wanted the best for you."

Although it is more likely to show up later, some kids in this age range begin to speculate about who their birth parents "really" were. It is usual for children at this time of life to add imagination to facts to try to understand things. Sometimes they dream up idealized biological parents who were famous, powerful, beautiful, talented, and very loving people. Children of this age see things in more extreme forms—either all good or all bad.

Such idealizing of the unknown may arise in response to the gibes of playmates who belittle your child's birth parents or emphasize his lack of knowledge of them: "You don't even know who your real parents are!" Not yet capable of dealing with the reasons why a birth parent would give her up, your child may well respond with a vivid description of what she has imagined: "My mother was a famous movie star."

What if you overhear your child making up a story like this? It's no cause for alarm. Your son or daughter is responding to a stressful and ego-threatening situation with the best weapon he or she now has: imagination. It's nothing to worry about. Stories about glorified birth parents are as harmless as the conversations children sometimes have with imaginary playmates.

Normal children of six or seven—adopted or not—indulge in a good deal of fantasy play, and some of it is about things that may trouble them: accidents, sickness, killing, and death in general. Seven-year-old Michael, for example, plays violent games with his Masters of the Universe figures. They kill each other, sometimes first cutting off their opponents' limbs. You might hear your child link such fantasies to adoption, imagining, for example, violence perpetrated on a birth parent—although it's not common. If you do hear this and it does not become obsessive—he does not become totally preoccupied with it or change his behavior as a result—you should not worry.

There is some disagreement among experts about whether adopted children of this age are likely to be ready—or want—to voice anger about the reality of their parents' rejection of them early in life. In our experience we have found that the expression of such feelings at this age is relatively rare. But the issue could arise.

Johnny Coleman, age six, flew into a rage one afternoon. When his mother managed to calm him, he explained: "A boy in my class said my mother didn't want me. She didn't like me, and that's why she gave me up for adoption. I hate her, I hate her!"

Should your adopted child say something like this, you will have to accept it. Your child *was* rejected; that's a fact of life from which you cannot protect him. It's OK for him to be hurt and even angry about it. If you hear these sentiments, acknowledge your child's pain and mirror what he says. It is important for him to be able to talk about how he feels. It is not important at this moment for you to explain anything, but, instead, to listen to him and comfort him for his perfectly normal feelings.

Some children like to be held when they cry, others prefer that you keep your distance, while still others get upset if you even look at them while they weep. Respect your child's style. Don't try to pretend that his bad feelings aren't there, because then he might doubt their reality. Don't tell him how sad he makes you feel when he is sad. It could seem as if you were trying to substitute your pain for his.

If you hear your son or daughter suddenly express strong feelings about adoption, or if your child has nightmares or anxieties that weren't there a few days ago, the cause might very well be something seen on television. Ask her about it; if she did see something on television, discuss it with her. You can use this to have a vivid conversation about adoption, perhaps more open than any you've previously had. Try to make the most of it, but be cautious not to push it too far. Your child will let you know when to stop, either by telling you he now wants to do something else or by visibly losing interest in the subject.

Adoption is a romantic, dramatic, and compelling subject, one that's ripe for television treatment. Not long ago, for example, "Punky Brewster," a popular TV show, featured a story about a kid who was put up for adoption but ended up instead in an institution. Finally, through some melodramatic plot turns, he found his way back to his birth mother and he confronted her. She refused to speak to him at first, but then she cried and apologized and the two were able to stay together. That's powerful stuff for a six- or seven-year-old adoptee.

"Mr. Rogers" and "Sesame Street" have also dealt with adoption. There's no reason to shelter your child from such broadcasts. They are sensitively and honestly handled. If you can, watch them with her. Do so in order to be aware of and sensitive to issues they raise. It is a wise adoptive parent who scans TV listings for such programs.

What if your child in this age group shows little or no interest in discussing his adoption? It would be a good idea for you to introduce the subject yourself once in a while if he doesn't initiate this conversation. However, ask yourself, are you sure that the reticence is entirely on his part?

A colleague of ours recently organized separate adoption support groups for several adoptive mothers and their six-year-old adoptees. The mothers, in their group, said that their children hardly ever talked about adoption—certainly less than they had expected them to. Their kids, on the other hand, painted a much different picture when they discussed their adoption among themselves. They said they didn't bring it up because they knew that it made their mothers sad and they "didn't want to hurt Mommy's feelings." One child even said that it might be a good idea if the videotape being made of their sessions could be shown to their mothers to help them feel more comfortable in discussing adoption.

"HAPPY" BIRTHDAY?

Birthdays had always been happy affairs for the Johnson family, who have two adopted children, Jeremy, eleven, and Jennifer, eight. On Jennifer's eighth birthday, Mrs. Johnson noticed that Jennifer seemed a little blue. That day, Jennifer chose to spend more time alone in her room than was typical for her.

Mrs. Johnson finally knocked on Jennifer's door and upon entering found her daughter staring out the window. "What's up, Jen?" she asked.

"It's my other mother, Mom. I think about her on my

birthday and I wonder if she's thinking about me. Do you suppose she remembers what day this is? Do you think she misses me?"

Though somewhat surprised by her daughter's questions, Mrs. Johnson reassured her. "Of course she remembers you; you were so important to her that she made a hard decision to let you go to another family who could love you and bring you up the way she wanted."

Jennifer seemed satisfied with this response, so Mrs. Johnson let it rest at that point even though she could see that Jennifer remained a little distracted for most of the day.

Birthdays are momentous events for most children. Pride, new freedom (for example, to stay up later and do more things without parental supervision), and increased status among their peers for being "more grown up" are some of the benefits that often accompany the birth anniversary. But for some adopted children, this is a day of intensely ambivalent feelings.

Put yourself in their place. What would this day mean to you if you had been adopted? Besides being a joyous occasion, it might be a powerful reminder that there is someone out there who gave birth to you and with whom you do not share this event. You could be acutely conscious that while other kids your age were celebrating a specific event about which they could learn all the details from the central characters in that drama, you were commemorating . . . what?

It's sometimes said that adopted children carry around with them a certain amount of sadness that birth children do not have. There may be an element of truth to this. It would not be unreasonable for some of them to have a sense of loss and incompleteness, because of a gap in their life history and because, in a sense, they were rejected. They are different from most other kids in an important way. And this is the day that, once a year, may dramatically confront them with this fact.

We do not mean to suggest that birthdays are melancholy affairs for all adopted kids. But it would certainly fall within the range of normal behavior if your adopted child had some mixed feelings about this day. *Where is the mother who gave me up?* she might be thinking. *What is she doing on this day? Is she thinking of me? Will she call?*

Adoptive parents should not diminish the importance of birthdays, since rituals and celebrations are important to everybody; and playing down your adopted child's birthday would single her out as different from her peers. Some adoptive parents, especially those who adopted older children, also supplement birthdays with another commemorative occasion: adoption day. This is the anniversary of the day your adopted child joined your family. It should never take the place of a birthday, but it's a special day your whole family can enjoy and be part of. In fact, some adoptive family support groups hold very moving candlelight celebrations each month to honor kids whose adoption anniversaries fall within that month.

FACTS OF LIFE

Alice walked into her children's bedroom and found her adopted son and daughter in bed together, touching each other's bodies. These were her first children, and Alice became deeply concerned that what they were doing was unnatural. She had heard that adopted children didn't develop incest taboos like everyone else. Now she became increasingly worried about leaving them alone together. In response to her anxiety, the children's behavior became more difficult.

We reassured Alice and her husband that kids were naturally curious about each other's bodies. What she had seen was not at all unusual with children close to one another in age, and that it had nothing whatsoever to do with adoption. We also told the parents that no research showed a likelihood that adoptees would engage in sex with their adoptive siblings.

Also unrelated to adoption, although sometimes mistakenly connected to it by parents, is the overly enthusiastic affection common to children of this age. Boys talk about marrying their mothers and girls act adorable with their fathers. A parent's misinterpretation of this normal stage of growth can lead to problems.

When Bill Roberts, a stockbroker, offered to read bedtime stories to his six-year-old adopted daughter, he wasn't quite prepared for the way she would cuddle up to him as she climbed on his lap. He was prepared even less for his response: an erection. The thought of discussing the incident with his wife gave him a chill. Preoccupied with what he assumed to be his unacceptable thoughts and feelings, Mr. Roberts began staying late at the office, channeling his anxieties into hard work. His wife felt confused about his attitude toward her and about the distant relationship that she perceived was developing between her daughter and her husband. That they had adopted because of her infertility made the whole situation seem even more painful. Before long, the Roberts had to seek counseling for their increasingly shaky marriage.

Had Mr. Roberts realized that flirtatious behavior by little girls with their fathers—and little boys' romancing of their mothers—is within the range of normal behavior for this stage of development, his family could have nipped this problem in the bud. Kids of this age may want to cuddle up in bed with you as well as sit on your lap. Aside from looking for affection and attention, they are also beginning to unselfconsciously mimic adult behavior.

Depending on the level of physical affection with which they're comfortable, parents' reactions to such conduct may vary from delight or amusement to fear that they are doing something wrong to provoke it. With a daughter, some people link this behavior to sexual irresponsibility they assume to have been part of the birth mother's traits if the child was born out of wedlock. They fear the same behavior is beginning to germinate in their daughter and that she may be a "bad seed." Fears of your child's origins coming home to roost are groundless—it just doesn't happen that way.

It is important if your child appears flirtatious to remember that such behavior is normal at this age. If you get ruffled and completely withdraw physically, your child will sense that something very disturbing has happened and you may begin to create a problem where none existed.

If you are uncomfortable with so much physical contact with your child as he or she grows older, gently move the child away. Substitute sitting next to her for holding her on your lap if this makes you more comfortable. Do it calmly and without alarm and your son or daughter will eventually accept these limits in the spirit in which you offer them.

Of course, there's the other side of the matter. If you enjoy extra attention from your kids (without, of course, actually encouraging seductiveness) you can just sit back and delight in being the apple of their eye, even if they occasionally overdo it.

Jill and Ron Melanick had three sons by birth. Ron recalls leaving for work every day with a " 'bye, Dad" from his sons and not much else. But when his adopted daughter reached the age of six, she made it clear that Daddy's departure was a terribly sad time, and his homecoming a signal for great demonstrativeness. Ron loved every minute of it.

DISCIPLINE AND LIMITS

Since your child is entering a period in which his interaction with people outside the family will increase significantly, it's important that he know and live up to the standards of conduct that you and others will require of him. Some adoptive parents have a bit of difficulty with this. They may still be unsure of how much "right" they have to discipline their child, since he was not born to them. They may also have heard that adopted kids, by nature, have low self-esteem, and they are thus wary of being too strict with their child for fear of giving him an "inferiority complex." And some adoptive parents, because they have worked so hard to get their child to love them as if they were his birth parents, fear that disciplining him could cost them that hard-earned love.

However, it is crucial that you come to terms with any ambivalence you may have at this time. If you tell him that he is doing something wrong and then don't follow up on it, your child will sense your ambivalence. Some parents convey their mixed feelings nonverbally. For example, a parent may laugh nervously while scolding his child, confusing her about the message he is trying to get across.

If you want to avoid fruitless power struggles in the years to come, be firm about standards of conduct now. Otherwise, before you know it, he will be too big to control physically, and you will have nothing to fall back on to help influence his behavior. Your child needs to feel confident that you know what you're doing. He requires standards at this age, so you need to impose them—unilaterally.

Avoid justifying your style of disciplining, since your child is still too young to do much abstract thinking. When you tell him what you're going to do and why you're going to do it, speak to him in short sentences. Say, for example, he stayed out late when you said he couldn't. You should say, "I want you to come home on time. As punishment, you can't go out to play tomorrow." Kids this age think very concretely and tend to obey older people, so it should not be too hard to establish your authority and respect for your rules in this way.

Most kids can behave reasonably well if they know what's expected of them and if the consequences for not behaving are clear, logical, and certain to follow misconduct. Emphasize consistency and fairness when you discipline. There is no single correct punishment for transgressions; most parents find that children of this age can accept any fair punishment. But keep it in proportion to what the child did wrong. For example, you wouldn't want to ground him for a month because he came in fifteen minutes late for dinner. One evening without TV is probably sufficient. Another reason to avoid excessive punishments is that they may require major inconvenience to yourself. You have to supervise—staying in, for example, to make sure that he stays in.

Remember that when you discipline you may hear some of the back talk that each adopted kid thinks he patented. Aside from the common "You're not my real mother" line, be prepared for something like, "Why did you adopt me if that's the way you feel about me?" Respond by saying that you will discuss adoption at another time, but right now you are dealing with the issue at hand and nothing else.

Sometimes families have so many rules that children can't tell what's really important. We saw one family in which an eight-year-old son seemed uncontrollable. After a few conversations with all concerned, however, we could see that the parents needed fewer, clearer rules if they wanted to develop their child's inherent ability to behave. To him, his parents seemed out of control, constantly making demands and criticizing and threatening punishment for all types of transgressions without any limits. To help the situation we asked his mother and father to pick out five rules that were important to them—for example, that their child get dressed for school promptly, keep his room neat, wash his hands after coming inside, etc.—thus helping them to create their priorities. Then we asked the boy to choose four out of the five that he could adhere to during the next week, which provided him with a sense of participation and control. They were to record each time he obeyed a rule rather than the times he broke them. It didn't work miracles, but it did enable them to start rebuilding a relationship of understanding and respect and to establish a basis for acceptable behavior.

Another issue that arises at this age is that kids try to stretch the limits you impose on them as they increase their demands for independence, such as, "Why can't I ride my bike past the corner? Betty's mother lets *her* do it!"

If you're not sure of where your restrictions stand vis-à-vis other parents, ask around. As a reality check, talk to other parents with children the same age as yours and see what sort of limits they set. You could also discuss the problem with members of an adoptive parents' support group. In addition to being a source of practical information, the parents will understand what you're feeling. And if, for some emotional or physical reason, you feel your child does need a little extra protectiveness for a while, give it to her and don't feel guilty about it.

OFF TO SCHOOL

In all likelihood, the transition from taking care of a preschooler or nursery school child to being the parent of a first grader will occur without a hitch, but don't be hard on yourself if it does give you a few jitters. (Nor should you worry if your child shows a little irritability, bed wetting, or cranky eating habits, which are not abnormal for this stage.) Giving up your child to the care and influence of strangers for a full day makes many parents—birth and adoptive—a little queasy, even though you probably share in your youngster's excitement over preparing for this big change in his or her life.

Adoptive parents may be somewhat more protective of their kids, viewing them as slightly more fragile than birth children. While it is natural to feel this way, try to keep from becoming overprotective both for your child's sake and your own. She needs to start the arduous task of making her way in the world, and you must begin the equally difficult job of letting go.

For some children, the prospect of going to school all day and separating from their mothers for that long is a difficult one. Your child may cling to you, implore you not to put him through the ordeal, cry, promise you he will be good, or imply that forcing him to go will harm him irreparably. If this behavior does not abate, discuss it with your child's teacher. Your son or daughter may need a smaller class or different kind of school for a while.

Most children don't have this hard a time, but if your child does, try to find out if adoption is involved. Perhaps someone has said something hurtful to her about her being adopted. Maybe other children have asked her about adoption and she's having a hard time explaining it to them without you there to help her. Or being away all day at school could be triggering some sad feelings about her birth parents that your child has yet to master. If the problem is adoption-related, it's still important that she know you can protect and comfort her at school by talking to her teacher about the difficulty.

Address your child's fears as he communicates them. For example, he may fear that the other kids or the teacher won't like him, that he won't be able to do the work, or that the school is too far away. He may even say that he needs a nap and a full day of school makes him too tired, or that there are too many kids in the class and they are too noisy. What he's really saying is that he fears the unknown and that it's the first time he's ever been somewhere for so much time where there's no one who loves him more than anything else in the world.

Assure him that you understand what he is feeling and that there are other kids who are probably feeling the same way. Talk to him lovingly but firmly, making it clear that he will have to go to school and will soon get used to being there all day, but will suffer no diminution of your love in the process. Explain to him that going to school is his "job," just like going to work every day is your job or that of your spouse. Point out that this is a difficult experience at first and that he will soon be able to handle it more comfortably.

Many schools allow parents to spend part of the first few school days with their child so that he may gradually acclimate himself to the fact of separation. If your child's school does not do this as a practice, you could ask for permission to be there at the beginning, maybe in the hallway rather than in the classroom. The drawback is that adopted children already have to deal with the fact of being different; if yours is the only kid whose parent has to tag along, you may set up a more difficult situation for him. You might try pointing out the possibility that other kids may make fun of him if he needs you with him (although you should make sure he realizes that you're not making fun of him). Kids at this age will do almost anything not to stand out in this way.

Should your youngster have a real problem with this separation, and if his birthday is near the cutoff for your school district, you may be able to keep him back in half-day kindergarten for an extra year. But don't opt for this too quickly, since it will separate him from kids his age who live nearby. Before you decide on this option, consult with school personnel about their experience with children who adjust to a full day of school more slowly. They may suggest a gradual process of building up to a full day for him.

If you do choose to keep him in kindergarten again, use the year to get him gradually involved in some kind of socializing activity in the afternoon and a full day of camp in summer.

TO TELL OR
NOT TO TELL THE TEACHER

Many parents wonder if it's a good idea to tell the teacher of their child's adoption. You could wait to talk to the teacher when your child starts school, hoping to get a good sense of her attitudes and character from conversations with her and from what you have been told about her by other parents. While talking to her, try to see how she regards people who are different—those who have disabilities, for example. Consulting other adoptive parents familiar with the school beforehand would be an even better way of coming to a decision. If you've met other adoptive parents who have children in the school, try to find out what they know about your child's present teacher and others she may get in the future. If you're a member of an adoptive parents' support group, seek out parents in your group who know something about your child's school and learn all you can. You will probably turn up some useful information.

The advantage of confiding in the teacher is that you can freely discuss with her or him any adoption-related problems that arise at school. For example, while it will not necessarily happen, your child could have a dispute with another pupil who taunts him with something like: "At least *I* know who my *real* mother is." If you informed the teacher of your child's adoption and she knew your feelings in the matter, she could handle such incidents as you would.

Still another reason to familiarize the teacher with your child's adoption is that you can talk to her about potential difficulties your child may have with the curriculum. A prime example is the "family tree" that third-graders often have to draw. For your adopted child, who should occupy the branches? Does she need two trees? Will hers look like an alien organism when compared with what her classmates draw? Does this project make any sense for her?

You and the teacher might have to do some intensive brainstorming to come up with a creative solution to complications like these—and you can only do it if you both understand what's involved.

If you feel comfortable letting school authorities know that you adopted your child, try to get him into a class with at least one other adopted kid, since that will take some of the edge off the important "difference" in his life. Even schools that ordinarily assign pupils to a class at random may honor your special request if you convince them that it would ultimately enhance your child's ability to adjust to school and his classmates.

BEHAVIOR IN SCHOOL

It's important that her teacher find your child's behavior acceptable. This is probably the first major encounter your youngster has had with any adult outside the family who she has to impress but who doesn't have to like her. Thus this interaction serves as a model for much of your child's future social activities. Also, a teacher's attitude toward her pupil colors the way she treats the child, which in turn will affect the youngster's chances of succeeding in school.

Influential factors here include your child's appearance—neat dress and haircut—her manners, her ability to listen to and follow instructions, and, in general, to play by the teacher's rules. Teachers are only human and do not like all kids equally, so it behooves your child, within limits, to learn how to get along with this important adult.

While attitudes are changing, if your child misbehaves in class you still may have to deal with teachers, guidance counselors, and psychologists who have prejudices about adoption or lack knowledge of the subject. For instance, in response to your son's cutting up in class, and with his adoption in mind, the school psychologist may say that your son has low self-esteem, a poor self-concept, or poor impulse control, or that he's hyperactive. But just as a person is not necessarily depressed because they are feeling sad, your child is not by definition any of these disturbing sounding things simply because he's a little rambunctious.

"Hyperactivity" is a typical behavioral problem that arises in the first grade: the teacher thinks your child simply can't sit still and pay attention for long enough periods of time. But one person's hyperactivity is another's liveliness and curiosity. It's not natural for a child this age to want to sit still and focus on something dictated by an adult he barely knows, especially when the process is new to him. After all, until now he has spent much of his young life running around, and it's hardly realistic to expect him to turn on a dime.

Such diagnoses, often considerably less scientific than they sound, may reflect the teacher's and guidance counselor's personalities more than your child's behavior. This is particularly true for adopted children. Because of the stigma attached to adoption, teachers are often as likely as others to blame adoption for behavior they find difficult to control in the classroom. In one study, teachers asked which kids in their class were hyperactive described 43 percent of the boys in the room that way. On the other hand, your child could end up in a class with many passive kids, thus appearing "hyperactive" or overactive by contrast.

We have seen so-called "hyperactive" children in our office who sit in their chairs and pay attention, leading us to conclude that somebody must be over-diagnosing their "condition." If your child is so labelled, speak to the teacher or school psychologist about it and insist that they specify the behavior on which they based their evaluation. If your child is overactive only at certain times or in certain places such as school, the overactivity is more likely to be due to stress or immaturity, both of which you can help him with. Ask them to define what's normal for kids this age in terms of getting up and walking around the classroom. This will help you and your child to set limits and to work for more self-control and a successful adaptation to the school's norms.

Even if her teacher errs on the side of too much self-control, your child will have to meet her standards in order to succeed in that class, unless you put her in a more progressive school.

Joanne, a second-grader, had been labelled disturbed because she was getting up from her seat and walking around too much in the classroom. We asked her to keep a diary (she loved to write and draw pictures), paying special attention to those times she was able to control her behavior. She soon noticed that she was able to control herself most of the time. She was already doing it. She just needed to do more of it. Joanne's mother told her daughter's teacher about this activity, encouraging her to expect positive changes in

Joanne's behavior. With the girl's efforts and her teacher's positive attitude, Joanne soon adapted to her school's standards of decorum. You could try the same technique if your child is having this kind of problem.

A small percentage of children—adopted and birth—do have acute behavioral or social adjustment difficulties at school. Jenny, for example, was by nature a shy child and had considerable trouble establishing relationships with the other pupils in her class. While her peers were beginning to engage in after-school activities with their classmates, she remained a loner. In fact, the occasional interaction she did have with the other children tended to be in the form of unpleasant confrontations.

What Jenny was experiencing may have been partly adoption-related. Adopted kids, if they are in the common position of being the first or only child in their family, have grown up primarily in a world of adults. They would naturally have to work harder to establish peer relationships, since at this age they have had less practice with them. But this is also true for biological children who are first or only children. Jenny's parents dealt with their daughter's social awkwardness by inviting a neighbor's child Jenny's age over for several minutes every few days, gradually increasing the time the children were together and gently intervening when it seemed that the friendship they had hoped for was in danger of foundering. Over time this technique worked, and Jenny was able to begin making her first tentative moves toward friendship with other kids, first with one child, then with two at a time, and then with a larger group of children.

If your child has behavioral problems in school, it is best not to act too quickly if school guidance personnel suggest individual psychotherapy as the solution. Some practitioners will zero in on adoption as the root of her problems, which isn't very useful as it is a fact that can't be changed. We suggest that you first speak to the teacher and family and friends about practical, limited ways of dealing with the difficulty. Then check with an adoptive parents' group. If none of what you try works and you and your child do seem to have a legitimate problem, search for a family therapist who understands how members of families can interact to resolve problems and who will help you to find solutions for the immediate difficulty at hand, rather than attribute everything to adoption.

LEARNING DIFFICULTIES

While there are such things as learning disabilities, a more common phenomenon is often mistaken for them. Some kids, because of their temperament, just take longer than others to pick up basic learning skills. They achieve educational milestones at a later age, the tendency for which may be inherited. But this is a matter of tempo— nothing more. It does not reflect on their intelligence or foreshadow any future inability to learn.

Like temperament, varying styles of thinking can also mislead parents into thinking that their child has a learning problem. Bob and Sheila Worth have encountered this phenomenon with Harry, their adopted nine-year-old son. Bob, a school principal, and Sheila, a CPA whose score on her certifying exam was one of the highest in the country, have expressed some concern about Harry's B's and C's in school. Given their talents and background and the A's that their two younger birth daughters consistently earn, they find it hard to see why Harry doesn't do better.

But Harry literally sees things another way. At this stage he shows more of a flair for drawing than for words. His style of learning differs from his parents' and sisters'. While it is still too early to know if his affinity for art will mature into real talent, clearly he marches to the beat of a different drummer, and his individuality is not a cause for concern.

We each tend to perceive the outside world with a little more emphasis on seeing, hearing, intellectualizing, or feelings than others might. We all have a little bit of each of these four major styles, but lean more toward one. Anyone can have a child who takes in the world differently than they do, but the odds of this happening may be greater with adoptive parents, since genetics may play a role in determining a child's predominant style.

Parents often come into conflict with their adopted and birth children who may have different cognitive styles—ways of understanding things. A couple who value high intellectual achievement and who find it easy to conceptualize when dealing with problems may feel frustrated with a child who spends little time reading and is indifferent to the pursuit of high grades, even though he's willing to devote several hours a day to socializing with friends. His largely intuitive approach to navigating past the pitfalls of life is also likely to be disconcerting. It can be even more annoying when his siblings manifest a style with which their parents are more comfortable.

If you find this happening with your adopted child, first remind yourself that there's more than one way to interact with the world. Then enjoy it, because your child is going to be his own person no matter what you do, and his differences from you and your spouse—and possibly from his siblings—on this account can enrich your family life.

On a mundane and very practical level, pick up cues from him when misunderstandings arise. For example, if you tell him to do something and then ask, "Do you hear what I'm saying?" and you get a halfhearted response, it could be that you're trying to get a visually oriented person to respond to an auditory metaphor. Listen to the way he talks. For example, if he frequently uses the word see, you can assume that he thinks visually. If you know he's visually oriented, say instead, "Do you see what I mean?" or "Let me show you how I want you to do it." Believe it or not, cognitive styles actually operate on this level and you'll have a better chance of making your point.

If you have more than one child, it's easy to fall into the trap of using the style most often used by the kids stylistically closest to you. Make an effort to relate to each child using the style, expressions, and imagery with which he or she is comfortable.

REAL LEARNING DISABILITIES

Misunderstanding aside, there *are* such things as learning disabilities. What's more, adopted children, according to one study, seem to have them in a slightly higher proportion than children raised by their biological parents—roughly 20 percent of adopted boys (it occurs in boys much more often than in girls) as opposed to about 10 percent of birth kids. What's the reason for this? We don't know for sure, although with adopted children it may have something to do with the birth mother's high anxiety during her pregnancy, poor nutrition, drug and alcohol use, or poor hospital care at birth.

Learning disabilities include dyslexia, audio perception problems, language-based difficulties (in which the child has trouble expressing what he thinks or interpreting what he hears), and short attention spans. Dyslexia, for example, is a disability that may affect speaking, reading, and spelling. The child may read from right to left, have trouble telling a d from a b, and, therefore, find it hard to concentrate.

The odds are that your child has none of these disabilities, or will learn or can be taught to compensate for minor ones. A diagnosis of a learning disability could be more indicative of poor teaching, many unruly kids in the class, or an overcrowded classroom. You might also be hearing the familiar overreaction to any learning difficulty—no matter how slight or brief—involving an adopted child. Even if the teacher or guidance counselor cites examples to show you how the disability has manifested itself in your child's work, you should retain some healthy skepticism. But don't ignore it, because your child could become demoralized by how difficult his work can be for him.

The school will probably suggest a series of tests. To

take them, your child may have to travel to the nearest regional medical center and be tested by strangers, which could intimidate him and affect his performance on the tests. Or he might just be having a bad day when he takes the tests. Don't hesitate to have him tested privately to give you a second opinion in the matter. For information about where to have him tested, call the local chapter of the Association for Children with Learning Disabilities. If you can't locate it, send a self-addressed, stamped envelope to the Association for Children with Learning Disabilities, 4156 Library Road, Pittsburgh, Pennsylvania 15234.

What if he does have a learning disability? Sometimes learning difficulties are not related to overall lowered intellectual functioning, a worry that frequently plagues adoptive parents. They can be compensated for. Albert Einstein, for example, was late in learning to speak and may have had dyslexia. Leonardo da Vinci, another well-known genius, probably had the same condition. You can take specific action to deal with learning disabilities. Your child will probably need supplemental instruction (or a different school) in a class with a low teacher-to-student ratio. The Association for Children with Learning Disabilities can provide you with information about where to find such instruction.

In other cases these learning difficulties are associated with lower measured intelligence. Special schooling may be required to enable your child to achieve his full potential as well as maintain his self-esteem.

QUESTIONS AND ANSWERS

My eight-year-old, who's usually talkative and open with me, has been much more secretive lately. I have a feeling that he's been thinking about his birth mother. What should I do?

There are times when adopted children do think about their birth parents, and they are often hesitant to share these thoughts with their adoptive parents. If you sense this is happening, make it clear to your child that you are receptive to a conversation about his biological parents, but don't push the matter. You could introduce your child to books about adoption, or attend a family event at an adoptive parents' group as a way of stimulating a discussion.

Adopted children are often more curious about their birth mothers than their birth fathers. There is a simple reason for this. Adoptive parents usually know more about their child's birth mother, and can give more information about her to the child.

Birth fathers have rarely been involved in the decision to place an infant for adoption for a variety of reasons. Most babies surrendered for adoption are born to unmarried women. Married fathers always had clear rights concerning the surrender of a child for adoption. Only recently have unmarried fathers been given rights related to the adoption of their babies. In some cases fathers didn't even know that a baby had been conceived. In others they denied paternity in an effort to avoid responsibility for the mother and infant. It is also much less expensive and time consuming to an agency and attorney if the mother states that she does not know who the father of her baby is when she gives the baby up for adoption. Otherwise the father would have to be consulted which would cost time and money. He might also, if consulted, decide against adoption. For these reasons most adoptions occur with little real knowledge of who the birth father is.

☐

I overheard my son telling his friend that his "real" father was a famous baseball player. I happen to know that his birth father was a high school dropout who was successful at very few things, and baseball was not among them. Should I tell him what I know, or just let him think what he wants to think?

It's common for adopted children to idealize their birth parents (as well as any parents) at this stage. It's their way of coming to terms, over time, with the fact that they know little about these people. So let him tell the story the way he wants to—for now. You could speak to him *alone* and assure him that his birth father has many positive qualities because you can see them reflected in your son, but it isn't likely that being a famous baseball player is one of them. It will only be a problem if he can't let go of the fantasy as he grows older.

☐

I'm very concerned because I keep catching my son in lies. When I ask him a direct question, he will frequently lie to keep from getting into trouble. I've tried punishing him, but nothing—taking his bike away, not letting him watch TV, etc.—seems to work. I ask him why he's lying, but he won't tell me.

Most children do lie a little; if you follow the lie with punishment you can usually make the point that this is unacceptable behavior. Clearly, you need a different approach. In our experience, a child can't say why he's been lying, so it's best not to pursue that course. Also, it's usually not a good method to ask your child questions for which you already have the answers; when you do this you're just setting yourself up for a disappointment when you don't get the truth. Instead, tell him that you already know what he did and discuss that; don't give him the opportunity to lie his way out of it. It's also helpful to look at times when your child might have lied but didn't; point them out to him and commend him for them each time they occur, to further reinforce the fact that he is already truthful, he just needs to be truthful more often.

☐

After a difficult beginning in first grade, my daughter is finally going to school without a fuss. However, the teacher tells me that she is not socializing well with the other children. I'm worried that she would still prefer to be home with me.

She could still be adjusting to school, which for some kids takes a while. If this persists beyond the middle of the year, she may need a different kind of school with a higher ratio of teachers to children to help her with this difficulty.

□

We believe that it's particularly important that our adopted daughter feel accepted at school. However, she has a teacher who seems unusually strict and overly critical of her. What should we do?

One thing children have to learn as they grow up is how to survive all kinds of teaching. You could turn this apparent adversity into a positive experience by helping your daughter to devise a strategy for getting along with her teacher while acknowledging that this person may very well be unpleasant. To help your child, get her to record each time she interacts with her teacher when the teacher is not being awful. Your daughter could also watch what the other kids do to get the teacher to respond positively to them. Have her pay attention to what she or another child are doing to make this interaction positive. When she can pinpoint what works, she will feel more in control of the situation.

If the conflict between your daughter and her teacher seems to be getting out of hand, ask for a conference with the teacher and a guidance counselor or the principal. (We have been told by people who have had this experience that schools respond more readily to parents if the father as well as the mother comes to school. While this is not how we would like it to be, it is nevertheless the reality.) Should that not work, try to get the principal to transfer your child to a different class. Aside from dealing with the problem of an excessively strict teacher, this would also help keep your daughter from getting an undeserved reputation as a troublesome child, a tag that she could find hard to get rid of as she proceeds from grade to grade.

□

Having learned that our adopted son has some learning disabilities, I'm wondering how to talk about this with members of our extended family—especially my brother-

in-law, who thought adoption was not a good idea in the first place and who will now probably say, "I told you so."

Is it necessary to discuss this with your brother-in-law or other relatives? If your child needs extra tutoring, how likely is it that they will know? It is not uncommon for parents who have children with learning disabilities, whether adopted or not, to have a difficult time trying to help relatives understand these difficulties. Learning-disabled children often complain that they have been called stupid and lazy, even by their teachers. There are a number of organizations that you can contact for assistance with the many issues that you will be facing, such as adequate diagnosis, finding an appropriate educational program, and dealing with some of the family issues. The first is the Mayo Clinic, 200 First Street, S.W., Rochester, Minn. 55905 (507) 284-2511. This is ideal for families who want a complete evaluation by a number of specialists under one roof. They will confer with one another and report their comprehensive findings to you. Another is the Association for Children and Adults with Learning Disabilities mentioned previously: 4156 Library Road, Pittsburgh, Pennsylvania 15234 (412) 240-1515. A national association with local chapters, membership is open to parents and professionals. Information on educational programs and support systems for families is available from local chapters. Two other organizations that could be helpful are the Foundation for Children with Learning Disabilities, 99 Park Avenue, New York, New York 10016, and the Churchill Center, 22 East 95th Street, New York, New York 10130. Remember most learning-disabled children are not adopted and most adopted children aren't learning disabled. Resources for Children with Special Needs is an organization that can recommend schools, camps, and other activities to parents who have children with a wide range of physical, emotional, and developmental handicaps. They are located at 200 Park Avenue South, Suite 816, New York, New York 10003.

5
Ages Nine to Twelve

Welcome to the age of divergence. Children between nine and twelve years old mature physically and emotionally at widely dissimilar rates. Differences between the academic progress of your son or daughter and his or her friends may also become evident. It's also likely that your child's activities will coincide less and less with yours and, if you're married, your spouse's, as your youngster's relationships with his or her peers take on greater importance.

At this stage, each child begins to come into her own. Her physical, mental, and emotional maturation make her stand out as an individual, separate from her parents. Her skills, talents, and idiosyncrasies become clearer to outsiders as well as family members. By the age of twelve, aware of this budding maturity, she will begin to move toward a greater autonomy.

Birth parents can often predict with some accuracy certain aspects of their offspring's likely physical characteristics, maturation rates, and intellectual or artistic tendencies. For some adoptive parents, however, this drama can resemble watching a mystery movie where you feel as if you have few clues about how it will turn out. Yet it's just that mystery that can make being an adoptive parent interesting as you watch your child develop talents and skills you might not have yourself.

For any parent who worries about how close his or her adolescent's development approaches the "norm," this can be a complicated time. Your child can be "too short," "too tall," "too developed" (or "undeveloped"), or "too babyish"—and yet still fall within the broad range of normal for her age.

School becomes more of a challenge in this period. Students, having acquired basic skills, begin to deal with substantive subjects. Now the school can identify "underachievers" and start putting bright kids on the fast track to academic success. Families oriented toward high achievement may find this particularly trying if their adopted child does not show the same level of interest or ability in academics.

It's important to maintain some perspective on your child's performance in school. If his grades are not what you think they should be, is it perhaps because he is more mechanically or artistically than academically inclined? Find out from the school if your child is performing up to capacity. If he's not, you can get tutoring for him or help him with his homework yourself. If he is doing all he can, make sure you convey to him your pride in his motivation and accomplishments even if they don't match your aspirations. In fact, work on obliterating any sense of disappointment by remembering that each child has different—not inferior—capabilities.

Preadolescents also begin to move out of the family's orbit. Friendships, hanging out, music lessons, scouts, 4-H, dance classes, and organized athletics take up more of their time. They may begin to read more—girls often love biographies at this age—and daydream. This is also the age of the true friendship, when same-sex pals share confidences, hang out together, and form cliques which, unfortunately, can sometimes lead to the exclusion of others.

THINKING ABOUT ADOPTION

Your child now realizes even more clearly than he did when he was younger that he has two sets of parents. Yet, believe it or not, in spite of the conversations about adoption you may have had with him, he is still quite likely to have some doubts about his permanent status as a member of your family because most kids under the age of fifteen can't fully grasp the complex principles that underscore the legal process that has terminated the relationship between him and his birth parents and created a legal bond between him and you.

Nightmares or fantasies about his birth mother returning to reclaim him are still possible and within the range of what is normal. If you encounter this phenomenon, let him know that other adoptees have this fear, too. Remind your child that you love him, that he is yours forever, and that someday he will be able to fully understand the laws that make this so. Show him the adoption decree or certificate of adoption which says that he is your legal child.

More likely, your child will express increased interest about her birth parents. For example, she may want more information about what they look like, what they like to do, what talents they have. She may also want to know about the size and makeup of her birth family, especially whether she has birth brothers and sisters and who they live with.

In this period of renewed interest, your protestations that you don't know more than a few bare facts about her background may no longer satisfy her. To respond to her curiosity, you might try going back to the adoption agency to learn more about her birth parents. Sometimes, parents forget some of the information they did get from the agency in the excitement of finally receiving their child. However, since rules and regulations have loosened in the last five or ten years, you may discover that the agency can now tell you more than they could at the time of the adoption. So this may be the ideal time to do some more investigating of your child's background.

If you haven't discussed adoption with your child for a while, this might be a good time to bring it up again. For example, you could give her *How It Feels to Be Adopted* by Jill Krementz (Knopf), to read. It's a collection of thoughts about adoption by teenage adoptees, written in the kind of honest language with which kids are comfortable.

STIRRINGS OF REBELLION

Just after his tenth birthday, Jeremy announced that he would no longer wash the dishes, make his bed, or do any other "women's work."

Mr. and Mrs. Anderson, who equally shared household responsibilities, were taken aback since they saw themselves as good role models for their adopted son. Though they suspected that Jeremy's attitude was the result of the influence of a new friend, they did not challenge Jeremy's right to his views but rather told him that as a member of their family he was expected to do his chores. Jeremy said nothing.

Over the next two days Jeremy did his chores, though he grumbled a bit. His parents chose to ignore his comments and instead complimented him on how well he was fulfilling his responsibilities.

On the third day, Jeremy refused to make his bed. His parents simply reminded him that this was one of his tasks and said no more about it.

When Jeremy came home that evening, he found that his favorite video game was missing. When he asked where it was, his parents told him that because he had not lived up to his responsibilities they had removed it.

The next day, Jeremy made his bed and his parents returned his video game. This pattern of Jeremy refusing to do a task of his was repeated every few days for nearly a month, with each test followed by a consequence. By the end of the month, Jeremy's behavior was clearly improving and the discussion of what is or is not "women's work" was put to rest.

Parents of children this age may justifiably feel that their youngsters are testing them. Children may begin to come home late from play or from organized group activities. They might also talk back or act up in school, especially as they approach adolescence. It is even within the realm of normality to see one or two instances of petty theft at this stage.

Adopted boys, some research has shown, tend to temporarily act up a bit around the age of eleven, and it's possible that an incident or two of stealing could be one way a boy misbehaves. Perhaps this is how he is trying to master his feelings of sadness or anger over being adopted. But no research has pointed to theft as a characteristic of adoptees.

Adoptive parents may doubt their "right" to discipline their child or feel incompetent because the youngster might have "inherited" bad behavior traits, making it "useless" to even try to get the child to behave. If they feel that way they are not likely to be clear and firm when the child does something wrong.

What should you do if your child steals? This has no more significance than any other kind of misbehavior unless it becomes chronic, and it's important not to overreact. Remember, this testing of the limits indicates that your child wants you to reestablish the kinds of limits and boundaries that will make him feel safe and secure. Let him know the rules. And make sure he understands that there are consequences for breaking them.

If petty theft starts to become a pattern, make sure your child understands the significance of what he's doing. Probably the best way to do that would be to make him return what he stole and apologize to the storekeeper. If he continues to steal, you may need some help. Family therapists are especially good at nipping this in the bud.

Life at this age can sometimes resemble a battle for control between parent and child. The battleground can vary from slowness in getting dressed that delays the child's departure for school to an overt challenge of your right to impose discipline. Kids who pose problems in this area are trying to find their limits. Should they gain the control they ostensibly want, they will not feel that the adults around them can take care of them. The best thing you can do for them here is to make sure those behavioral limits are present and well-defined so they can develop a sense of themselves through the boundaries you create for them.

For those rules which are absolute for you, this is not the time for ambiguity. If you've been a little tentative—perhaps a little less demanding of good behavior because your son or daughter was not born to you—it's important to get it straight in your own mind that you have a right and obligation to set behavioral standards and, if necessary, to punish.

The consequences of misbehavior do not have to be dire, just consistent. If you still hear lines like "My real mother wouldn't punish me this way," tell your child that while you have no idea what his birth mother would have done in similar circumstances, you've decided that this is best for him. Don't allow your child to bully you, and make sure that he or she can't play one parent off against the other. In fact, if your youngster has been behaving especially bad lately, look into the possibility that you and your spouse might be undercutting each other, with one parent criticizing behavior that the other is in some manner por- traying as cute either overtly or covertly; or perhaps one of you is giving permission for something that the other has banned. If you are a two-parent family, it is important that you function as much like a team as possible when it comes to setting clear limits on your child's behavior.

On the other hand, it's also important that you confirm your child's growing sense that you are not omniscient. It's always good for children to understand that their parents can make mistakes, and to expect an apology from these all-important adults when it's appropriate. If the adults they love and respect act that way, kids will grow up to do the same. Acknowledge that you've made an error and learned from it, as all people do from time to time.

By the time your child approaches adolescence—at the end of this age range—he will begin to realize that not all rules are absolute. He will see that different families have different ways of doing things, and may insist on an explanation and justification when you lay down the law as you see it. As he matures, acknowledge the points he makes when they're legitimate, and let him begin to play a role in negotiating behavioral limits that are not absolute. Possible activities now open to negotiation would include the hour at which he must come in from play, whether he can use public transportation by himself, and whether he can spend less time doing homework if he finishes his assignments accurately and quickly.

To the difficulties that some families have with disciplining, adoption can add a few extra twists. Fred Larkin couldn't understand what was happening between himself and his son; their relationship was degenerating into one of constant confrontation. It was especially painful to Fred because through his son's eleventh year, they got along so well. For his part, Bill complained that his father was picking on him, singling him out for constant criticism while his younger brother, a birth child, "got away with it."

To an outside observer, something besides the normal tensions between preadolescents and parents had clearly arisen in the Larkin family: their twelve-year-old's height. Bill was a slim but towering five feet nine inches in a family characterized by men of short stature. Fred Larkin, at five feet six inches, felt a little uncomfortable with his young upstart. He had not expected to have such a tall boy. Never totally sure of his authority over his adopted son, the height disparity between the two had put him on edge, aggravating whatever conflicts they might have had. Once aware of his feelings, Fred was able to see Bill's behavior in perspective and respond to it appropriately.

Sometimes an adopted child's good looks or superior

intelligence can cause her parents to have uncomfortable feelings toward her. As well as pride, an uneasiness could result, and this, too, could affect the way they discipline their child. They may be harsh with a child who is making them feel inferior by contrast.

On the other hand, adopted children sometimes get away with behavior that would bring down parental wrath on birth children. Biological children, of course, resent this patently unequal treatment. But adopted kids don't like it either, since it reinforces their sense that they are different. In fact, when we asked a large number of adopted children what advice they would give to adoptive parents on raising their kids, the adoptees all responded that they should treat the adopted children the same way parents treated their biological children.

At times, of course, differences in age, gender, and temperament may make it necessary to treat a child differently from her brothers or sisters. But on the whole, fair treatment should be your aim. How can you tell if you're treating each of your children fairly? It's not easy; you might think you're doing it when, in fact, you're not.

Janet Wilson thought Joe, her adopted son, was taking advantage of her. He rarely did his chores when he was supposed to and usually had to be reminded before he would start them. Joe said that she demanded more of him than his brother Frank. To help clarify this disagreement we asked Mr. and Mrs. Wilson to keep a chart for a week of all activity related to chores in the family.

One week later, Mrs. Wilson had graphic evidence that her perception of what was going on did not match the reality of her family pattern. She and her husband permitted the intellectual, bookish Frank to forego some of his chores if he was in his room reading, while they made Joe, who liked to spend his free time outside playing with his friends, more consistently fulfill his family obligations. The Wilsons were more likely to favor their birth son because his inclinations matched their own, while they saw their adopted son's activities as frivolous and not sufficient to excuse him from raking leaves or changing the cat's litter.

If you think that you might have a similar problem, first ask your children if you treat them fairly. If they don't think that you do, try keeping a record, like the Wilsons', of how you treat each child. Beyond that you could ask friends and relatives if they think you're even-handed when it comes to your treatment of your children. Outsiders can sometimes see things more clearly.

DIFFERENCES IN INTERESTS

Now that your adopted child is getting old enough to share some of your interests and activities—hobbies and sports, for example—it can be frustrating to discover a divergence over what you and he like to do with spare time. The Robinsons were having a great deal of trouble with this dilemma. Mr. Robinson, a computer consultant, liked nothing better than to take a busman's holiday after work and tinker with his home computer. Mrs. Robinson taught art and loved to paint whenever she could make time for it at home. Their eldest adopted son took after his parents and his favorite activity was simply to read. But their ten-year-old adopted son came out of a different mold. He wanted attention and action. He liked games and outdoor sports.

This is the sort of thing that could have developed into a real problem, alienating the youngest child from the rest of the family. But instead they decided to meet their younger boy halfway. The Robinsons found some active pastimes that everybody could enjoy together at least once in a while, and Mr. Robinson discovered that he could blend his interests with his son's proclivities by playing video games with him. They also spent enough time exploring what their youngest son liked to do to discover some quiet activities— playing Monopoly and card games—that would engage him.

Normality, of course, is not at issue here. What's

"normal" in terms of interests and talents varies with a person's temperament. When these tendencies clash within a family, as they well might in an adoptive family, there are usually specific and uncomplicated solutions that parents and children can work out together. That could be something as simple as encouraging an athletically inclined youngster to sign up for a supervised program at the Y or for an after-school gymnastics club so he can work off steam and do the things he likes to do and then be ready to participate in more sedate activities. If you have younger children, consider hiring a young, energetic baby sitter. This could give you the chance to pursue your own interests without always having to go along with the activities your child favors; you could continue allocating some periods of time to joint activities, and he could still have plenty of opportunity to engage in activities which suit him best.

OSTRACIZED

We're coming to an age that can be a danger zone for any child who is different. Children are now verbal enough to wound with their words but not yet old enough to appreciate the full impact that their words can have on others. Furthermore, they are in the clique-forming stage; and what good is a clique if you can't find somebody different from you to exclude?

Nevertheless, parents need to bear in mind that the ostracizing of a child is not always as simple as it may appear. Group dynamics can get complicated; sometimes a scapegoat plays a role in his own isolation. If your child comes home from school and tearfully relates how he approached a group of boys, asked that they include him in their games, and then was told to "get lost, we don't play with adopted kids," there may be more to it than that—especially if it happens more than once. Kids are usually not singled out just because they're adopted, although you can't discount the possibility that prejudice about adoption could be motivating some children. The kids who are excluding your child are more likely to be using adoption-related taunts and epithets when some other and more basic conflict is actually causing trouble.

Try to find out why the other kids won't accept your child. Get as much information as you can from your youngster about the background of the conflict. What's the history of his relationship with these kids? Exactly what did he and they say this time? What happened just before the incident? Perhaps he could talk to someone close to both him and them, maybe a teacher, to get an objective opinion about what occurred.

Some of the characteristics and behavior that may alienate kids this age are extreme silliness and immaturity, lying, exaggerating, sarcasm, bullying, buttering up the teacher or acting like a know-it-all, and snitching to the teacher on what other pupils have done.

Since you can't be with your child all the time to protect him against this kind of pain, it's very important that you help him to develop a workable problem-solving technique he can use to deal with or, better yet, to prevent such incidents in the future. For example, ask him to focus on how he gets along with these kids when there is no conflict—the times he's asked them to let him play and they said yes. How did he get them to let him into their games? What did he do differently and how can he do more of it?

Some kids gain acceptance by zeroing in on the things they have in common with others, such as following the exploits of a local sports team. Sometimes a child needs coaching on a particular sports skill that will impress the other kids. If it's your son who's having these difficulties, make sure his father gets involved in helping him work his way out of trouble, since fathers can often relate more easily to the ways boys of this age interact socially.

If the other kids know that they're getting to your child, they may step up their efforts. A sense of humor, on the other hand, will often deflate ribbing before it turns ugly.

The idea is to concentrate on those interests and skills that will earn him acceptance from his peers or at least blunt differences when they arise.

You can pursue other courses of action if a persistent problem develops and your child seems stuck in his isolation. If the situation requires it—and if it doesn't make you or your child uncomfortable—you could sign him up for karate lessons. These would help him to focus on self-protection and building up his self-confidence, not on revenge. Encourage him to look for other friends. If he attends a large school he can almost certainly find groups of kids with interests and temperaments close to his. If you're not part of an adoptive parents' support group, you might join (or rejoin) one, so he can meet other adopted kids his age.

Throughout this trying time, make sure your child knows that you're sorry this is happening to him and that you don't like it one bit. Echo the painful feelings he describes. For example, if he says, "I feel so lonely," reply with, "Yes, I can hear that you feel very lonely." But try to keep the emphasis on what he can do to change the position he's in. Stress problem solving over self-pity. P.E.T. (Parent Effectiveness Training) by Dr. Thomas Gordon (New American Library) offers good examples of this style of reflective listening and problem solving.

SUMMER CAMP

Many children in this age group go away to camp for the first time. For you, it may trigger thoughts of the time, not so far distant, when your youngster will go off to college or go to work and leave your home for good. But your child will probably be focusing exclusively on the separation at hand. Most kids experience some trauma when going off to camp for the first time. An adoptee is not likely to manifest anything different from her peers, although there's always the possibility that you will see something a little out of the ordinary.

As the end of June approached, Marsha Goldstein thought her adopted daughter, Cindy, wasn't going to make it to the camp bus. Although the idea of going away to camp had excited Cindy—who had, in fact, asked to go—the closer the big day came, the more anxious she got. She began to interpret her mother's willingness to let her go as a sign that she was no longer wanted by her family.

Mrs. Goldstein helped Cindy deal with her fears by first listening to them. She agreed with her daughter that going to camp for the first time is scary for all children, and she told her that even kids who have gone to camp before sometimes get scared when that first day rolls around again. She also pointed out that many kids get homesick and that the camp staff knows how to help children feel better when they get the away-from-home blues. And Cindy's mother reminded her that she would already know some of the other girls at the camp because they came from her neighborhood.

Finally, Mrs. Goldstein, knowing that homesickness usually runs its course in about two weeks, got Cindy to agree to try camp for at least that long with the guarantee that if she needed to come home early, her mother would come and get her. Aware of the possibility that her daughter's adopted status could influence the fantasies that Cindy might have about leaving home for an extended period, Marsha Goldstein reminded her that she would always be part of the family no matter what. She emphasized that wherever Cindy went—on a visit to Grandma's, away to camp, on a school trip, off to college, and finally into her own house or apartment—her family would always be there for her and their home would always be hers.

Though still wary, Cindy tearfully left for camp, and her subsequent letters told of her adventures and only occasionally mentioned her homesickness.

SEXUAL AND
EMOTIONAL MATURITY

Perhaps no other aspect of preadolescents' lives more dramatically reflects the theme of divergence than their physical development—and the disparity between it and their level of emotional maturity. Important anatomical and physical changes occur in girls at this stage: their bodies start to fill out and they begin to menstruate. Boys are generally about two years behind in their physical development. They are likely to begin to put on muscle and height after age twelve; by twelve and a half they may get erections, masturbate, and have wet dreams (it is normal for girls, too, to have masturbated by this age). These developments are occasionally disconcerting for parents, and can be particularly jarring for some adoptive parents.

In well-nourished, middle-class youngsters, the onset of menstruation is, to a great extent, genetically determined. Therefore, birth parents can estimate when this might occur in their daughter, but adoptive parents usually have no idea when it will happen. Generally, girls begin to get their period between the ages of nine and fifteen (on the average, at twelve or thirteen), with athletes and dancers often beginning to menstruate at the high end of the range. If you have a daughter, you should be prepared to deal with this important event in her life before she begins to menstruate. Since you are not her birth mother and therefore have no idea when she might begin, it's best to assume that she will start at the lower end of the age range so you can prepare her early. Try to have some discussions with her by age nine so that if she starts early it will not come as a surprise to her.

Mrs. Johnson had been meaning to do this with Emily, her ten-and-a-half-year-old adopted daughter, but just hadn't found the time. Then one day Emily frantically called her mother at work during lunch period from the school pay phone. "Mommy!" she screamed through her tears, "I'm dying, I'm bleeding to death!"

Though surprised, Emily's mother, with a few questions, quickly figured out that her daughter had started her period and told her to go the nurse's office and wait there for her.

Mrs. Johnson left work and after a quick stop at the drugstore drove quickly to her daughter's school where she found Emily still sobbing. Putting her arms around her daughter, she rocked her gently until the sobs subsided. Then she explained briefly what Emily had to do to take care of herself, showed her how to use a sanitary napkin, and answered her questions.

After some time, Emily was calm enough to return to class and Mrs. Johnson went back to work. Before they separated, her mother told Emily that they would have a special dinner out to discuss the changes Emily was experiencing and to celebrate her growing up.

While this manifestation of growing up is not likely to cause much of a problem for you, some adoptive parents do find it brings up some uncomfortable feelings and memories. If infertility is still a painful subject, this evidence of your daughter's possible ability to reproduce could leave you with mixed feelings, perhaps even a little jealousy. For some parents, it is a reminder of what they once considered to be their failure.

For others, it may awaken thoughts of a birth mother who bore their adopted child out of wedlock, and the fear that history will repeat itself. You need to remember that there is no connection between a birth mother's past and your child's own future sexual conduct. The only thing that might produce this linkage would be if you treated your daughter as if she "had it in her." In fact, the most important element in the formation of her sexual values is your communicating to her your beliefs about what constitutes a responsible attitude toward intimacy and sexuality.

If you do have some fears that your daughter will repeat her birth mother's experience, talk them out with your spouse to avoid putting too much emphasis on them and having them influence the way you interact with your child.

Try to convey a lack of tension in discussions with your daughter. It is an important goal as you help her understand her changing and maturing body.

The beginning of menstruation does require some frank talk with your daughter. If sexuality and bodily processes are difficult topics for you to discuss, as they are for some families—and your daughter is not yet studying these subjects in school—you might want to ask your pediatrician or some other competent adult to discuss it with her. In big families, older children sometimes tell the younger kids. Or your daughter might feel more comfortable talking to an aunt if she has one whose age falls somewhere between her own and yours. You might also take a look at these books: Planned Parenthood's How to Talk with Your Child About Sexuality (Doubleday), Lynda Madaras's What's Happening to My Body? Book for Girls (Newmarket Press), Lynda Madaras's What's Happening to My Body? Book for Boys (Newmarket Press), and Ruth Bell's Changing Bodies, Changing Lives (Random House).

If you do feel comfortable talking about sex, the best approach is to wait for your children to come to you with questions and then to answer them matter-of-factly.

Adopted children sometimes wonder about the sexual relationship between their parents. Your youngster, at this age, knows that she was born to another woman, and that the act of procreation involves sex. If you don't have any birth children, she might ask you if you and your spouse ever have sex. It's a good idea to decide beforehand how much of your privacy you are willing to have breached to satisfy your child's curiosity should this question come up. Acknowledge that married people have sex, but you can answer questions about specific details with, "That's a private matter between your father (mother) and me." However, do explain to your child that people who are unable to conceive children still have intimate relationships and that sex can be for pleasure as well as reproduction.

Occasionally, parents, whether adoptive or birth, overreact to their children's sexual curiosity. For example, it's perfectly normal for a ten-year-old boy to peek through his sister's bedroom door as she undresses if she didn't close it all the way. If you encounter this behavior and it is unacceptable in your family, make it clear to your son that such conduct is unacceptable and that there are consequences for repeating it, and ask your daughter to close her door when undressing. But don't make more of it than you would if he had broken any other family rules; and, if you can handle it, offer to answer directly any questions he might have that provoked the peeping. Most important, we can assure you that such behavior is not adoption-related, but rather normal curiosity in a developing child.

Adopted kids are no more sophisticated than those raised by their birth parents, so it shouldn't surprise you if you get fantastic questions about sex and reproduction that seem totally absurd. For example, one ten-year-old we spoke with was absolutely convinced that when a baby was born the mother's vagina came out with the infant. (He was an only child!) Another was certain that boys, too, had periods, and felt sure that all the grownups were trying to keep it a secret from her. Whatever the question, try to be as patient and honest as you can be. Sex and intimacy are confusing topics for almost everyone, so understand that developing a healthy and mature attitude is a complicated process for your child.

QUESTIONS AND ANSWERS

We feel it increasingly necessary to discipline our eleven-year-old. However, we now realize that when she was little we never made it clear to her what our values were. Is now too late to start?

No. In fact, she will be able to understand your values and standards more easily now than she could have at an earlier age, when children obey rules because the people setting them are older and more powerful than they are.

Eleven-year-olds, on the other hand, are on the verge of understanding the intrinsic merit of a value system.

However, you have to start being very specific about your rules and what's expected of her and realize that it will take time for her to adapt to this new order of things. If your child is going to become active in Girl Scouts, for example, establish a rule that she has to come straight home. As she gets older and stays out more often, either set a curfew or at least make it clear that she must call and tell you where she is if she's out past a certain time. She may test you, and you will have to be prepared to deal with this. You and your child both have to believe that your rules will not be broken without consequences. You have to convince yourself that you mean business and will pursue the matter.

☐

My twelve-year-old adopted son is ashamed because his six-year-old adopted sister tells people that they are adopted. Does this mean that he has some emotional problem related to adoption?

It doesn't sound like there's anything wrong with your son. Twelve-year-olds don't like to have attention called to the things that make them different from their friends. Sympathize with your son; acknowledge that little sisters can sometimes be a "real pain."

☐

My nine-year-old daughter sometimes likes to pretend that she is my birth child. Is there any harm in my going along with her?

There's nothing wrong with your daughter having this fantasy—it's a compliment to your parenting that she feels that way—but it would be harmful for you to play along with it. The next time she expresses these feelings, try responding, "It sounds to me like you feel like it would be nice if I had given birth to you and you weren't adopted." Then repeat back to her what she says without making any judgments so she will feel safe expressing these normal feelings.

☐

I told my ten-year-old daughter that if she wanted to find her birth mother, I would help her. That seemed to make her a little uneasy. Did I make a mistake by suggesting this now?

Yes, your offer was premature. She is still too young to understand the legal connection created by adoption. She may be worried that if her birth mother appears she may have to make a choice about whom to live with. Tell her that you meant that you would help her look some day—if she wanted to—when she's much older. Assure her that you are the mother she will live with until she leaves home.

☐

In our family, it's normal for girls to get their period for the first time at age twelve or thirteen. My adopted daughter has just started her period at age ten. What will this mean? Should I treat her any differently?

The timing is more related to genetic factors than anything else. It has no significance for predicting her behavior, nor does it mean that she will be prematurely sexually active. These days a lot of parents feel they have to follow a biological time clock. But just because she got her period doesn't mean you have to start treating her as if she were a mature woman—any more than you would just because she has started to use cosmetics. She's still a girl, with the emotional makeup of a girl—it's important to treat her like one and not as if she's suddenly more mature.

☐

My nine-year-old adopted son, who has never had behavioral problems, has suddenly become impossible to handle. He beat up his little sister, threatens to run away at least once a week, and has started to misbehave in school. Is this something that adopted boys tend to do at this age? It's a little frightening.

While it doesn't necessarily happen, it's not unusual for boys of this age, adopted and nonadopted, to act up as your son is doing. Paradoxically, he may respond to feeling confused and out of control by testing your willingness to maintain control of your family and, especially, of him. Winning this battle of the wills would be the worst thing that could happen to him. It's important now to reestablish clear limits for him and not let him think that he is more powerful than you. For example, if he refuses to go to school, take him firmly in hand and transport him to the school. If you have been a little lax in asserting your authority over him, you need to insist on it now. The child wants you to use a firm hand, reassuring him that you are able to take care of him.

Be reassured that this phenomenon can occur in any family. We recently treated a family with four children, three birth and one adopted. Both parents have Ph.D.s. But that didn't help them with their adopted child, who was driving them to distraction. When either his parents or sisters gets mad at the boy, he says, "You don't want me to be in this family and I don't want to be a part of it." Then he goes out into the garage to sit in the car for a few hours. We explained to the parents that, contrary to his actions, he wanted them to stop him from acting out this way. What they had to do was not let him leave the house and reach the car. Instead, they had to sit him down and explain in a clear way what his place was in the family and what he could and could not do.

□

My ten-year-old adoptee behaves well at home but misbehaves terribly at school. We've been to his school to talk to his teacher and guidance counselor, but his misconduct continues. What's going on and what should I do?

Kids this age have a lot of nervous energy; and as we just noted, many of them, especially boys, may act in a very disruptive manner. It's not likely to have anything to do with adoption. Since your child is acting this way only in school, unless he has a particular problem at school, it sounds like it's just easier for him to blow off steam there than at home. This often happens when a family is highly structured and fairly strict and the school is a somewhat looser environment. The child chooses the path of least resistance, acting out where he knows the consequences will be minimal. If your child is well behaved at school and acts out at home, the situation is probably reversed.

Since you have more control over your home environment, try making some adjustments there. A more relaxed family structure in which your child has a greater voice in what limits you impose on him—say, in how late he can stay out and play during the summer—might take some of the steam out of his rebelliousness at school. Also, try enrolling him in an after-school program that emphasizes physical activity so he can harmlessly burn off some of the energy he's now channeling into disruptive behavior.

☐

Every year our family has vacationed together but this year our adopted daughter wants to go away to camp. My husband is willing to go along with this, but I'm upset because I've always looked forward to these family vacations.

Peer relationships become more important to children at the upper range of this age group and will build to a crescendo by age fourteen or fifteen. Many of her friends are now probably going away to camp, and she may not want to be the only kid who still has to vacation with her family. Since she's adopted, being like her peers may be very important to her. So there's nothing wrong with her wish to go to camp. And for you, it's the beginning of a letting-go process. Now would be a good time to start to confront and prepare for the fact that in a few years she will be moving away from joint family activities in even more substantial ways.

□

We are a two-career family and caring for our three-year-old birth child has become quite a burden. Our nine-year-old adoptee has volunteered to help out, but we wonder if he's old enough to take on this type of responsibility. What do you think?

Nine-year-olds are quite competent to help out in this way with adult supervision. Child care calls up the best in these youngsters. It also gives them a sense of responsibility and reinforces the notion that adoptee or birth child, they are a highly valued and integral part of the family.

6

Young Teens, Ages Twelve to Fourteen

—F—amilies begin to undergo a basic change when their children reach adolescence. Until this time, most families operate upon the principle of a parent's authority. For the most part, you set rules of behavior for your child and you made sure that your youngster obeyed them. But with the coming of adolescence your child needs—and will often demand—more autonomy. At this stage your son or daughter must also develop a greater sense of responsibility. You will have to arrive at a point where you begin to trust her to make good decisions for herself. All this is in preparation for a time—no longer so distant—when your youngster will leave home and be responsible for herself.

The successful completion of this transition is a tall order under the calmest of circumstances. Unfortunately, many of the conditions and experiences that characterize adolescence make for turmoil. Hormones often appear to be running rampant. At the same time that adults ask them to be more independent and to develop more internal controls, adolescents' bodies and emotions may feel most out of control. In junior high school, the nurturing, constant presence of one teacher—usually female—is suddenly replaced by a group of subject teachers, men and women, who have less focused contact with your child. Your child is increasingly influenced by his peers, and the misunderstandings between parent and child, which are anything but amusing, begin to cloud your family's life. And there are the heavy issues regarding sex, alcohol, and other drugs to contend with.

An added complication is that as your child gets older, he will have less need for your supervision. You have to begin to let go and prepare for the empty nest that may now be no more than six or seven years down the line. Sometimes adoptive parents find this harder to do than birth parents.

Marge Jones, a forty-five-year-old housewife, couldn't understand what was motivating her twelve-year-old adopted son, Bobby, to disobey her. After school he went out to play with his friends for about three hours before he had to come in to have dinner and do his homework. She thought it perfectly reasonable to require him to check in with her every hour or so during his play time. He thought that was ridiculous at his age and responded by not only not staying in touch but often coming in late for dinner as well.

When faced with such unrealistic demands, kids tend either to comply, stifling their appropriate urge toward more independence, or they defy almost all parental limitations, meeting overprotection with an overreaction. Marge could have checked with other parents in her neighborhood to determine the norm for kids Bobby's age. However, she and her husband, a fifty-one-year-old automobile dealer, after years of battling against infertility and enduring a long wait to become adoptive parents, were holding tight to what they thought was best for the child they had worked so hard to get.

Adoptive parents, who had to go through a struggle to get their child in the first place, may have more of a need to try to delay their child's independence than do birth parents. When the time comes to begin the separation process, they are likely to be older than biological parents at a similar stage of their child's development, and thus possibly a little less flexible in their adaptation to change. They may also wonder how strong their ties to their child will be once he moves out into the world, and if those ties would endure were he to look for and find his birth parents.

For some families, an additionally troublesome factor at this stage could be one of the very features of their family that the adoption agency was so pleased with at the beginning of the adoption process: a wife as full-time homemaker. Until recently it was rare for an adoption agency to place a healthy infant in a family in which the wife worked. In rural areas this still often holds true. Thus women who adopted more than one child may have been required to remain at home for many years, making it difficult for them to begin a career. One could easily understand why, without a career outside the home, a mother might feel especially reluctant to part with the person who has occupied so much of her life.

When parents don't deal with their feelings about their child's moves toward autonomy, they could end up inappropriately drawing their youngster into the part of the family transition that is rightfully their job. Their child, responding to his parents' inability to let go, reverts to immature behavior, thus justifying continued "mothering." It can become a vicious cycle, with the actions of parents and child provoking more of the same from the other. Parents who have difficulty with this process should discuss it with their mates, friends, or, if it really gets sticky, a professional trained to help with such obstacles.

A DAY IN THE LIFE

Life can seem like a whirlwind for parents of an adolescent. A thirteen-year-old comes home five minutes before dinner, gets on the phone almost as soon as she's in the front door, with barely a "hi" as she goes by. You thought you knew all her friends, only to find one Saturday evening that the cast of characters has undergone a sudden and inexplicable change. Just when you felt familiar with her likes and dislikes, she sounds like she's borrowed another person's tastes and sensibilities. Even the way she dresses can be disconcerting at best and absolutely disturbing if she chooses to pursue the far(out) fringes of teenage fashion. What's more, she may claim that she wouldn't be caught dead participating in the family activities that she formerly enjoyed so much.

Emotionally, she may seem totally incomprehensible. She's up one minute, down the next, short-tempered, and passionate about everything. She may come home from school devastated by something one of her girlfriends said to her; yet when that same girl calls, your child gets off the phone smiling. When you ask her what happened to the sworn enemy she was denouncing ten minutes ago, she doesn't know what you're talking about. She's capable of responding to a new style of pants with, "I would *never* wear *that! No* way!" But when she sees her best friend wearing it the next day, she has to have it or she'll "die."

Boys, too, can experience mood swings in this period. Many parents of sons of this age complain that their once cheerful, talkative boy now acts sullen and doesn't speak much of the time. Sure, he's as vocal as can be when participating in or watching a sports event, but at home he spends more time in his room than with other family members, just as an adolescent girl may do. If your family tends to be gregarious, you might view this as strangely uncharacteristic of your family style. But rest assured that this could happen in any family, adoptive or not.

What happened to the sweet and somewhat predictable kid you knew? No wonder our popular culture is full of images of uncomprehending parents trying to fathom the ways of these aliens in their midst. Almost all parents find this period at least a little trying, and adoptive parents perhaps more so, since they may wonder if this adolescent turmoil is really a symptom of emotional disturbance arising from their child's genetic background.

Parents also sometimes interpret their adolescent child's occasionally erratic behavior as symptomatic of something they did wrong in raising her. But if your teenager's conduct strikes you this way, it's more likely that you are looking at coping mechanisms, not pathology; she's struggling with her mixed feelings about the rapid changes in her body and the world that adults expect her to master. The easiest way for her to respond to these pressures is to accept the marks of meaning and belonging that our culture offers her—the dress, music, language, hair styles, ways of interacting with parents, and super-attentiveness to the attitudes of her peers.

If she was having serious problems beyond the ordinary travails of teenagers, you would probably know it. For example, spending a good deal of time at home in her room without her friends is not necessarily a cause for alarm. But if that were combined with other unsettling behavior, such as a sudden change in her eating habits, a hysterical response to your simplest request, no peer relationships, a refusal to go to school, an inexplicable and abrupt decrease in her grades, and/or an unwillingness to obey family rules when she had not acted this way before, it would suggest a problem. The key is the presence of more than one symptom over time.

If your adolescent's behavior starts to look like this, you could say to her, "I see some changes in your behavior and I wonder what they mean. Is there anything you'd like to talk about?" If she seems reluctant to open up to you, you could add, "If you don't feel like talking about it now, I hope you'll feel free to sit down and talk when you're ready."

Bear in mind that a certain amount of turmoil and unhappiness naturally accompanies the experience of adolescence. These are transitional years, and change on this scale rarely comes easily. Fights between friends, rejection by a boyfriend, a party that flops, or a breakout of acne are part of the pain of being an adolescent. You can't completely shield her from pain—negotiating difficulties is part of growing up—and you certainly should try to avoid becoming more upset about whatever is bothering her than she is.

As an adoptive parent, it's crucial that you realize that adoption in itself does not cause any serious adolescent difficulties. Yet adoption can have a bearing on almost every major aspect of adolescence, and while the connection may be more subtle than it was in earlier stages of growth, it is just as important to understand it now as it was when your child was younger.

HORMONES OUT OF HARMONY

Puberty is, first, a physically unsettling time. If you looked at a graph showing when girls first got their period, the curve would peak at ages twelve and thirteen. A similar graph demonstrating when boys first experienced ejaculation would hit a high point between ages thirteen and fourteen.

Kids grow proportionately as much at this stage as they did in infancy. It's not unusual for them to begin their twelfth year retaining the characteristic look of their early years, and to approach their fifteenth birthday already beginning to resemble the way they will appear when they are full-grown adults.

However, unlike the beginning of their lives, they are now very much conscious of how they are changing. Girls, who may yet see themselves as children, must come to terms with bodies that increasingly suggest maturity and sexual awakening, while many boys must deal with increments of height and muscle implying a manhood that, they usually sense, is still a fiction.

There is a good deal of research which suggests that taller, handsomer, and earlier-developing adolescents are more popular with their teachers and peers. Since looks have an important bearing on popularity and self-image, anything that mars an adolescent's appearance is a serious matter. Acne, crooked teeth, mousy straight hair, shortness, and breasts that are either too big or don't appear on schedule are just a few of the obstacles along the way. Most parents offer advice to their children to be patient because, with age, these worries will pass. But your child doesn't have your experience and may find it hard to accept on faith, no matter how much he trusts you, that there really is a light at the end of the tunnel.

Your adopted child is in a somewhat tighter bind concerning certain physical flaws of adolescence than are other kids. We know that inheritance plays a role in the manifestation of physical characteristics that often trouble children in this age group—for example, the oily skin and the production of certain hormones that forms the basis for acne. Nonadopted children often get some measure of comfort when they hear from a relative how he, too, had this problem but outgrew it by the time he reached his twenties. A family photo album may offer graphic proof to back this up. Indeed, such facts give children some reason to hope that their development will follow a similar course.

Adopted children don't have these kinds of experiences to fall back on. Unless you were fortunate enough to get detailed information about your child's birth parents, you can't reassure him about his short stature because his father and uncles all shot up at about the age of seventeen; maybe they did, but you have no way of knowing it.

However, even without a family tree from which to draw comfort, you're not helpless in ameliorating the effects of these adolescent difficulties. Boys can compensate for their lack of height with extra muscle or athletic skill, to name just two ways. If your son is short for his age, you might buy him a set of weights—they make them for younger kids—or sign him up for gymnastics classes at the Y or at the after-school center. The girl who seems too tall and feels awkward can take dance classes and develop a sureness and control of her body. If she's overweight, don't criticize her; rather, assist her to devise a workable diet and an effective exercise regimen. Don't buy tempting snacks. Attractive and appropriate clothing can help take the edge off her disappointment at not developing the way some of her friends have.

If your son is not being picked for basketball choose-up games or your daughter is negative about her height because most of the boys won't dance with a girl who is taller than them, you could point out short men or tall women whose accomplishments and renown your child admires—perhaps Woody Allen and Michael J. Fox for boys, Lauren Hutton and Grace Jones for girls. Ask your daughter, also, to notice how other tall girls she knows get along and to make note of the specific things they do that seem to work (from style of dress to the ways they carry themselves) and help her to review these characteristics from time to time.

For either sex, acne is, to some extent, medically treatable, so get a referral to a good dermatologist. Orthodonture, also, though expensive, can improve your teenager's appearance over the long run. Despite the fact that braces are not exactly attractive, they are often considered a status symbol at this age.

Sometimes, these complications can lead to sibling rivalry. If your adopted daughter's skin is broken out and she has still not developed breasts, while your older birth daughter went through this period just two years ago without a complexion problem and with an attractive, lithe body that even her friends envied, your adoptee may have one more stress to deal with.

If your adopted child is comparing herself unfavorably to her sibling, you are not without ways to comfort her. For example, you could show her pictures of movie stars looking no more glamorous than her when they were her age (magazines such as *People* often run such pictures). But if her sibling is making this comparison, you should act decisively. Make it clear that such teasing violates family rules. Should the brother or sister bring adoption into the teasing, consider it a punishable offense.

JUNIOR HIGH SCHOOL

It might be comforting at this tumultuous time in their child's life if adoptive parents could at least think of the intense ups and downs of adolescence as occurring within the supportive framework of a nurturing educational institution. Unfortunately, just when they really need stability and close attention, adolescents enter junior high school, which reflects the outside world much more than did their elementary school.

The transition from one type of school to another seems to be an especially vulnerable time for some adopted boys. They are slightly more likely than nonadoptees to have behavioral difficulties in school at ages eleven and twelve, although their problems are not monumental and usually fade by the time they reach high school. Why this happens is not altogether clear.

For all kids, the change from elementary to junior high school is a revolution and thus a major stress in their lives. Socially, it is almost an instant end to their childhood. They may not yet be going to coed parties and dating, but now they are surrounded by kids who do and who talk about it a great deal. Although the pressure to get good grades so they can get into college is not yet upon them, it's in the air; they constantly hear that by the ninth grade their marks will start to "count."

Adoptees face additional pressures. In junior high, they no longer stay in one room all day under the watchful eye of a single teacher. Now they move from room to room and from subject to subject every hour. Their teachers emphasize subject matter, not general educational and social skills. While teachers encourage them to their full potential, they are not as concerned with making their students feel good as elementary school teachers probably were. Losing the close contact with one teacher they had in elementary school might evoke fantasies some adopted children have of abandonment. Further, the sudden plunge into a world of adolescent cliques and the necessity of making a new set of friends may also enhance their feeling of being different from other children.

Your interaction with your youngster's school and its staff also changes. If you used your child's primary school teachers as allies in dealing with adoption-related complications, you will find yourself likely to have a more distant relationship to this new set of teachers. Unless your child has become a problem in their class, they will want to discuss his achievement, not his social adjustment.

Your child is less likely to require the protection of grown-ups, so you will probably not need his teacher as an ally to keep adoption from becoming an issue at school. The exception would be something serious, such as harassment from a bully. But while that represents progress, it may also undermine any feeling you had that by staying in touch with the teacher you had some control over how your child did in school.

If your child does have some difficulty at school, try to narrow down the possible source of the trouble. Until Jill Worthington took this approach, she thought her daughter was developing some kind of complex.

Jody Worthington was getting stomachaches in school. While the school's cafeteria hardly rated four stars, it certainly wasn't that bad—and her pediatrician had eliminated a medical basis—so her mother figured that the sudden illnesses must be emotionally based. She decided to do a little detective work and charted the occurrences of her daughter's malady. In less than two days she solved the mystery. Jody was all but doubling over when confronted with Ms. Wilson's social studies class. The teacher was demanding, sarcastic, ironic, and judgmental, while Jody was gentle and straightforward.

To help her daughter cope with this situation, Mrs. Worthington asked her to play observer for two weeks. She told Jody to note the specific things that Ms. Wilson did that upset her and anything that Jody was able to do to make things easier on herself. Jill also told Jody to see how the other kids managed to deal with the teacher. It turned out that Jody was very bothered by Ms. Wilson's sarcasm when she called on Jody and she did not know the answer. The kids who were not bothered by this unpleasant practice were those who had taken extra time to prepare for the class and were able to volunteer before being called upon. Jody took the hint, and her little bit of extra preparation time cured her stomachaches.

Home routines not conducive to studying could be the cause of poor performance in school. Perhaps you have two youngsters sharing a bedroom. If so, make sure each has access to a quiet area for enough time each day to do homework. In one family we know of, the parents solved this dilemma by allowing one of two brothers who shared a bedroom to do his homework in the bedroom temporarily vacated by their older sister, who was away at college.

Another boy, Timmy, seemed like two different people at his junior high school. He was either alert and on top of everything, or else virtually inert and out of it. The secret ingredient turned out to be informal after-school choose-up sports. On days when he engaged in them, he would come home, have his dinner, do his homework, watch TV, and go to sleep, awakening the next morning rested and ready for another day. On nonathletic days he was restless, stayed up late, and paid for it the next day with a bleary-eyed presence in class. When his parents brought him to us and we saw the pattern, we encouraged them to get him into an organized program of athletics to help him work off the excess energy that's natural for a boy his age.

In other words, the first thing to look for when school difficulties arise is connections. What time of the day does the trouble occur? Does it seem to coincide with particular activities or teachers? Sometimes family tensions, such as an argument with a grandmother who lives with you, play a part in how your child will behave or perform academically in school the next day. Also, focus on the good days and see what happens then to find out what your child did to cause things to go right. If you can figure out what happens when things go well, you will be able to increase their occurrence, thereby improving the situation.

School performance in the junior high school years starts

to take on added significance for many teenagers: college looms on the horizon. As an adoptive family, you may feel the pressure even more than other families. People who have adopted often think they must try a little harder to be good parents; they really work at it. While this is a good thing, the down side is that they sometimes see their child's academic progress and achievement as a measure of whether they have been doing their job well. That's why we would like to put the question of schoolwork at this age in some perspective.

For the most part, kids this age do not focus on their studies. As we have already pointed out, they have a good deal to contend with outside the classroom; and they are very much aware that their grades, at least until the ninth grade, "don't count" towards college admission, if this is their goal.

In the past, experts have discussed the subject of motivating children in early adolescence to like school and to want to study. Parents subsequently believed that if they could just find the right emotional button to push, they would see results. But in recent years we have come to realize that any such approach is questionable, at best, simply because there's no good reason for children to enjoy their studies now—they would most likely enjoy doing other things. That's not true for the few kids who always place in the top percentile of their class but, remember, they are the exception, not the rule.

On the other hand, at this age, children must learn the basics of a broad range of subjects and must develop good study habits if they want to go on to higher education. So you do need a way of getting them to fulfill their responsibilities. One approach is to think about your child's homework and getting good grades as his tasks, as his work. Happiness is not the issue here. Think of these responsibilities as akin to your family's rules for behavior. They are what he must do and he simply has to do them to the best of his ability.

Christopher Davidson wasn't doing *any* homework at home in his first year of junior high school. When his parents questioned his lack of homework, he said that he finished it in school. But when the first marking period brought C's rather than the solid B's their son had earned in elementary school, they began to worry. They had adopted him as an infant and they knew that his birth parents had not done well in school. Did they expect too much from him academically?

The Davidsons conferred with Chris's teachers, asking them what grades they thought he should be attaining and how much homework he should be doing. The teachers thought the youngster could be getting B's and they felt that two hours of homework per night would bring him to that level. Consequently, Chris's parents told him that they would expect him to do two hours of homework every night. They would supervise it, and if he didn't have an assignment, they would give him one from his textbook. After that, his time would be his own. The result: beginning with the next marking period, solid B's.

Having noted that academics are not a high-priority activity with most teenagers, we should also point out that school does have great significance for adolescents. After all, it's in the school hallways and at the lockers that they interact with some of the most important people in their lives: their peers.

FRIENDS

It would be hard to overstate the influence of her peers on this stage of your child's development. They will have a lot to do with how she talks, thinks, and dresses. They define what's "in" and what's "out." When you think it necessary to counter their influence on any given issue, you may find yourself swimming upriver against a very strong current.

Kids at this stage have a deep-seated need for acceptance by their peers. For adopted kids, this may be all the more reason for them to push their birth circumstances into the background if they aren't friendly with peers who are adopted. They know that kids their age are quick to categorize others, so they are not likely to make much of their adoption, for fear of being introduced to their friends' friends as Jane or Johnny, "who's adopted."

One thing all adolescents share is the experience of sometimes feeling out of control. Their bodies and emotions just won't cooperate. This phenomenon is at the root of many teenage customs: they try to create a safe environment so they can know what to expect. It can mean making their room look a certain way; hanging out at a familiar place, like McDonald's (their home room in junior high school fulfills somewhat the same purpose); carrying their music with them in the form of personal stereos; and blending into a familiar background of clothing styles, such as cutting out parts of their tee shirts, that you might regard as weird at best.

Your adopted child might seize upon these and other badges of identity with an even greater relish than his friends. He may feel that his world is more out of control than theirs, since he knows less about himself. He may welcome any way open to him to create stability and familiarity, so don't worry about weird haircuts or clothing fads he adopts because they are in.

An adoptive parent who has been enormously involved with her child may find it difficult to acknowledge that her youngster is now taking her cues from her peers. Are they the right bunch for her? Do they drink or fool around with drugs? What are their families like?

All parents, of course, have some of these anxieties about their child's friends. But for adoptive parents, extra anxiety could enter the picture. For example, if your child came from an ethnic or racial group different from yours, he may now seek out friends with whom he has that characteristic in common. That's only natural. We are all, to some extent, drawn to people who are like us in some way. While your child does share your family's "culture" with you, there are certain traits he may want to identify with that you simply can't supply.

This may be difficult for you to accept. His friends could

look and speak differently than you do, come from another social class, practice a different religion, have values that clash with yours. They may aspire to be carpenters and mechanics while you hope your child will go to college.

When an adolescent does seek the counsel of an adult, he may sometimes go to the parent of a friend, rather than to you. This has nothing to do with adoption. Kids tend to hang out at one house in particular, and adults in that family are sometimes convenient sounding boards and sources of advice. If this happens, try not to view it as a rejection of you. There is just enough distance between your child and these adults to make it possible for your youngster to raise issues he might not be able to with you. For him, it's a safer way of dealing with topics that might literally hit too close to home if he brought them up with his own father or mother.

One way you can get some control over this situation is to get your child's friends to spend more time at your house. In general, kids will go where they feel comfortable and accepted. If you have delicate antiques and white carpeting, they may take that to mean that they're not welcome. But even if your living room is not conducive to hanging out, you could set up other areas of your home in such a way that your child and her friends will feel welcome.

A finished basement, for example, oversized pillows on the floor, a good stereo system, a Ping-Pong table, and a VCR well stocked with movies appealing to this age group should serve as an effective enticement. If you have less room, another attraction is a kitchen that always seems to have all the right foods. Potato chips, chocolate chip cookies—whatever is currently in—will make your home appealing. You could also encourage your child to bring his friends over on a Saturday night to make pizza, franks and beans, or whatever people in your section of the country consider a fun food. If your youngster hosts a pajama party, you might feed the kids pancakes made from scratch for breakfast.

On the other hand, you'll have to be very discreet if you encourage the kids to hang out at your house. If you appear

HOW TO RAISE AN ADOPTED CHILD

to be a little too anxious to have them around, it could backfire and turn them away. Adolescents don't like to have adults fuss over them, try too hard to be friendly, and, especially, ask them too many questions. So while you're understandably interested in knowing as much about your child's friends as you can, you'll probably have to remind yourself once in a while that much of their relationships will have to remain a mystery to you.

What if you know enough about one or more of your child's friends to know that you don't like them? The first thing you should ask yourself is whether this friend represents a real danger—does she use drugs or alcohol?—or is this just a matter of chemistry and you don't like her because of her personality, values, or something even more undefinable. Unless this friend does represent a clear danger to your son or daughter, you're better off withholding criticism. It's good for your child to get to know all kinds of people. You can't protect her from everything, and if you've given your youngster a clear sense of right and wrong, you can be confident that she will probably not get too close to the wrong kind of people.

PRIVACY—AND YOUR WORST FEARS

The privacy issue occupies the border area between your need to know and your child's compelling desire to carve out an increasingly larger part of her life that is hers alone. She is struggling for control and autonomy; you're trying to let go gradually and graciously, all the while knowing that you still have to do much of the steering until she can safely take over directing her own life.

Parents must accept that their children have some feelings and facts which they need to keep to themselves. You have to respect that need. As an adoptive parent, you might find this a little hard to do. In our experience, adoptive parents, more than birth parents, tend to be concerned with what their child is thinking. They may feel that if they knew more they could help more. But this only works when your child wants to talk to you about something.

With fewer role models than birth parents have, adoptive parents may want reassurance from their child that everything is going fine in her life, that they are doing a good job of parenting. But it's not a child's job to reassure her parents. If you have these feelings, seek the reassurance from your peers—friends, relatives, or an adoptive parents' group.

Though it may be tempting, especially if you're feeling anxious, never try to read your child's diary or eavesdrop on his phone conversations. It might also be a good idea to tell him to lower the volume on his telephone answering machine, if he has his own, so that you don't inadvertently hear something you'd rather not.

Serena Martin, thirteen and a half years old, turned her answering machine off when she went to the country for a weekend to stay with a friend. Her mother, thinking her daughter had forgotten to push the "on" button, turned it on. The volume was high enough for Mrs. Martin to hear what she took to be a juicy message from one of Serena's friends, bragging about the hot time she had had the previous night with her boyfriend and alluding to Serena's similar relationship with another boy. In fact, the message was ambiguous, and it could as easily have been referring to necking on a park bench as to anything that might have been occurring in a bed. But Serena's mother now had to live with considerable anxiety, for to question her child would mean acknowledging her eavesdropping.

If your child were drinking or using drugs on anything more than an experimental or occasional basis, you would certainly know it without having to overhear references to that fact. Observation of your child's behavior is the key here, not your behavior, which your child could interpret as snooping.

Having accepted this, how do you stay in touch with what your child is doing and thinking? Contrary to notions fostered by our popular culture, parents *can* communicate with adolescents. One way to go about this admittedly difficult task is to avoid conversations that are really one-way interrogations. You might begin by being open yourself. Show your child that you're willing to talk about things that have happened to you and how you felt about them. Even if you've never tried this approach before, you can start now and probably get a good response.

Carla Hopkins, in trying to empathize with her son's dismay at being falsely accused of cheating on a test, said to him, "It's funny, I was thinking about what happened to you the other day and remembering a weird experience I had when I was your age. I also had a teacher who thought I had cheated on an exam. To see if his suspicion was correct, he gave our class two different tests, but he didn't tell us. When he checked the answers he discovered that my girlfriend, who sat in the row next to mine, was the one who was copying the answers." She commiserated with her son about the unfairness of it all and about how hard it was to get somebody to listen to your side of the story. While her youngster remained somewhat upset, the raw pain did ease a bit and he appreciated his mother's response.

You might try talking to your child while you're both engaged in the same activity, like cooking or making repairs around the house. Establish lines of communication with talk about subjects that interest both of you, such as planning trips and family weekend activities, politics, sports, what's going on with your relatives, and the like. By establishing the habit of talking freely, you make it more likely that he will approach you if he has something more personal or urgent to discuss.

Recent studies indicate that a tendency toward alcoholism may be an inherited characteristic. In fact, adoptive families have participated in a few of the studies on the subject. We emphasize the tentativeness of the results of these studies and that we are dealing with a *tendency*, not an inevitable fact. If you know that one of your child's biological parents was an alcoholic, you should make an extra effort to teach your youngster that drinking is inappropriate at his age. Alcohol can disrupt the process of hormonal change during puberty, exacerbating an adolescent's normal ups and downs. It can also keep a child from learning and performing up to his capacity. Set an example by not making alcohol too much of a presence in your home. If you do not know of any alcoholism in his family background, there's less reason to be concerned, but keep an ongoing awareness of this issue. Controlling alcohol intake is an important lesson for all youngsters.

Some signs that your child may be abusing drugs and alcohol are certain behaviors that have lasted more than one month. They include:

- impulsive behavior

- suspiciousness

- aggressive behavior, provoking family arguments

- inability to meet important responsibilities to friends and family members

- failure in school

- money difficulties

- legal difficulties related to the illegal purchase of drugs or alcohol

- accidents, especially in automobiles

If you note these behaviors in your adolescent, it is important to seek advice and assistance immediately from a drug and/or alcohol program. Again, remember we are not talking about occasional experimentation, but rather a clear pattern of developing dependence on highly addictive substances. The current drugs of choice among today's teens are alcohol, marijuana, cocaine and cocaine derivatives such as crack, and amphetamines. Because of the highly addictive nature of some of these drugs and the serious damage they can cause, often in a very short time, it is important for parents to become educated about the signs of substance abuse.

SEX

Girls in this age group daydream a lot. They may talk—especially among themselves—of having a family. For adopted girls, an especially poignant aspect of these thoughts relates to the possibility that some day they will finally have biological relatives they know and can love. While this is of course also true for adopted boys, we've observed that girls seem somewhat more interested than boys in this subject. However, this could change as the role of the male in our society shifts more toward that of nurturer.

Having their own family can also give adoptees a sense of increased control over their lives, something they experienced even less of while growing up than did other kids. Even if they were adopted as infants, they knew less than did nonadoptees about where they came from and about what they could anticipate from their future. Their own biological child would provide a connection to both past and future.

Most adoptive parents can sympathize with such thoughts; the only problem involves their worry about the timing of the family creation process. By the time they are fourteen, some girls are beginning to approach the age at which their birth mothers conceived them. That's enough to make some adoptive parents a little uneasy. Could their daughter follow in her mother's footsteps?

As we have pointed out, early sexual activity is not an inherited characteristic. Your daughter's sexual behavior depends on what values you have instilled in her. But since it's not unnatural for parents to have at least a few fears that there might be something to a genetic connection, when your daughter reaches this age it could be helpful to remind yourself that there's no correlation between her future sexual activity and her birth mother's past.

It's also important that you do not criticize her birth parents' sexual indiscretions. Adolescent adoptees are often sensitive about such criticism, hearing it as an attack on themselves. If you do insult her mother or father, even without meaning to, she may not tell you. Should you realize that you have hit a sensitive spot, by all means apologize and attempt to clarify your concerns.

During these years, the interaction between boys and girls is uneven. By age fourteen there are often dances and coed parties, but the girls—adoptees and nonadoptees alike—are likely to be more on the lookout for relationships than are boys in the same age group. As a result, fourteen-year-old girls sometimes seek out older boys, increasing the chances that they could become sexually involved.

How should you talk to your adolescent about her sexual maturation? Don't hesitate to make your views clear on what you consider appropriate social behavior for your daughter: she should know your standards. Emphasize the difference between being a child and being an adult. Point out to her that she simply hasn't had enough experience of life to make certain judgments—about the difference between love and infatuation, for example. At this age, your child *is* capable of understanding that such guidance is for her own good and the setting of rules in this matter can actually relieve some of the peer pressure on her to get prematurely involved with someone.

What if she's stubborn about not conforming to what you say is best for her? If she says, "All the other girls are doing it," say, "I feel that you are too young now and will be too young for some time. There's a difference between being thirteen or fourteen and being eighteen; you're just not ready." If she replies that "you don't know, I am ready, you just don't know me," you could respond: "We may disagree, but I'm the adult and I've been there. I was your age, and I know about it. It would be too hard and complicated if you got sexually involved while you have a lot of growing up to do."

Make sure your child knows about birth control. While schools are handling this issue at the junior high level in some parts of the country—and thus your child may even know more than you about this subject—that may not be true for your area. By the time your daughter reaches fourteen, you can send her to a gynecologist with the assurance that she will get straight information from a professional. You could also give her *Changing Bodies, Changing Lives* by Ruth Bell (Random House).

Impress upon your daughter the seriousness of abortion—no matter what your particular views on the issue—and that she should not regard it as just another means of birth control. This is particularly important for adoptees, since there are indications that frequent abortions may affect a girl's fertility. Should your youngster impair her ability to bear children through too frequent recourse to abortion, she could destroy the possibility of ever having a blood relative she knows.

And don't neglect your son. Male adoptees often speak of their desire to have children—blood relatives. It's important to protect your son from and educate him about those things which appear to decrease male fertility, including diseases such as mumps and drugs like marijuana and cocaine. Aside from making sure that he knows about the mechanics of birth control, and the importance of using condoms, you should impart a sense of personal responsibility to him about the prospects of possibly creating another life.

YOUR EVOLVING FAMILY

Although it may seem like a minor aspect of your adopted child's life compared with some of the other issues we've just discussed, the sharing of household chores at this age plays a major role in the successful evolution of your family and your youngster's growing maturity. In fact, we prefer *responsibilities* to *chores*, since this word suggests the family role that your child is beginning to play: that of an autonomous yet contributing member of the household.

Occasionally there are adoptees who were spoiled because their parents felt that they had to bend over backwards not to make too many demands on them. With these parents, we point out that one of the greatest gifts you can give a child is a sense of responsibility. Knowing he can do what's required of him as he matures gives him confidence in his ability to take care of himself, enhancing the growth of his sense of autonomy, so necessary for a successful passage into adulthood.

What's more, parents who excuse their adopted children from household duties are depriving them of a feeling of belonging, of being truly a part of the family that has raised them. This often results in the child feeling singled out and different from other members of the family. In fact, adopted kids have come to us complaining that they were not being given enough work to do around the house. Since you and your child don't share a genetic history, the bonds that come from the sharing of responsibilities are perhaps even more important than they might be in a birth family: they are part of the necessary creation of family rituals and the establishment of a family history.

Even the process of deciding who will have which responsibilities in your family is integral to your child's development. At this stage, such decisions should come about more by negotiation than by fiat. By the age of twelve, children have begun to develop a sense of empathy. Until this point they had to be told to do something, simply because you said they should and you might punish them if they didn't do it. But now they fully understand the concept of fairness and they can imagine themselves in somebody else's shoes. They can understand that if they don't help you, you will have to do it all. The significance of this new level of comprehension for single-parent families and for parents of latch-key kids is of obvious importance.

There is no one "right" way of delegating responsibilities. A good general principle to bear in mind, however, is to try to match each person in the family to the tasks they either like the most, or to those jobs they find the least onerous. For example, maybe you don't mind doing the laundry but hate to shop. If so, see if your youngster is willing to take on some of the responsibility of bringing home the groceries. Remember that the process of dividing these responsibilities can be just as important as the actual assignment of specific tasks.

If you suspect that you might be expecting too much or too little from your child when it comes to these tasks, check with other parents, adoptive and nonadoptive, to see how this process works in their families. In a family with more than one child, a little sibling rivalry could show up over these assignments. If that happens, keep in mind that children of different ages *should* have different responsibilities, and if a twelve-year-old, for example, has to do more, then he should also have more privileges.

For adoptees, it can be especially valuable to have this sense of responsibility for shouldering one's share of work carry over beyond the family into the broader social realm. While it's always an admirable value to feel the need to perform community service, adoptees can perhaps derive an even greater satisfaction from such work than others. It gives them a sense of connection to the community, to a past and to a future, that the lack of blood relatives may have left them without. In fact, many of the adoptive families we see are active in church or synagogue affairs or other community activities related to religious groups. This work seems to give them a feeling of transcendence, an important but often overlooked component of emotional development.

MONEY

According to a certified public accountant recently quoted in the *New York Times,* many people feel "more comfortable talking to children about sex than about money." However, while your child can go elsewhere to learn about sex, she will have to come to you to learn about money, at least initially, since for her you are the only source of it.

This could be especially important for an adoptee. Everyone feels more secure if he can handle money. Since the fact of adoption leaves some adoptees with question marks about themselves and their origins that nonadoptees do not share, it behooves you not to leave your adopted child uncertain about this important part of life.

Also, the feeling of having been given much without much being asked of them is an observation that some adoptees have made about their lives. They say this made them feel never truly part of their families. So it is especially important for adoptive parents to make sure they teach their child the value of money.

As with family duties, the interaction on this subject between you and your child should be changing as she passes through early adolescence. When she was younger, you probably just gave her what you thought she should have, and that was that. But now allowances become more a matter for negotiation. Here, too, she should develop a sense of responsibility—and a feeling for the relationship between her allowance and your family's income.

Many adoptees live in adoptive families with far higher income levels than those of their own birth families. Adult adoptees have reported that this has troubled them and often made them feel that they were "rescued" from poverty and should feel grateful. Some don't feel that they rightfully should share in the family wealth. By teaching your child control over money you are reinforcing not only her sense of personal responsibility, but also your confidence that she can handle "family money" as a "family member."

One of the things you could negotiate with her is the matter of which purchases she would like responsibility for and which you will still buy with or for her—clothes, for instance. The advantage to giving her money to buy her own clothes is that it forces her to budget her funds and make choices from several possibilities, thus preparing her for adulthood. On the other hand, this arrangement may not work if she is not yet able to delay gratification. You might try adding such money to her allowance on a small scale; perhaps it could initially just cover shoes or sweaters. As she proves her ability to handle her funds, she could have more responsibility for her own purchases.

Kids this age should also have savings accounts to help them begin to see the connection between current income and future needs. But don't be surprised if your child resists the idea of putting away a sizable amount of money earned from a part-time or summer job. She's still too young to have a true intellectual and emotional grasp of that connection.

Should your child work? Notwithstanding economic necessity, we think it's a good idea to encourage adolescents, but not to force them, to get a part-time or summer job, such as having a paper route, baby-sitting or lawn-mowing. Besides offering them more control over their destinies, it also gives them a better sense of life. Just as your child's initial foray into the world of school made him cope with adults who would not necessarily love him automatically, dealing with a boss is a good preparation for interaction with people who will judge him primarily on his performance.

THEIR THOUGHTS ON ADOPTION

For some children at this stage, adoption begins to fade into the background as a source of confusion in their lives. Most likely by the time your child reaches fourteen he will have a full legal and psychological understanding of adoption's significance. But if he ever had any overt preoccupation with the process, he may have put it behind him. The odds are that in the place of the adoption questions he might have asked in earlier years, you now will hear silence.

QUESTIONS AND ANSWERS

The shock of junior high school has been too much for my child. She did very well in elementary school but she seems isolated and confused now and can't establish relationships with her teachers.

It might be a good idea to talk to the guidance teacher at your child's school. If your child has just entered junior high, she may just need a little extra time to adjust. This is more likely to happen with only children, a category that includes many adoptees. It also crops up more often in families that have moved recently, or to children whose friends from elementary school have gone on to private or parochial school. If the trouble persists, she may need a different school that offers more individual attention.

☐

My son has been coming home later and later. We tried setting a formal curfew, but he's just ignored it. We're worried and running out of things to say to him. What should we do?

When adoptive families have come to us with a child who stays out past his curfew, it's almost always part of a pattern of misbehavior—and not the major part at that. If lateness is not a temperamental characteristic with your child—for example, is he simply less attentive to time when making appointments?—then you should sit down with him and try to see what's bothering him.

As to the mechanics of setting a curfew, it's often best

accomplished when parents get together and establish a community norm. For example, when Arthur, Bob Franklin's son, reached the ninth grade, Bob and his wife, Kay, joined with the parents of Arthur's friends to establish a common policy on parties, dates, and the like. They decided that 12:30 A.M. on weekends would be a reasonable limit for this age. Parents were encouraged to telephone the parents of kids having parties to determine if adult supervision would be present. By going public and acting together, the parents were able to get better cooperation from their kids, who knew where they stood and who couldn't play one set of parents off against another.

□

Every time my husband and son sit down to negotiate anything from allowance to studying and acceptable grades, it ends in a fight. I'm worried that this has something to do with our only son being adopted. Could there be a connection?

The transition to the negotiation style of family interaction is difficult for many parents. There may or may not be a connection between adoption and the difficulties you are experiencing, but try this negotiating technique and perhaps you won't need to make the connection. Have your husband and son each argue his case for five minutes. Your son could go first, with your husband taking notes while your son talks. Then it's your husband's turn to present his case while your son takes notes. Now each spends five minutes talking about what the other has said. At this point, they might want to separate and come up with list of solutions before coming together again.

The intent of this exercise is to get them to listen to each other, something that few people who argue do. Once they've established the habit of listening, they can begin to narrow their differences and seek areas of compromise, since they know what's important to the other and why.

□

My adopted child had a drink at a party this past weekend and got very giddy—more so than the other kids. We heard that there is a genetic predisposition to alcoholism. We know virtually nothing about our youngster's birth parents and we are worried. Are we overreacting? Should we discuss the possible connection between alcoholism and his genetic background with our child?

Treat this matter as you would if there were a possible history of diabetes in his birth family. His adoption is a legitimate issue here and you should be vigilant if your son exhibits a special sensitivity to alcohol. It's appropriate to discuss this with him, and you might find it easier to do this by introducing an expert into the discussion. By going as a family to see a genetic counselor, you can remove this subject from the realm of moralizing and give it a medical-scientific context—thus adding some distance when you need it. He will find it easier to hear what he needs to hear in this objective setting.

□

I've heard there's nothing to worry about if your child doesn't talk about adoption. My thirteen-year-old adopted son has nothing to say on the subject, and I am worried. Could you help me to feel better about this?

You can never be sure what's on a child's mind. Assuming you have been open and honest about his background, you have to trust that your son would come to you with anything that now significantly troubled him about his past.

□

I have two adopted daughters, eleven and twelve. The other night they were watching a TV program about a girl who discovered that she was adopted and searched for her birth mother. My children burst into tears, left the room, and have since refused to talk about it with me. All my subsequent attempts to get them to talk it out have failed. What should I do?

While this must have been upsetting for all of you, it's highly unlikely to have caused any permanent problems for your children or any change in their feelings about you. But if you want to be sure that no harm was done, perhaps you could ask one of your relatives to talk to them. Also, ask other adoptive parents if their kids had similar reactions and how they did or would handle it.

☐

I wish my daughter had more friends; she's so shy. I've heard that adopted kids have lower self-esteem than other kids. Could this be the source of her isolation?

Some recent studies suggest that adopted kids' self-esteem is at least as high as other kids'. Unless there are some other problems and if this is not new behavior, you just may have to accept shyness as her temperamental style. Shyness appears to be characteristic of the inborn temperaments of some people and may have to be accepted as such by parents both adoptive and not. It is important for parents again to respect their children's unique personalities. A shy individual can be encouraged to be a bit more outgoing, but to expect her to change entirely is unrealistic. If this is a change in behavior, however, then you should worry. If it is more of the same and just bothering you more, then you should sit back and observe the ways in which your daughter interacts with friends and whether this is satisfying for her. You should then accept her for who she is and encourage her to do more of what works for her.

7
The Late Teenage Years

Matt Thomas, a lawyer and CPA, never thought he'd have to deal with this particular adoption-related complication: there he was, a man in his early fifties, walking down the street with a vivacious and attractive 17-year-old girl on his arm. Had she resembled him, nobody would have looked twice. But Laura, his adopted daughter, did not look like him, and the two drew more than one or two inquisitive stares from passing strangers.

It wasn't the first time this father had encountered insensitive behavior by strangers. For adoptive parents, that sort of thing comes with the territory. But this day Matt was in the mood to deal with it with his sense of humor. When he caught a disapproving look, he nodded, smiled, and put his arm around Laura. She was delighted to go along with this bit of playfulness, participating in their private joke by throwing him an adoring glance.

Matt's wife grinned when he told her about the street byplay. It seemed just like yesterday that they were agonizing about when and how to first start discussing the subject of adoption with that delightful three-year-old child who had entered their lives via an agency. For them, the "problems" of adoption had certainly changed.

TIME FLIES

Where did the years go? Chances are the child you once picked up and carried around is almost big enough to carry you. By late adolescence your youngster has completed most of his physical growth. His emotional development has also progressed, although more unevenly. On some days his good sense may make you forget that you're still talking to a child, while at other times you may wonder if he'll ever be able to get both feet into adulthood.

Your child needs you less now than when he was younger, and he decides when he requires your attention. Some adoptive parents may experience this as a rejection and begin to worry about how their youngster will regard them once he achieves his independence. But if your relationship with him as been solid, there's little to fear. Your ties to him need not be any less deep and satisfying now that he's older, just different. You will be less a caretaker, your discussions more intense and egalitarian.

Don't be surprised if you feel sadness as well as relief at your child's maturing into adulthood. You've been through a lot with this almost-adult, from dealing with scraped knees to soothing emotional hurts (not to mention the mountain of laundry you've done over the years!). Before long you will hardly see him around at all.

Much has been asked of you. As we pointed out in response to one of the questions at the end of chapter 2, it is often said that adoptive parents have to establish "claiming" behavior when they first get their child, that they must possess their child, make him their own, not see him as the "other," an outsider. Yet for your child to grow into an autonomous human being, you also had to begin to redefine that claim by the time he was six years old, as he took his first steps outside the family, differentiating himself from you. Less than two decades later, you have to relinquish the remnants of the claim you worked so hard to establish.

The fruits of your labor, once your adoptee has grown up,

are likely to be continuing love and close family ties. Now your child is fully capable of understanding the significance of adoption—and the central role that you have played in his life. At this point, the fact that he was born to someone else and possibly spent some time with a foster family is heavily outweighed by the many years you have spent nurturing him. He knows that you are his parents. We have, in fact, often noticed he may even be more appreciative of your efforts than birth children are of their parents' labors.

With your child approaching the point where he will leave home as an independent person, you can also look forward to the next stage of family development, in which you can be more independent, as you were before you began to raise your child. You can anticipate peace and quiet around the house, fewer responsibilities, and more free time to pursue your interests.

Adoptive parents are typically a few years older than the average birth parent when their child joins their family. If that description fits you, you are now even more likely than the parents of your child's friends to be entering your peak career years and may be especially looking forward to your youngster's autonomy. You could probably use more time and energy to apply to your job—or to a full-time career if you interrupted work to be a homemaker.

As the time approaches for your child to leave home, particularly if she is an only child, you may need to work at making a smooth transition into the next stage of your marriage. A good part of your relationship with your spouse has been bound up in the process of child rearing. That period is ending.

If the thought of an empty nest unsettles you, try focusing on specific issues. Then you'll start to realize how much you can do about shaping your life once the kids are on their own. For example, if you've played the role of full-time mother and homemaker, start planning for new activities, a renewed career, or an entirely new line of work. Look into the possibility of taking refresher courses at the local college; make an appointment to see a career counselor to discuss the possibilities open to you. You can find professional career counselors in most cities; and don't overlook the books and pamphlets in the careers section of your public library.

Many fathers who have been heavily involved in their child's athletic activities suddenly find themselves at sea when their youngster moves on to college. But that needn't make for empty Saturdays. What did you like to do with your spare time before your child was old enough to need you to help the team? This is also a good time to explore new interests and activities as well as to resurrect old ones.

It may occur to you that without day-to-day, child-centered activities, you and your spouse will have less to talk about. But that needn't be the case, especially if you're both active pursuing new projects. And now you have the opportunity, with fewer distractions, to redefine and enjoy your identity as a couple. Dinners out, weekends away, heightened interest in new careers—all of these can add new sparkle to your relationship and solidify it.

CREATING
THEIR OWN IDENTITY

Of course, your child-rearing work isn't quite over yet. As we pointed out in the previous chapter, the teenage years are formidable for parent and child for good reasons. At this age it can be very unsettling when the child you thought was becoming more mature and independent suddenly reverts to juvenile behavior. But contrary to what you may have heard, your youngster will not have to pass through some kind of pathological version of a teenage identity crisis, just because he was adopted.

In the past—and in a few pockets of resistance today—some mental health professionals suggested the inevitability of serious problems for adoptive families, caused by their adolescent's Herculean struggle to establish her identity and autonomy with respect to two sets of parents, birth and adoptive. In our extensive experience with adoptive families, we find no basis in fact for these theories.

Indeed, to the extent that all adolescents have to come to terms with who they are, adoptees may have a heard start on other kids. Because of some of the complications built into adoption—especially the most basic one: being different—your adoptee has probably already had to deal with the identity question and has had practice figuring out who she is in relation to her parents and other families. It began when you first told her that she was adopted.

We would also like to emphasize that tension and conflicts between parent and teenager are not as inevitable as they are often portrayed. In fact, we've often observed that parents and their teenage adoptees have less trouble with each other than other families do. We suspect that's because many adoptive parents have fewer expectations about how their child will turn out than the mothers and fathers of birth children. Because of this they are less likely to try to force their adoptee into a mold dictated by their family traditions. They find it easier to stand back and give their child breathing space, room to find his own way.

While teenage adoptees do not necessarily experience an identity crisis, and may even have a head start on determining their identities, they still have a few more complications in their lives to deal with than do other teenagers. These kids are still trying to figure out who they are, and why they were given up. Sometimes that leads them to, say, act out a bit in school. Then parents might bring the youngster to a therapist thinking their child was experiencing a major crisis when in fact it just might be something that needs to be talked out and handled in one or two sessions. Adoptive parents tend to have more education and income than the average parent and that also disposes them to take advantage of therapy for dealing with such difficulties. The bottom line is that preoccupation at this age with adoption-related identity issues will not make your child crazy, but some kids need a little help in sorting things out.

It is important to realize that even if your teenager has little to say about adoption, it may still be on his mind. One sixteen-year-old teenager responded strongly to a question about what her feelings were when she thought about her birth mother: "When I think about her, it's with anger or sadness, never with benign curiosity. I am sad that she gave me up and angry at her for getting pregnant before she could take care of a child." Other teenagers have answered this kind of question just as fervently, and in almost the same words.

Your role in this stage of your adolescent's process of coming to terms with herself is similar to what it has been for some time: be there for your child, offer her support, listen to her, and bring up adoption from time to time.

DISCIPLINE AND CONTROL

Whenever possible, the way to resolve differences with your child when she reaches late adolescence is through negotiation. We can't say this too often. Even more than when she was younger, your child now needs to realize that she can sometimes make a point and "win" if she gives you good enough reasons, that you did not predecide an issue before you discussed it with her.

Parents sometimes have trouble maintaining the flexibility required to make this give-and-take mode of family interaction work. They may have been more comfortable and effective when their child needed them to lay down the rules unilaterally. But such firmness, which once served the purpose of creating much-needed limits for a preadolescent, may now take on the character of rigidity in this new stage of family development.

Some kids will rebel if their parents persist in imposing hard-and-fast rules at this point in their development, creating problems between parents and child that need not be there. On the other hand, some adoptees are generally less rebellious than their nonadopted peers at this age

because of excessive gratitude for all their parents did for them through the adoption process. And here parental rigidity may aggravate their passivity and acquiescence.

What if you simply don't feel comfortable exercising less parental control after it's functioned so well for you for so long? First, if you can monitor yourself and acknowledge that you're having this difficulty, you've already won half the battle, since what's required is not a change in your personality but simply a change in the way you act under some circumstances. You don't need to *become* more flexible, but you do need to *act* that way.

It isn't magic and it is workable. Here's how to do it: Every time you hear yourself dictating something to your teenager simply because you think you know what's best, stop yourself. If there's a bone of contention, instead of saying, "You must" or "You have to," you could say, "It's more comfortable for me that you do————this way, but I also realize that you feel more comfortable handling it the other way; so let's talk about it." Remember that you have to decide each time that you'll listen to and consider what your child says and not just pretend to negotiate and then hand down the law.

For example, suppose your daughter wants to come home from her Saturday date at 2 A.M. but you think midnight is more reasonable for someone her age. You could begin your negotiations by going over the facts of the matter: the standards for your community and her "crowd" in the activity in question, whether the event is chaperoned, the weather (if she's driving or being driven), how responsible she's acted with other privileges you've granted her lately, whether she's going out in a group or will be on an individual date, and anything else that's relevant.

Besides letting the facts influence your agreement, always look for opportunities to engage in a little give-and-take. For example, resolving the disagreement over a curfew might involve the child having to give in a little this time but, in return, getting an extra, different privilege or permission to stay out later for something scheduled next month. This give-and-take process can be as important as resolving your differences, since it builds trust and a sense of fairness that will strengthen your overall relationship with your child.

Adoptees, especially, need to know that they are trusted to act reasonably well outside the home, particularly if they've given you no cause to think they will do otherwise. They may interpret the lack of trust to mean that you do not quite consider them a full member of your family. If you're finding it difficult to extend this trust, you should discuss it with your mate and consciously work on it.

Are we asking you to totally give up your standards and make everything negotiable? Not at all. Every parent has—or should have—bottom-line values about basic safety and health, especially when it involves things like drugs and alcohol, and other issues, such as school attendance, that are nonnegotiable. But we are saying that when your child is this age you can't be everywhere, acting as a constant monitor, so it is purely practical not to fight it out every time you disagree. Besides, by now you need to trust that you've done the job of imparting your basic values to your child.

What if you've made a mistake and either haven't given in when you probably should have or have given in when you shouldn't have? The sun will still come up the next morning. Don't be hard on yourself. For both you and your teenager, each little crisis of adolescence is a learning opportunity, and you rarely learn something without making mistakes.

IF THE GOING GETS TOUGH . . .

The typical teenager thinks he knows everything, at least some of the time. "Mom, you don't know *anything*," he may reply, rolling his eyes, to what you thought was a quite cogent observation on your part. It's best to deal with this type of remark with a sense of humor whenever you can.

However, he still needs discipline when he breaks family rules. If anything, he may need it a bit more than his nonadopted peers, since reasonable nos, with sanctions for transgression, add clarity and structure to his life, which has already had enough haziness.

What if you run into some serious behavioral difficulties with your teenager and he does not respond at all to appeals to reason? After all, you can't ground him forever without imprisoning you and him in the house. What do you do when all else fails?

Battles for control at this stage of your child's development are not a good idea. He's certainly too big to control physically. Rather than engage in a struggle to get him to do something specific—such as coming home at a reasonable hour—if nothing else works, try changing the rules, making your behavior unpredictable.

Here's an example of what we mean: the Loftons were having trouble with fifteen-and-a-half-year-old Tom, their adopted son. He seemed to be two people. At times he acted, if anything, slightly mature for his age, and was a pleasure to be with. Then there were the periods when he behaved as if he were writing the rule book for teenage behavior as he went along, acting as he saw fit. *This* Tom was especially evident in his unwillingness to pick up his sneakers from the living room, the one room his adoptive parents especially wanted to keep neat.

Tom's mother, after trying everything reasonable she could think of to get her son to cooperate, took his sneakers, which he had dropped next to the coffee table while watching TV the night before, and hid them in the refrigerator. The next morning, when Tom reached into the refrigerator for some milk to pour over his cereal, his hand brushed against something that was not on his breakfast menu. From then on his sneakers were to be found neither in the living room nor in the refrigerator, but rather under his bed, where they bothered no one.

While most parents worry about their kids rebelling,

disobeying, and running a little wild, the opposite kind of behavior is at least as much cause for concern. When a child does not rebel it is often because his parents have had a hard time allowing for more individuality and independence to emerge. Occasionally, one parent, especially, will try to maintain a child's dependence, encouraging the youngster to stay within the family orbit rather than move out into the world.

While some adopted children respond to this situation with rebellion, others take the path of submission. They may fear a withdrawal of parental love if they dare to be too different. Their unwillingness to buck the wishes of their parent may be reinforced by guilt at wanting to become more independent when they know how much their adoptive parents have done for them. These adolescents do not talk about their future plans, have few ideas separate from their parents', are a little too cooperative. They spend too much time at home and relatively little away with their friends; in fact, their social life is nil.

If this describes your child, or if you notice that your mate is having trouble giving up control over your maturing youngster, then you should seriously consider at least some short-term family therapy to resolve this difficulty before it creates serious problems for your child.

SCHOOLWORK: NOW IT COUNTS

Although your child is now making many decisions for himself, there are still some things about which you know more than he does. No teenager, for example, is capable of fully appreciating the significance of dropping out of high school—any more than he can fathom the idea of his own mortality or just how bad drug or alcohol dependence can get. It goes without saying that high school dropouts in this society start adult life with the odds heavily against them; staying in school and doing as well as he can is something that you will have to impose as a matter of discipline if necessary.

However, if your teenager is not doing well in high school, it may be because his school is not tapping his talents. He may have more of a flair for the graphic arts than for strictly academic work. Perhaps he has an intuitive rather than an analytical bent, with an aptitude for creative writing that his school's standard English curriculum is stifling. He might not score well on standard tests, but could possibly shine in a program that stressed creative skills.

You could investigate alternatives to his school's regular program of studies. For instance, "City as School" might be just the thing for him. This increasingly popular program, which uses the community as a classroom, allows kids to absorb and apply knowledge in the outside world by serving as an editorial assistant on a newspaper, for example, or as an apprentice at a theater. If he's bored because he's not being challenged enough, look into the possibility of his taking courses for advanced placement at a nearby community college, where he can study just about anything that interests him.

College, however, is another issue, one that sometimes unsettles adoptive parents. Your adopted child may not have the intellectual bent that you think of as characteristic of your family. Or perhaps she'd like to see a little bit of the world before committing herself to another four years in the classroom. Should conflict arise over this issue, negotiating a compromise that preserves her independence while keeping her on a course that you know is best for her is the key to helping her to keep her options open.

While you have to be careful not to confuse what you want for your child with what she wants for herself, you can insist that she work hard enough in high school so that she will still have the choice of whether or not to go to college. And the only way to insure that, as we have noted, is to make sure she does at least several hours of homework each night. If she's having trouble with a particular subject, get her a tutor. To find one, call one or more of the colleges in your area and arrange to have their placement office put your requirements in their listings. If public school is really overwhelming your teenager, you might want to consider putting her in a private school—perhaps only for a year—where she can get more individual attention.

Remember that if she decides against going to college when she graduates from high school, it's not necessarily the end of her academic career. Many eighteen-year-olds take a year off from school at this point and go to work to see what life is all about. In fact, in Europe this is fairly standard procedure. The ones who return to school often do so with better motivation and a clearer idea of where they're going than do their peers who went directly to college from high school. Or she could take courses at night at a community college while working during the day, giving her a taste both of work and higher education.

The costs of adoption and the values that guide adoption workers and attorneys who place healthy infants make it likely that you and your spouse went to college and, therefore, may expect your child to do so, as well. It is important to remember that your child is a product of both inherited tendencies from her birth family and the environment you have raised her in. A son or daughter's talents and aptitudes may lead the child in a different direction. Vocational or technical training programs may prepare a person better than college to do what he or she likes or is good at—for example, word processing or auto repairs.

An example of a child who found a happy career without college training is Susan Ryan, whose adoptive parents both have Ph.D.s. They were not entirely comfortable when their daughter, a bright, hard-working young girl, opted not to go to college. During the summer before her senior year in high school she worked at a clothing store, part of a large chain. Two weeks before graduation Susan took a full-time position at the store. Within a month she was promoted to floor supervisor. She worked hard and she loved it. Now the chain has offered her an opportunity to join their management program. Not only have her parents overcome their misgivings, they've started to brag about their daughter's accomplishments.

IF YOU HAVE
YOUNGER CHILDREN . . .

If your family includes younger children, adopted or birth, you may face the necessity, and the opportunity, of having your teenage adoptee act as an assistant caretaker. For most of the world's families, the economics of survival dictate such an arrangement, although we often tend to see this as somehow impinging on the natural freedom of the child asked to help out. It is also, however, an opportunity. For an adoptive family, the need to have an adolescent look after younger siblings enables parents to tell their adopted child in the most basic way any parent can that you trust him and that he is an essential part of the family.

If your adoptee cares for a younger brother or sister, make it clear to the younger child that you've authorized your teenager to act in your name. Set clear limits about what punishment the older child can mete out for misdeeds. "Debrief" your adolescent after he has spent time supervising his charge, pointing out any corrections in his supervision style that you feel are necessary. Don't criticize mistakes he's made in front of his younger sibling. Emphasize ways he can do his job better. Remind him of the successful strategies he's used when his task has gone smoothly.

In arranging for your teenager to share in child care, keep in mind that between school, after-school activities, and homework, kids his age often have a very long day. Depending on how rigorous the schools are in your community, that could account for as much as thirteen hours of his time each weekday and a good part of the weekend. Also, he is in the midst of forming his own identity apart from the family—a necessary task at his age—in preparation for complete independence. So you will have to balance these demands on him with your need for help with the younger kids.

If your teenager serves as the family baby-sitter, he deserves compensation as well as recognition for his work. That could be money—a raise in his allowance—or increased perks. Since he is showing a high degree of responsibility by caring for a younger child, you could reward him with a later curfew or increased access to the family car.

What if your child really hates taking care of a younger brother or sister? Unless economic necessity forces the issue, don't make him take on the job. If you have more than two children, try letting the middle child do the baby-sitting. Your eldest can fulfill his family obligations in other ways.

DATING

Julie Edwards, a conservative, somewhat shy woman, almost didn't have to describe her fears. She arrived at our office with her fifteen-and-a-half-year-old adopted daughter, Mary, whose heavy makeup, tight, revealing clothing, and affected air of sophistication was causing her mother a great deal of anxiety. While she didn't get straight to the point, it wasn't long before Julie reached the crux of her concerns: the possible relationship between Mary's adoption and what her mother viewed as her daughter's sirenlike demeanor.

Julie Edwards's situation was somewhat unusual. Parents don't usually come to us saying that they're worried about the effect of adoption on their teenage daughter's sexual behavior. It's not often that obvious and straightforward, yet it's sometimes there in the background. We can occasionally hear it in their voices. Their anxiety level about their daughter's sexual habits has a different quality to it than that of nonadoptive parents.

We would therefore like to make it clear that there are no scientific studies which indicate that teenage girls act out sexually because they were adopted. That doesn't mean that no adopted girl—or boy—has ever acted irresponsibly in matters of sexuality. When it comes to sexual activity, today's teenagers live in a world that differs substantially from the one in which you grew up. The opportunities and pressures to get prematurely involved have increased enormously. Contrary to what many people think, the teenage pregnancy rate has not risen, but the average age at which teenage pregnancies occur has dropped. No study shows that adoptees are more likely to get pregnant than nonadoptees.

If anything, the adopted teenagers we've known, boys and girls, as a group tend to be somewhat more responsible and straightlaced than their peers about sexual involvement. When we got a few of these kids together for a discussion of this subject, we heard remarks like: "I think people should be more careful about having babies," and, "People should consider how they're going to be able to feed and take care of a child before they have one. They should be more responsible."

Adopted kids have been conscious of issues of relationships and intimacy since childhood because of their awareness of the importance of these subjects in their family history. Consequently, they may be more likely to feel clearer on where they stand about sexual relations, and more self-confident that they can deal with it.

Nevertheless, we realize that most adoptive parents have special concerns when it comes to teenagers and sex. These days that's only natural. The core of the matter usually turns out to be communication. Parents would like to know where their kids stand on sexual limits, what they've been doing about birth control if they have decided to be sexually active, if they are now having sexual relations with anyone, even what their children know about sex (it's amazing what some kids don't know, even at this age). Their children, not surprisingly, volunteer none of this information.

The first thing we do in this situation is to point out that sex, along with other loaded subjects such as drugs and alcohol, is an issue that parents can discuss with their children, just as they speak to them about other areas of life. If you're having trouble dealing with these matters, or your child is approaching these years and you're anticipating some problems and can't imagine how you would bring up topics like these, you might find it helpful to look at this interchange we recently had with a concerned parent.

When Ann Bronson came to us, Joan, her sixteen-and-a-half-year-old daughter, had been acting a bit more secretively than had been characteristic of her in the past. The daughter also had recently acquired a steady boyfriend:

THERAPIST: It seems to me that you're a pretty concerned parent and I can understand why, what with the way things are these days, you have some concerns about this issue. Is your daughter a fairly responsible girl?

Bronson: Yes, we've given her what we think are good values, and for the most part she's lived within those guidelines, at least in other areas of life. But somehow, we're feeling a little uneasy when it comes to Joan's relationships with boys and the possibility that she might get sexually involved.

THERAPIST: Has she cooperated in family matters and manifested no more than the normal amount of teenage misconduct?

Bronson: Yes, we couldn't say that she's been a "bad" kid, that's for sure.

THERAPIST: Well, then what would have to happen to reassure you about your fears? How could your daughter set your mind at rest?

Bronson: I'm not sure.

THERAPIST: I'm hearing from you that Joan is a pretty cooperative girl; it sounds like she would be willing to talk to you about her social life, at least to some extent, if you bring it up in a respectful and unprying way.

Bronson: Yes, I suppose so, although it sounds like a very touchy subject to bring up in any way with a teenager.

THERAPIST: Do you *want* to know how she feels about it? Enough to ask her?

Bronson: Do you think she would actually discuss how she feels?

THERAPIST: Well, you know her better than I do.

Bronson: I guess that while we don't let it all hang out all the time around our house, we tend to be honest and open in our family when the occasion calls for it.

THERAPIST: How do you bring up other touchy subjects in your home?

Bronson: Nothing fancy; one of us just says something like, "Gee, I've had something on my mind, can you spare a minute to talk?"

THERAPIST: And it usually works?

Bronson: Yes.

THERAPIST: It sounds like you have your method.

Ann Bronson got mixed results from her conversations with her daughter about the teenager's love life. Joan did start sleeping with her boyfriend, although her mother tried to talk her out of it. But on the other hand, Joan was willing to discuss it with her mother, she did use birth control, and she kept her head about the whole situation. When the boy started pressuring her to spend too much time with him, causing her schoolwork to suffer, she broke off the relationship. If anything, Ann Bronson's determination to "be there" for Joan, offering advice but also listening to her child and not trying to control her life, brought mother and daughter closer.

If your teenage daughter is determined to get sexually involved with someone, it's almost impossible, short of locking her in her room, to prevent it. But you can point out that just because she's had sexual relations with a boy, it doesn't mean that she has to continue to be sexually active. You can insist that she take a responsible approach to birth control—which these days means the use of condoms and spermicide containing Nonoxynol 9. And you still determine what happens under your own roof. You have a perfect right to say no if she wants to have her lover sleep over at your house.

Talking about sex with your child or providing her with information will not increase the chances of her becoming sexually active. Knowledge is always helpful, not an incitement to harmful behavior.

Adoptees (and their families) also have some anxieties about dating with which nonadoptees never have to contend. Jill Rosenberg's parents felt strongly that their adopted daughter should date Jewish boys, and for more reasons than one. They hoped that she would marry within their faith. But they also thought that confining her dating to Jews would avoid the chance that she might end up on a date with one of her birth siblings, since her birth parents were not Jewish.

The possibility of an adoptee dating her birth sibling isn't just theoretical: it's happened. Teenagers tend to gravitate toward people who are like themselves. And if an adoptee lived in a medium-sized city or town, was brought up there and adopted nearby, and had several birth siblings, her chances of having this experience would increase.

Even the remote possibility of this incestuous scenario occurring should alert adoptive parents to the importance of doing everything they can to secure from their adoption agency as much information as possible about their child's birth siblings. It's also one of the reasons why New York State is moving toward giving adoptive parents an opportunity to adopt any birth siblings of their adopted child who come into the state foster-care system.

Adoption may enter a teenager's romantic involvements in another way. Roberta thought she was saying something totally innocuous when she referred to her cousin Bob's adoption while talking to Sue, Bob's girlfriend. But when Sue's mouth dropped, Roberta realized that she had just spilled the beans: Bob had never discussed his adoption with Sue.

By adolescence, adoptees must decide for themselves who they will tell about their family origins and when and how much they will tell. Bob's parents might have had some ideas on the subject, but it was no longer in their hands.

There are sometimes reasons to hold back this information. Prejudice against adoptees still exists in many quarters. Enough scare stories appear in the media to provoke anxiety in some people about a "bad seed" repeating her birth mother's behavior, or possible genetic defects resurfacing from previously unknown generations. It would not be a good idea for an adoptee to hide the circumstances of his birth from someone with whom he had become seriously involved romantically. But how about her parents? What if he sensed possible prejudice on their part? If they seemed inordinately curious about his family background, already speculating about their potential grandchildren, he might feel on his guard, since some people still obsess about "blood lines."

Unfortunately, no one can lay down hard-and-fast rules about how to handle such a situation. Each person must decide for him- or herself what feels right.

LEAVING HOME

Do you sometimes feel like you're running a motel? The car is a fitting symbol of this stage of your child's life. With a car—whether it's your child auto, the family car she borrows, or a friend's—she can put distance between herself and the rest of the family, stopping by occasionally to grab a bite to eat and change her clothes. The automobile also represents the emotional distance from the family that she must be creating for herself if she is to successfully break away and lead her own life as an adult.

The process of breaking away could be a bit more difficult for your adoptee than for other adolescents. He knows, on some level, the extra work that you did in getting him. Even more important, he realizes that you really wanted him; unlike birth parents, you weren't forced to keep him. That's a heavy responsibility to place on the shoulders of a young person. The child may view his impending departure from the family as an ungrateful act, even disloyalty.

These thoughts may also reinforce an adoptee's feeling that he has known less about himself than his friends have about themselves. Who in his family did he look like? From where did he get his red hair? What if his adoptive parents had not taken him? When he needs to begin taking control of his own destiny, he may not feel entirely secure at the wheel.

There is a type of activity we recommend that helps prepare many youngsters, including adoptees, for the time when they must stand on their own. Wilderness programs, such as Outward Bound, give kids a sense that they can master their environment and gain control over their lives—prerequisites for independent living. Through activities such as rock climbing, long bike trips in which they must fix their own flat tires, and sleeping out in tents in cold weather, these programs force kids to push themselves physically beyond what they thought were their limits. You can find such programs in the advertisements for summer camps in your Sunday newspaper. You might also try attending a camp show, since these programs often take space at the shows.

SEARCHING FOR BIRTH PARENTS

June Tyler remembers when the thought first hit her. Her adopted children were nine, ten, and twelve years old. She had just seen a human-interest feature story on the evening news about an adoptee who spent seven months trying to find her birth parents, only to discover that her birth mother lived in the next town, a mere ten-minute drive away. "My God," June thought, "what if my kids want to look for *their* birth mothers?" And then she quickly suppressed the thought because it was simply too painful.

Fortunately, with time, June realized that she had no control over whether her kids decided to search, and that if they did search it would do her and them no good if she feared what they might find. So she read all she could on the subject to make herself feel as comfortable as she could be with it and to be able to offer help and guidance if her kids asked for it.

Of all the aspects of adoption that adoptive parents may have to deal with, searching for a birth parent is one of the most loaded ones. Few adoptive parents approach it with complete peace of mind. The questions it raises are almost unavoidable:

- Will my adoptee find someone she likes better than me?

- Will she still consider me her parent?

- Will I have to establish some kind of relationship with her birth parents if she finds them?

- Should I help her if she asked me for my help?

- Will she play me off against a biological parent?

- Will we both discover something about her relatives we would just as soon not know?

It is understandable that an adoptive parent's imagination might simply run wild at the various possibilities. But only a small percentage of adoptees—perhaps fewer than 10 percent—ever go through with a search, although our society's increased openness toward adoption records may eventually result in a rise in the number. Among adoptees who try to find their birth parents, women seem to outnumber men. In fact, women appear to have so much more of a desire to know about family roots than do men that when a married male adoptee decides to search, it's often at the prompting of his wife, regardless of whether she is an adoptee or not.

Not every adoptee who says she will search fully pursues the sometimes arduous task of looking for someone who may have left a very faint trail. For many adoptees, simply finding more information about their birth parents may be enough to satisfy their curiosity, and they never carry it through to the final step of actually locating a birth parent. Discovering their original name, for example, is often a momentous occasion, making their birth parents seem much more real and diminishing their interest in continuing the search. On the other hand, some adoptees who intend to do nothing more than uncover facts they don't know have their curiosity piqued and decide to go on and look for their biological parents.

Searching is neither "good" nor "bad." It's simply something that some adoptees do and others don't. We should point out, though, that a recent survey of adult adoptees who had searched suggested that, whatever the results of their search, most were glad they did it. They also felt that *the search brought them closer to their adoptive parents.* Interesting, isn't it?

Even if your adoptee is among the relatively few who engage in a search, the odds are that he will not pursue it until he is at least in his twenties. The Adoptees' Liberty Movement Association (ALMA), the most well-known organization that assists adoptees looking for their birth parents, won't help an adoptee—unless her adoptive parents agree—until he or she is at least eighteen years old.

Adoptees most often initiate a search either when they plan to marry, when they're thinking of having a child, or when their adoptive parents die, possibly because they might have felt disloyal if they had begun a search while their adoptive parents were alive. That last occasion is particularly poignant, highlighting the irreducible fact that, in at least a narrow sense, the child did have two sets of parents. And it's another reminder that birth parents are likely to be younger than adoptive parents, usually by at least ten years.

If your adoptee wants to make the effort to search, offer to help, but don't push your help on her if she doesn't ask for it. Adoptees who look for their birth parents are going through an emotional process that must unreel at its own pace. The timing and the agenda of this profound experience must be the adoptee's alone.

The mechanics of the search may vary from state to state, depending on local laws concerning such activities. In Connecticut, for example, adoptive parents have to give their permission before the state will grant adoptees access to their birth records. We know of one fifty-year-old man whose eighty-year-old adoptive parents stymied his desire to seek out his birth parents when they refused to approve his search.

There are about 250 search and support groups in the U.S. who help adoptees find their birth parents. For example, Orphans Voyage was founded in 1953; ALMA, in 1973. An adoptive parents' organization, the North American Council on Adoptable Children, only began in 1974, and Concerned United Birth Parents (CUB) got its start in 1975. That last group shows the increasing organization of birth parents looking into what happened to the children they gave up.

There are twenty-eight state-operated adoption registries containing information from both adoptive children and birth parents, but their usefulness is severely restricted because regulations governing their use vary from state to state and there is little cooperation between registries. The International Soundex Reunion Registry is more helpful. This data bank, begun in 1975, has 43,000 registrees and has already matched 1,750 adoptees with a birth parent. Adoptees can register at any time, but their file is not activated until they reach their eighteenth birthday.

The actual search may produce results in a week. Or it could require months, even years of spadework. Some people hire private detectives—there is now a subspecialty of professional searchers—to assist them. Others need only the additional information they can get by going back to the adoption agency and asking more questions. A typical clue would be the name of the hospital where the child was born and the date of her birth. Even at a major metropolitan medical center, there's a limit to how many babies could have been born there on one day.

If the agency from whom you received your child told you that her birth parents had died, don't assume that to be the final word. Return to the agency and find out on what evidence they based this assertion, because it may not have been accurate. By the way, this is an excellent reason not to tell your adopted child that her birth parents had died unless you know this to be the case.

For some people, life goes on hold while they search; occasionally the investigation becomes a little obsessive. And the process can get bumpy. Early in their search they may experience an emotionally bruising encounter with an agency or court. It's not uncommon for personnel at these organizations to suggest that an adoptee should be grateful for her adoption and that she is wrong to be curious about her past.

What if the search is successful? What might be its consequences? Steve Brady began his search for his biological mother after the birth of his first child. Four months of checking hospital records, local newspaper files in the library, and numerous telephone directories, led him to the woman he was looking for. She had married about a year after giving birth to him and had since had three children—a family much like the one in which he grew up. He was gratified to have found her. It gave him a sense of having closed an important gap in his life. Yet, somehow, he was also a little let down.

There was nothing special about her. If anything, after the initial encounter, he felt he had very little to say to her.

The results of these searches, even when they are successful, are often less dramatic than you might imagine. The birth mother, who by now may have assumed almost mythical proportions in an adoptee's mind, is likely to prove very ordinary. If the child to whom she gave birth is now a teenager, the birth mother was probably just a college or high school student who "got in trouble." That's the way it was especially before abortion became widely available.

Meeting the adult child she never knew may, of course, be a deeply moving experience for the birth mother. Just because she gave the child up for adoption doesn't mean that her baby hasn't occupied a big place in her thoughts through the years. But that doesn't mean that she and your child will necessarily establish a close, intense, and continual relationship. Remember that in searching for birth parents, your child is trying to fill in a gap in her or his life. What role might there be for the birth mother in your adult child's life now if she is found? It's very hard to predict. Your son or daughter already has a mother: you. Or as a teenager who met her birth mother remarks in Jill Krementz's *How It Feels to Be Adopted* (Knopf): "In my view I have only one mother and that's the mother who raised me and mothered me—who gave me food and shelter and love while I was growing up. That's my definition of a mother."

Another adoptee recalls of her search: "I had a very happy adoptive home. I wasn't looking for anyone to replace the family that raised and loved me. But I felt as though there were a lot of questions I wanted answers to about my background. When I went to have my own children, I couldn't tell the doctor how much I weighed when I was born—things like that."

Occasionally both adoptive and birth parents can share an adoptee's pleasure at a reunion. One adoptee we know of spoke on the phone to her birth mother from 10 P.M. to 4 A.M. after she finally was able to discover her phone number. The adoptee wanted her adoptive mother to meet her biological parent, and eventually they agreed to a get-together. The two older women became so engrossed in looking over family photos—from both families—that they didn't notice it when the daughter who brought them together quietly slipped out of the room, leaving them alone to reminisce about their lives and the very important person they had in common.

An adoptee might also run into difficulties with the birth mother he had worked so hard to find. She may want more involvement in his life than he had anticipated giving her. If this happens, it's important for the adoptee to establish clear boundary lines so there will be no confusion as to what the nature of the relationship will be.

If your adult child does establish a close relationship with his birth family, it is more likely to involve his birth siblings than his birth parents. And even that may be a mixed bag. Al Dawson, one of three adopted children, at the behest of his wife, sought out and found his birth mother and four half-brothers. Two of his brothers welcomed him warmly and became his friends, while the other two have never given him anything but the cold shoulder. Of his two sisters in his adoptive family, incidentally, one has no interest in searching and the other has always expressed some interest but never bothered to proceed beyond the talking stage—even though their mother made it clear to all three that searching was fine with her and that she would help if asked.

Sometimes the search ends with a relationship established not with a birth parent but with a birth grandparent. This can occur when a woman does not want to tell her husband and other birth children about the child she bore out of wedlock and gave up for adoption. Perhaps she became pregnant while her husband was in the service, or a similar circumstance. There is no place in her life for even a casual relationship with the child, but the woman's mother may feel entirely different about it.

Cindy Roland's birth mother rebuffed Cindy's attempt to establish a relationship with her when the adoptee located her after an eight-month search, although her birth siblings welcomed her. Periodically, Cindy would try again to interest the woman who had given her up for adoption twenty-eight years before to at least maintain casual ties, but to no avail. When her birth mother died a few years later, Cindy went to the funeral and poignantly recalls feeling like a "shadow" at the service.

We even know of situations in which an adoptee found his birth mother within his adoptive family. A birth uncle and aunt might have served as adoptive parents, raising the child because another woman that the child now calls his "aunt" was, unbeknownst to the boy, actually his birth mother. She may have been a high school girl who got pregnant, could not deal with the stigma of "illegitimacy," and worked out a solution with her family that enabled her to maintain ties with her son.

Occasionally it's the birth parent—usually the mother—who searches for and finds the adoptee she brought into the world. This is still relatively rare, although it may happen more often with increased consciousness raising in birth parent groups. Although the chance of it happening to your child is remote, remember that if it does, you are still your child's legal guardian. You don't have to relinquish any control just because the birth parent has appeared on the scene. In every sense except the strictly biological one, you are the parent. Especially at the initial contact, you would have no idea of the birth parent's state of mind or needs. So you must play a role in supervising any contact the birth parent has with your child.

Should this happen to your family, determine what the birth mother has in mind. Does she just want to know how your daughter is doing? Does she want a relationship with her? If so, what kind? What does your daughter want? A child could feel overwhelmed trying to negotiate two sets of parents, especially during adolescence. You and the birth mother, in establishing the terms of her participation in your child's life, must therefore make sure that everything you agree to is in the youngster's best interest. If you are having trouble reaching such an understanding, you, the birth mother, and perhaps your child might want to seek counseling from someone experienced with adoption matters.

QUESTIONS AND ANSWERS

I have children ages ten, thirteen, and fifteen. The fifteen-year-old is adopted. I work full-time and I'm a single parent. My thirteen-year-old is better than the eldest child at caring for their ten-year-old brother when I'm not home, but someone told me that I should put the older boy in charge of the preadolescent simply because of his seniority. Also, won't the fifteen-year-old, because he is adopted, feel less than a full member of the family if I bypass him for this important responsibility?

Ideally, each child's responsibilities should mesh with his temperament, abilities, and interests. You may not have a real problem at all if you can come up with important tasks that you can entrust to your fifteen-year-old that make him feel that he is an important family member. For example, since a fifteen-year-old is usually more mature than a thirteen-year-old and better able to handle emergency situations, you could put your oldest child in overall charge of the house while you're away, with the thirteen-year-old specifically assigned the "lesser" task of caring for the youngest child. You could also have the oldest child do most or all of the shopping, showing him that you trust him with money responsibilities.

☐

Believe it or not, I've never found the right time to tell my sixteen-year-old daughter that she's adopted. When she was little I wanted to wait till she was older and could understand it better. But as she got older, it became harder and harder to tell her. What should I do?

It's never too late to tell a child that she was adopted. If you doubt your ability to handle the task, consult a family therapist for help. Some time ago a couple came to the Center for Adoptive Families for help with belatedly telling their fourteen-year-old son that they had adopted him. We worked with them, practicing the way they would talk to their youngster. When the big moment came, the boy responded, "Big deal, I've known about *that* for years. I just knew you didn't want to talk about it." And when you think about it, between neighbors, friends, and relatives, a lot of people knew about the adoption and could have let the child know, purposely or inadvertently.

Of course, once the boy's parents had gotten their "secret" out into the open, the hard work had just begun for them. Now they had to build a relationship of trust with their son, gaining his acceptance of their promise that they had not kept other serious facts about his life from him.

This kind of thing happens more often than you might think—and at later ages. We spoke to a therapist who was treating a family with two adopted daughters, ages twenty and twenty-one. When the daughters had to miss a session, the parents took that opportunity to inform the therapist that they had adopted their kids but had never told them the truth about their origins. The therapist pointed out to the mother and father how much energy they had wasted keeping such a secret and showed them how it had affected the way they had interacted with their children. After a few more sessions without the kids present, the parents were able to share with their children this important fact about their lives.

☐

My oldest child, who we adopted, has chosen to go to a college halfway across the country rather than to the one nearby that we thought he would attend. It's making me feel very sad. Should I mention that to him, or keep it to myself? His adoption has never really given him any trouble and I certainly wouldn't want him to have any second thoughts about how much my husband and I support him.

There's nothing wrong with telling your son that you have mixed feelings about his going away—that's not an adoption issue. Let him know that you're happy about his increasing maturity and ability to function independently, but that you'll also miss him.

□

My eighteen-year-old daughter came home from her first Christmas vacation from college expressing interest in searching for her birth mother. My daughter is so far away most of the time now that I wonder what it will mean for our relationship if she goes through with her search and it's successful.

If this were happening while your adoptee was living at home, you could be supportive and let her know how much you stood behind what she was doing. But the geographic distance between you and her puts her more on her own, complicating matters. Still, ask if she'd like you to help in any way with the search process—perhaps you can check some records that are easier for you to get to. Also tell her that if her search brings up any feelings that she'd like to talk out with you she should feel free to call about it any time.

□

I've read your chapter on the late teenage years and I recognize my son in the child who doesn't rebel at all, who makes no move to break away from the family and seems to have no plans for the future. I also see myself in the parent who has trouble adapting to a relationship with a child based more on negotiation than authority. What can I do about this?

It is encouraging that you can see the problem and not pretend it isn't there. That shows that you're already on the road to dealing with it. Have you talked to your son about what he plans to do as an adult? That would let him know that you expect him to start acting on his own more in the near future and might prompt him to start thinking along those lines. Also, begin trying to be more conscious of any signals you might be giving him to stay a child and remain dependent. Work at building some distance from him. Take progressive steps to encourage his independence—say, for example, encouraging him to do his own laundry. And when he disagrees with you on anything, even mildly, make a point of acknowledging your differences but show him that you respect him and his opinions.

□

I understand that our sixteen-year-old adopted daughter needs the freedom to go out and date but my husband is resisting. He's more conservative than me and comes from a strict background. He also keeps mentioning to me the fact that she was born out of wedlock and he doesn't want to see history repeat itself. I know we can trust her. How can I handle this?

From what you tell us, it sounds like you have come to a basic disagreement over an important issue in child rearing, one that couples often take to therapy to hammer out an acceptable solution. However, before taking that step, why not try finding out from your husband what it would take to convince him that he could trust his daughter to have the kind of social life most kids her age have, and to act sensibly? For example, maybe he'd be more comfortable allowing her to go to parties if he knew there was at least one adult in the house. Ask him what your daughter would have to do to earn his trust, and then have a family discussion about it. This might make the problem for him more one of evaluating information than of abstract moralizing and vague suspiciousness. And by all means get him to read the parts of this book that discuss parental fears that their adopted child will repeat a birth parent's unwise behavior.

□

We've just moved to a new neighborhood and our teenage adoptee has asked us whether he should tell the kids he meets here that he was adopted. What do you think?

The one course that is never helpful is to keep adoption a secret under any circumstances. Other than that, at his age, it's something he must decide for himself in each instance. For example, let's say that you've been to his high school and met his homeroom teacher. She tells you that from your appearance she would have never guessed that you and he were related. The thing for you to do would be to change the subject and afterwards ask your son if he would be comfortable having her know about his adoption.

□

My husband and I think that some of the kids our adopted daughter hangs out with experiment with drugs. One of my teenager's birth parents was a heroin addict and our daughter was born addicted and had to be kept in the hospital until she withdrew from the drug. I read about the possibility that alcoholic parents may pass on an enhanced sensitivity to alcohol to their children, and I'm concerned that my adoptee could now be especially at risk for drug addiction should she ever try even a small amount of the stuff. Is my anxiety justified?

We don't know of any long-term studies that have yet established a tendency of kids born to addicts to be especially sensitive to drugs when they grow up but it seems logical to assume that this might be the case. However, until we have more knowledge of the long-term effect of prenatal exposure to narcotics, it would be a good idea for you to take extra precautions to alert your daughter to the harmful effects of drug use, just in case.

□

My adopted daughter has been insisting that I buy her expensive clothes that she says she just has to have. I get the feeling that she thinks I should do this to make up for the fact that she was adopted and never knew her biological parents. She even once said that "if you were my real mother you would get them for me." I have been feeling guilty and I was wondering if there's a way for me to get a handle on this before it goes too far.

It's all right to say no. If you do, she may react rather strongly, but she has to learn that there are limits to what she can have—that's part of growing up. It's also important that you not fall into the trap of confusing the giving of material objects with getting your child to love you. If she continues to demand those purchases, tell her that her birth mother would have set the same limits.

□

My son has no interest in looking for his birth mother, but I am curious to know what she is like. Would it be harmful for me to search for her?

We can understand your curiosity, but this is a dilemma. You could be opening up something that has repercussions for your child. Maybe he's not interested now in searching, but he might be when he gets older. If you had already done it, you would have foreclosed the possibility of his experiencing the process of seeking her out. We think your best course of action on this matter is no action.

□

I'm a foster parent. I expect to adopt the seventeen-year-old boy placed with me once the twelve-month waiting period is over. My problem is that I don't know how to establish a father-son relationship with him. I've read your chapter on older teenagers but it doesn't seem to speak to my situation.

Little that has been written about adoption addresses your concerns. Separation from caregivers and establishing an individual identity are at the core of what your boy needs to do at this point of his life, and you will build a relationship with him against this backdrop. Try to aim for an ongoing friendship with him, and then see what else develops out of the mix of your personalities.

8

Special-Needs Adoptions

At the ripe old age of twelve, after six years in foster care, Jessica was a veteran of five foster homes. Her wanderings through the world of foster care began suddenly, two days before her sixth birthday. With guns drawn, the police had arrested her mother's boyfriend, a drug dealer, and his accomplice, Jessica's mother. A policewoman handed Jessica a large plastic garbage bag, gave her a few minutes to fill it with possessions—she didn't even need the whole bag—and hustled her off to the nearest child-welfare shelter.

Social workers in the state's foster-care system described Jessica as a child who found it difficult to trust anyone, especially an adult. She was combative; when told to do something, she often responded by yelling. She had a hard edge for a girl her age, and a seriousness and intensity that belied her youth.

But Jessica was also feisty, carried herself with dignity, had a droll sense of humor, and projected a certain vulnerability despite her toughness. She showed a tender side when in the presence of younger children, taking it upon herself to protect the youngest and most vulnerable. Jessica was a fighter—and a survivor. While many people thought she lacked any charm whatsoever, there were others who could appreciate the good qualities that could make for an engaging child if only they were given the chance to flourish. A family finally did adopt her.

The population of children available for adoption through agencies has changed substantially since the mid-1970s. All too often these children have heartbreaking stories to tell. Jessica is not necessarily the typical special-needs child readily available for adoption today; but, unfortunately, she is far from extraordinary.

About 90 percent of children available from agencies now have special needs. What almost all of them have in common is that they are older than the babies that most people prefer when they seek to adopt a child, and that many of them have been through the wringer. It's not for nothing that they ended up in foster care, and their experiences in the foster-care system itself often add to the stresses that have burdened their young lives.

Eddie, a fifteen-year-old, has seen many foster families, and he put it this way:

> It bothers me that everyone except me has
> control over my life. It bothers me that I am
> the way I am. If I could change my ways I
> could be able to live somewhere. It bothers me
> when people trap me or use past history
> against me to make me feel bad. And it really
> bothers me the most that they always seem to
> change my life around every time I get into a
> relationship with someone special. But to put
> this into its simple terms, life bothers me.

In everyday language, *special needs* refers to youngsters who are not likely to join a family and then just blend in effortlessly after a brief, uneventful period of adjustment. Too much has happened to many of them; they often have psychic wounds that need time to heal.

If adoptive parents have to work harder than birth parents, then parents who adopt children with special needs must work harder still. The number of complications are greater, and sometimes there are real problems, ranging from immaturity to violent behavior. These children differ from adoptable infants in a crucial respect: they have a difficult history, much of which they remember. That fact will make a difference in their relationship with their adoptive family.

We are not suggesting that a child's past defines her future possibilities. That her father deserted his family and her mother was a drug addict who neglected her daughter doesn't tell us how a youngster will do in a loving, nurturing environment. But neither can we tell you what you can reasonably expect as she grows up, as we have done for children adopted as infants. Because of the difficult environment from which she comes, this child may not act according to the ages and stages outlined in child-development books—her behavior may not even correspond to the typical behavior of other adoptees that you've read about in this book. Some of what you know about child development will apply to her, but you would be mistaken to rely too much on her chronological age in anticipating her behavior and responding to her needs at any given time. Her particular life history and how she acts in your home are better indications of what she needs from you, especially for the first few years she's with you.

Older children may have lived with one or more foster families. They may have survived physical or sexual abuse or both. Under the best of circumstances, you have to assume that their emotional development has suffered at least temporary setbacks because of the instability and stress they've experienced. We can't emphasize that too much. Even if the older child you adopt has remained emotionally intact after being abandoned, taken from her home by the police when her family had deteriorated past the point of no return, or survived the death or imprisonment of one or both parents, these terrible experiences will have taken a toll. There is always a price to pay.

"All you need is love" does not suffice as a guideline for raising a special-needs child. If there is a rule of thumb in raising these children, it is: hope for the best, but don't count on it. Anticipate problems, and be willing to work long and hard to alleviate them.

THE OLDER CHILD: FORMULAS FOR FAILURE AND FOR SUCCESS

If you are thinking of adopting an older child but have not yet done it, you should know that people who have adopted older children, despite the difficulties involved, tend to think that they made a good decision and would do it again. For example, in a survey of 177 families in the Midwest who adopted children with special needs, conducted by Katherine A. Nelson, 93 percent expressed satisfaction with their experience, and 20 percent of these described their experience as excellent or good. How do you think a similar group of birth parents might respond to such a survey about how they viewed parenthood?

Good agency preparation of these parents and a close match between the child's characteristics and what the parents felt they could cope with often had a lot to do with this high level of parental satisfaction. But it also stemmed from patience and hard work on the part of the parents. As an adoptive parent of one of these children, you will have to telescope into a brief period of time much child rearing that other parents can spread out over many years. Contrary to what some theorists still maintain, you will not have to repeat every stage of childhood that you missed experiencing with your new son or daughter. However, it can go slower than you expect or hope.

Some people flounder in this job because they seriously miscalculate the amount of work required to successfully parent a special-needs child. Among the people most likely to have a hard time raising these kids are those who may think that in adopting an older child they've skipped his most dependent years and thus most of the work. Similarly mistaken are couples who married at a relatively older age and think that not having to deal with an infant will minimize the demands on their energy.

Others run into trouble because they know little about child development and child rearing in general, not to mention the unique requirements of raising a special-needs child. That's why families that already have at least one child, birth or adopted, and have been through the development process in some way before may have a slight advantage.

For example, the infant and five-year-old that the Henrys adopted together were their first children. Almost immediately they ran into difficulty with the five-year-old. Whenever Jeffrey misbehaved, his parents asked him, "Why did you do it?" He either said that he didn't know or else made up a reason. That happens to be normal for any kid his age, but his parents had no experience with such a response, assumed he was lying, and that this had something to do with his life before he joined their family. They brought him to a therapist, creating a problem where there had been none.

The age of adoptive parents may also work against them. People who adopt older children are themselves often older than the average adoptive parent. They are further removed from their own childhood and may find it harder to empathize. Few adoptive parents have personally experienced the traumatic childhoods of their children and may find it difficult to understand entirely how a child might feel when exposed to some of the stresses that kids adopted beyond early childhood have had to experience.

We have worked with parents who had enthusiastically adopted and effectively raised older children whose behavior had made their placement very difficult: fire-starting, inappropriate sexual behavior, and chronic bed-wetting, to name a few kinds of disturbing conduct. One of the secrets of being able to transcend even these extreme problems is making a good match with an older child in the first place.

Parents who did well were often those who found out everything they could about the child offered to them. If you are currently in the process of adopting an older child, tell your agency that you have read that these adoptions work best when parents have every bit of information about the child that can legally be given to them.

Successful parents also tended to be honest with themselves about any characteristics that they probably just couldn't stand. For example, some people, if they had to, could tolerate bed-wetting, but fighting would be the last straw and could cause them to seriously reconsider the adoption. Similarly, some parents may be more comfortable with a child who responds to difficulties by withdrawing; other parents are more comfortable with a child who is more active, even if it is in a negative way. Many others drew the line at lying or stealing. They would not take a child with those traits, even if they feared the agency would not offer them another youngster. Many agencies use the Achenbach Child Behavior Checklist to help potential adoptive parents rate their tolerance for specific misbehavior. If you are at the stage of choosing a child and your agency has not provided you with this guide or something like it, ask them to do so.

Successful special-needs adoptions are also usually found among parents who make sure that bringing an older child into their life does not erode their intimate relationship with each other. They do not allow the adoption to overwhelm their marriage, forcing them to give up their own lives to be with their kids all the time. They let their child know what adult couples are about by acting the part.

However, such couples also tended to be somewhat more child centered than other adoptive parents, taking more of their identity from being parents. Often they were people who had already raised other children, birth or adoptive, to adulthood, and responded to their now empty nest by adopting one or more special-needs children.

Those who have been manifestly successful in raising special-needs kids can get a lot of attention from agency social workers, desperate for good homes for new children coming into the system. The special-needs child that Ed Baron adopted was thriving, so although he never returned to the agency to adopt another youngster, he kept getting calls from them offering him other kids. Fortunately, like many of the more successful of these parents, he knew when to say no. Ed realized that he had enough work and didn't want to risk putting too much stress on the child he already had. He knew his limits. Bringing a new child into your family is always stressful. Be certain that the members of your family can tolerate such stress before you do this. List some recent stressful experiences and think about the ways your family members responded to these events.

THE IMPORTANCE OF PREPARATION

Information about your child's background is one important thing that will give you a clue about what to expect from him. So make sure you get all the general medical, neurological, dental, psychological, and educational data the agency has. You also need to know what experiences he's had in foster care. Get all this in writing or tape record all discussions with your social worker, because when you go through the adoption process you may be initially overwhelmed by the experience and forget the details. Agencies often tell us that they gave adoptive parents the necessary facts about their child when the parents can remember no such thing. Both may be right.

If it's at all possible, arrange to have your doctor and dentist examine your child right after you get him. To be an effective parent you should know for sure what your child's health needs are. Is he a child who will need special medical treatment or close observation of a condition that may require future care? Since the agency has legal custody until the finalization proceedings, they may be unwilling to pay for your own physician and you may have to do so, so bring up this issue with your social worker.

It's by no means a sure thing that the social worker at the agency will tell you everything you need to know. In a big urban agency, the social worker who arranges the adoption may not be the same person who has had direct and continual contact with the child. The person you deal with may be working from a sketchy case record.

If you are dealing with the person who has worked with the child, her loyalty may be to the child, understandably enough, who she may have been involved with for several years. She may be anxious to get him into an adoptive family, since that's probably the only chance the child will have of leading a satisfying and productive life. She may, therefore, withhold some negative information—perhaps that a grandparent was schizophrenic or a parent a drug addict—thinking that revealing such information might turn away prospective adoptive parents.

Jan and Robert Stone had undergone difficulties with their adopted daughter, Melissa, from the age of five months until she entered school. Their pediatrician, whom they consulted, was as confused by Melissa's behavior as they were. The Stones blamed themselves for not giving Melissa all of the love and attention she needed. One evening, they accidentally met their adoption worker at a social event and asked her whether there was anything she could remember that could shed light upon some of their daughter's difficulties. The worker, who had been a pioneer in special-needs adoptions, admitted that Melissa had been born addicted to heroin and had undergone withdrawal from the narcotic over a four-month period in a municipal hospital where it was unlikely she received more than custodial attention. When the Stones asked her why she withheld the information the social worker admitted, "I was afraid you wouldn't take her if I told you about this and I knew a loving family would make up for her early experience."

The big turnover at many agencies often makes for a

young and inexperienced staff who may not be fully trained about the development of even the average child. Schools of social work rarely offer courses on older-child adoption, and the literature on the subject is still very thin, so these social workers are not likely to have even much theoretical knowledge or practical experience with the issues involved.

However, the bottom line is that the adoption may not work if false or missing information colors your expectations about the child. Also, a social worker with whom you do not feel comfortable will unnecessarily add to the work you are already taking on. Between the home study process, placement, and supervision, you may be dealing with this professional for as long as two years. You don't want a difficult and burdensome relationship with her. If you feel you're not getting the whole story, or if the chemistry between you and the agency's social worker is way off, request a new worker or try a different agency with which you can cooperate more easily. For help in finding a Family Builders Agency, specializing in special-needs adoptions, write to the National Resource Center for Special Needs Adoption, P.O. Box 337, Chelsea, Michigan 48118, (313) 475-8693, and enclose a stamped, self-addressed envelope.

We would like to note an encouraging recent trend among some agencies toward not only freely providing the information they already have, but also making extra efforts to fill in the gaps by bringing together in one place bits and pieces of data that make for a comprehensive picture of what has happened to the child so far in her life.

Families usually act as their child's historian, providing her with a record of her life, her roots, as she develops. Photographs of her document much of what her parents say about her early life. All kids in families also share memories with their parents to see if they are based on reality. But children in foster care often have, at best, a hazy notion of where they've been and what has happened to them. Unless someone in the system has been careful to compile a comprehensive account of the child's life history, the child may, in effect, have none.

Now some adoption agencies are taking the admirable step of recording the life history of their children as far as they know it. This often takes the form of "life books" for the kids. These scrapbooks include information about foster families the child has lived with and the circumstances under which the youngster left, places she's visited, and things she's done. They contain photographs as well as text, creating a substantial biography of the child. Since youngsters under the age of six sometimes have trouble separating fantasy from reality, the books help them to develop a sense of their real past, performing a therapeutic function for them, as well as giving you a fine introduction to your child. But at any age, life books are a good idea.

Ideally, the agency should do this task before placing a child. But since the social worker has to see your child monthly after making the placement, she could also do it then. If your agency doesn't perform this service at all, press them to do it. Be persistent. If the social worker says she's overloaded with cases, doesn't have the time, and can't pass on the task to someone else, ask to consult with her supervisor (going through their chain of command should help you to avoid unnecessary confrontations).

Adoptive families we speak to tell us that several services are important in the successful adoption of older children. Adoption subsidies pay for medical and other services and may help you defray costs you are more likely to incur with these kids than with other adopted youngsters, such as tuition for special school, or after-school activities. Make sure your social worker explores every kind of financial help for which your child qualifies because of her status as a hard-to-place child or her handicaps.

Also make every effort to get counseling from the agency on the problems involved in adopting an older child. One of the factors related to the success of older-child adoptions in a recent study was group preparation of the parents who were going to adopt these kids. This "group home study" process evolved in response to pressure from parents' advocate groups who realized that people about to adopt special-needs kids needed better training than they were getting.

In group preparation, prospective parents meet in weekly sessions—typically about ten. They view videos showing why kids come into foster care, learn parenting techniques such as P.E.T. to make them feel competent and less helpless, and discuss special-needs adoption with adoptive parents who have already successfully raised such kids. At this point, people who had an unrealistic notion of what they would be contending with in a special-needs adoption have the opportunity to change their minds while it's still relatively easy to do so. The process also enables adoptive parents to start forming their own informal support networks. And joining with others like themselves gives adoptive parents a feeling of strength and empowers them to view the agency social worker more as a partner than as an adversary who can arbitrarily affect their lives.

REALISTIC EXPECTATIONS

In the Nelson survey of parents who adopted older children, 62 percent of the adoptive parents said their child had at least some emotional or behavioral problems. Some adoptable older children do not manifest dramatically negative behavior. But anybody who adopts an older child should realize that expressions of grief, anger, hostility, manipulativeness, or overt aggressiveness are well within the range of normality. Such children may cling to you and express excessive gratitude for the most trivial favors; or they may be exploitative, or perhaps hell-bent on constantly provoking other people into confrontations.

Boys, especially, are often restless, jittery, unable to do anything for more than twenty minutes at a time except watch TV. If they are truly hyperactive, they may give the impression that they are motor-driven regardless of the event: they may constantly try to climb on objects and not be able to await their turn in group games. Such children may be bossy and stubborn and have trouble tolerating any kind of frustration. Sometimes they can also fool you with their street-wise sophistication into treating them as if they were older than their years. To survive in very difficult environments, many of them learn to mimic adult behavior and they often know how to "play" an adult, manipulating to get what they want.

Children who have survived traumatic experiences such as sexual abuse, rape, physical abuse, removal from their birth family because of the violent behavior or criminal activities of their parents, or constant moves in foster care, may exhibit symptoms of posttraumatic stress disorder (see page 242) or clinical depression. Adoptive parents can't always predict when normal family activities might resurrect the child's memories of that trauma. A family move, for example, could set it off.

Most adopted older children will exhibit behavior in their adoptive families that is at its worst mildly or moderately disruptive—and that mainly in the first two or three years of the adoption. The worst of it may show up only at school and not be evident in your home at all, or only at home and not at school, or everywhere. Usually such conduct is the consequence of what worked for them in the difficult environments in which they lived. That behavior helped them to survive, but although it is inappropriate in their current circumstances, it has become a habit they need to unlearn. You will need to show them good reasons to unlearn it, and that takes time.

In view of their background, to expect too much from adopted children with special needs—and to expect it too soon—is to set up both you and the child for disappointment and possibly failure. One of the most potentially disastrous expectations would be that you and the child will quickly come to love each other after a brief getting-to-know-each-other period. If you think about it, how could that happen in the initial stages of your adoptive parenthood? You barely know the child, and his first reaction to his placement with you is likely to include considerable wariness, at the least. Would you really expect him to walk into your home and start loving you, a stranger, almost immediately?

We've heard heartrending tales from these youngsters. For example, a child may be told by a foster family that she will stay with them permanently, only to wake up one morning to find her bags packed. Or a social worker may have come to her foster home and told her she was taking her to visit the child's aunt, only to have the destination turn out to be an institution. No wonder the child has learned not to trust anyone over the age of eighteen. Only in the movies do people shed the weight of such a past in one sudden and dramatic catharsis, although your family environment will eventually begin to bring out her best.

An added complication: more often than not, a child's primary caretaker in her adoptive family will be the mother. Unfortunately, many of these children trust women the least, since they may already have been given up by several foster mothers and had to deal with female social workers who they felt had let them down—not to mention whatever mixed feelings they have about their birth mothers.

That doesn't mean that the older child you adopt can't learn to trust you. Think of his capacity to trust as a muscle allowed to atrophy, or perhaps never used at all. You wouldn't begin to exercise that muscle by lifting two-hundred-pound weights; instead, you would start slowly, gradually working it into shape.

The most practical initial approach is to concentrate on appreciating those characteristics of the child that caused you to adopt her. Let yourself grow to like her first. Draw your satisfaction from the tiniest progress she makes. That could be as simple as the first time she lets you read to her at bedtime and hold her hand while you are doing it. If love follows, it will do so in its own time. Sometimes, with difficult kids who have been brutalized by adults, it may take you a long time to get past the "like" stage; in truth, developing nothing more than a workable caretaker relationship constitutes a success with some of the most difficult older children. And that is a success to be proud of!

NEITHER HERE NOR THERE

As in any adoption, you face a period before the adoption of a special-needs child is made permanent—usually six to eighteen months. This may last longer than the similar wait before the adoption of an infant reaches completion because there is more counseling involved.

Your interaction with an older child is considerably more complicated than it would be with a baby, and ideally you would have much more freedom of action than you will actually have during the preadoption period. Unfortunately, you will have to take on the job of a parent for that time—probably of a child with some problems—without some of the usual parental responsibilities and decision-making powers.

Legal custody of the child still rests with the agency. They have the final say in everything from how you can discipline your child to what kind of therapist your child visits. In an emergency, your child's school may contact the adoption agency, and may not call you. We came across an appalling incident in which a school that had information about an adopted child's birth mother called *her* when a problem arose, even though the child had already been legally adopted. Also, you may need your social worker's permission to take your child out of the state or even to have him stay over at his adoptive grandparents' house. Emergency medical care must be approved by your worker as well.

Establishing a good relationship with the social worker will help make the adoption process easier for you. Sometimes adoptive parents, discovering the abusive treatment their child may have received in foster care, and already forming a bond to her, vent their fury at the social worker, who they think should have protected their child. But you're not likely to know the full story of what happened to your child, nor how much, if anything, the social worker you're now dealing with had to do with it or could have influenced the child's treatment. Scapegoating the social worker is not in your interest, and you should do your best to avoid it.

The social worker on your child's case is required to see her alone periodically. This could possibly hamper your ability to parent the youngster, encouraging her to think that she can keep secrets from you, discussing them only with the social worker. Should you and the youngster come into conflict, the child could play up to the social worker, getting her to place further limits on your ability to use your discretion in caring for the child. This is a difficult but not uncommon problem among special-needs adopters.

Try to get the social worker to share with you any important information she gets from the child during this period. Ask her to discuss with you, away from the child, any problems and conflicts that arise, to bolster your authority. In matters that directly concern the child, urge the social worker to bend the rules a bit, if necessary, so you may be present when they're discussed. Tell her you want to do things in a family context as much as possible. Acknowledge that she is still in charge in that she is responsible for monitoring the adoption, but try to negotiate with her a gradual withdrawal of her status as the authority figure in the child's eyes. She's probably overworked, so she may be quite agreeable to this.

If the finalization process seems to lag, press your attorney to get the court to set a date. When that day comes, don't assume that you will find a festive air in the courtroom. While it is not frequent, some judges fail to make it easy or joyous for anybody at the end. Sometimes judges are prejudiced about adoption and concerned with the sacredness of blood ties. "Judicial discretion" allows them quite a bit of leeway. For seemingly no reason judges can, and occasionally do, order an additional home study after all work preparatory to adoption had been thoroughly done. Believe it or not, in one recent case in a large city, a judge would not permit a child with AIDS to be part of the adoption finalization in his court and he ordered psychological tests for the adoptive parents to probe their "motive" for the adoption. We've also observed judges who give parents a hard time when they adopt children of another race. An attorney who handles a large number of child-welfare agency adoptions can protect you and your family from these experiences.

Your child may be anxious as the time for finalization approaches, partly because every transition is stressful and also because he most likely has never had anything good happen to him in a courtroom. For this reason, many adoptive parents feel it's important for them and their child to plan a small celebration for him at home or at their church or synagogue after the legal proceeding. Some religious groups are developing ceremonies for families who adopt, and if you haven't inquired at your place of worship about this practice, it might be a good idea to do it now.

WELCOME TO THE FAMILY

The best general advice we can give you about how to act with the older child you've recently adopted and brought home is to go *slow*. Don't crowd in on him. He's been through a lot in his few years. Your warm home and good intentions notwithstanding, entering yet another environment is stressful to him, and it may not take much to overwhelm the youngster.

His room should not be overstimulating. Keep it sparsely furnished and paint it in a subdued color. You needn't feel that you have to make up for all the toys he never had. Leave only a few toys out if he's young enough to have them, and store the rest, introducing them into his life gradually. He probably does not know how to care for his toys—you'll have to teach him.

If he's your only child, remember that only-child status is probably something new to him. He may have been part of a large birth sibling group, or had brothers and sisters in the foster homes in which he's lived. Living with other children would have allowed him to share complaints about the adults in the house, getting confirmation of his feelings and allowing him to blow off steam. He may feel more at ease with children than with adults. Suddenly, if in your home, he finds himself the focal point of the family with no other children to distract attention from him, it may be the first time he's ever experienced having nowhere to hide.

Anger may be the most usual kind of emotional intensity he has ever experienced from adults, provocation the only way he's ever learned to get attention. So even if your instincts tell you to take him right to your heart, back off a little and let him signal when he's ready for closer ties and something approaching the parent-child relationship with which you're familiar.

Have you assumed that she will start off calling you "Mom" and "Dad"? She might, but let it be her choice. Some special-needs kids will begin calling their adoptive parents by their first names. As soon as you can after she's placed with you, ask her how she wants to address you—let her know she can call you Mom (or Dad) if she wants to—and what she'd like you to call her if she seems to have a nickname.

As an overall approach to finding and adapting to her rhythm of fitting into your family, use the observation method we introduced in chapter 2 (page 44) when we discussed how parents can deal with their anxieties about how an adopted infant will develop when they may lack important knowledge about her family history. Give yourself an assignment to note when your child seems most satisfied, most content. In time, you'll develop a profile of your child that may help you predict how she'll react to most new experiences.

Most parents want to be physically affectionate with their children and to have that affection reciprocated. But since your child may have received mostly painful physical contact from authority figures, you will have to move carefully here. See when your child comes to you. Does he like it when you physically reach out to him? Does he respond positively to your arm around his shoulder? To a hug? Some kids like to be kissed, some don't. If your child doesn't, don't press the issue, because that certainly won't get him to accept your affection. Sit on a chair next to his bed and read bedtime stories to him. After a while you might try touching his arm as you read. With some kids you may never be able to have close physical contact, at least until they're bigger and feel more self-confident and less afraid.

Observe which activities your child enjoys; see when he takes the initiative to join in and when you have to invite him to participate. When you find something he likes, do more of it. If bike riding is what he likes rather than talking, for example, emphasize that activity. Many adoptive families have found that camping trips are a special way of relating to a special-needs child. The family has a chance to interrelate away from the normal distractions. They work together at the simple tasks which camping requires and ones which each family member can contribute to in some way. She only has the family to relate to. It is also unlikely that there will be any environmental cues to remind her of former experiences of abuse or neglect.

Try a variety of activities to draw him out. For instance, he may not feel up to joining the conversation at the dinner table, but a board or card game after dinner might make him talkative. Pick something simple that will not make him feel like a failure, and remember that he may have a short attention span at the beginning, so be willing to suspend the game when he appears to lose interest.

These kids often have a lot of physical energy, so try some activities that focus on movement. Individual athletic games are a good bet, although stay away from team sports at least at first if your child finds it difficult to relate to large groups of people as many special-needs adoptees do. You might also do something like baking bread that requires a lot of physical exertion (without a food processor, so you have to knead the dough).

It may sound strange, but your first job as a parent adopting an older child is to teach him to be part of your family. Every family is different, and their dissimilarities range from the seemingly trivial—are kids allowed to eat while watching TV? are they required to make their bed as soon as they get up in the morning?—to basic values concerning manners, cleanliness, acceptable language, and religion. Don't assume that your new child will know what's "natural" around your house, no matter how normal it seems to you.

Kate Simpson, then six years old, was already a veteran of several foster families when she was placed for adoption with Ellen and Harry Simpson. Things were going reasonably well in the first few weeks but the Simpsons still got the feeling that something was on their daughter's mind. When Kate didn't say anything, Mr. Simpson casually asked her if there was anything bothering her. There was: how to make the bed. Every family she had ever lived with had different rules about this mundane duty. Kate was confused and concerned, since she liked the Simpsons and wanted to fit into their family. When Mr. Simpson demonstrated their version of hospital corners, Kate had one less thing to worry about.

Nothing is too obvious for you to explain. Your child will not be hurt or insulted when you point out your family customs, since by doing this you are in effect telling him that you want him to be part of your family. In fact, we urge you to be as straightforward and as authoritative as you can about how you like things done. If morning showers are the house rule, let him know it from day one. If you care how the table is set, show him the right way. But don't flood him with too many new customs at once. Let him master one or two at a time.

You never know when rituals that seem obvious and appropriate to you will take your adopted older child completely by surprise. For instance, you could have knocked Frank Sheridan over with a feather when he greeted his nine-year-old at dinner on the boy's birthday with a birthday cake on the table and a gift-wrapped present set down next to it. Richard, who had lived with Frank for only three months, was startled and didn't know what was going on. He had no experience of this ritual, didn't know how to act, and seemed very uncomfortable. Frank, of course, had expected to see his son's eyes light up.

To your older adopted child, the activities your family enjoys as well as your rituals may seem like they come from another planet. Do you celebrate Thanksgiving? Do you like to go to museums, plays, concerts? Do you take it for granted that most people at least occasionally eat in restaurants? Don't assume that your child has done any of these things— even once—or that he will take to them in time simply because you like them.

By all means introduce your child to these new experiences, but do it gradually. The first time you take him to a museum, for example, limit the visit to fifteen minutes or a half-hour; unless, of course, he takes to it with relish, in which case let his enthusiasm and your physical endurance set the limit. Take him to a Little League game as a spectator and see how he reacts before signing him up for a team. Share with him anything you like, but do so with subdued expectations so that if he's bored, you won't be sorely disappointed.

Eating in a formal restaurant with your child might be a trial more than a treat unless you acclimate her to the experience first. It's quite possible that she's never seen the inside of any restaurant other than one that serves fast food. Why should she know how to act? She has no precedent in her life for this strange activity.

Fortunately, you can practice at home how to act at a restaurant. First, don't bring the food right away. It may not have occurred to you that waiting for food involves a kind of delayed gratification, which always entails trust that something you want or need will come to you if you are patient. Little or nothing in your child's background may have proven that to be true for her.

If you frequent better restaurants, place cloth napkins, maybe even candles, on the table. Is it the custom in your family that children first tell their parents what they want, and then the parents tell the waiter? If so, explain it to her, since there's no reason she should be able to figure it out for herself. Once she seems to get the picture, you might want to do a "practice run" by going to the restaurant just for dessert.

Meeting your neighbors, friends, and extended family is also something the child should experience a little at a time. It's natural to want to throw a big party to celebrate the arrival of your child. After all, it's a proud moment in your life. But it's hardly likely that the child will be easily able to handle it. Think back to your own childhood. Can you remember a social function at which friends or relatives of your parents, people you didn't know or couldn't remember, came up and all but overwhelmed you with their attention, questions, and comments? Imagine how your adopted older child would feel about meeting a flood of people when she is still trying not to see you as a stranger.

People outside your immediate family will feel a little differently about your adopting an older child than they would if you had taken in an infant. You may hear questions like, "Aren't you afraid his character is already formed and that you won't have any effect on him?" To that you could reply with information about special-needs kids—their difficult past and their potential for growth and achievement once they are secure in a nurturing environment. If they tell you you're a saint for putting up with such a child, you might want to respond with humor and tell them that your child is a saint for putting up with *you*.

SCHOOL

Should you get your child in the middle of the school year, he will have to endure still one more stressful situation. Not only will he be the new kid—always rough on any child—but he may also have a name different from yours, since you will not yet have finalized the adoption. In a small town or close-knit neighborhood, where families often know each other at least slightly, his status as an adoptee will make him stand out, accentuating the last quality he needs right now: difference. You might be able to avoid this problem by arranging for the school to call him by your last name, assuming that's all right with your child and the adoption agency.

Parents adopting older children should prepare for the distinct possibility that their child will need special attention in school. Many things may have adversely affected your child's ability to concentrate and learn. For example, special-needs children may have had mothers whose use of alcohol or drugs during their pregnancy affect their child's ability to learn as quickly as other children. If your youngster moved around a good deal, he may have had big gaps in his education. Good grades on his academic record might be deceiving, especially if he spent time in institutions such as residential treatment centers, where the emphasis was probably on controlling emotional and behavioral problems rather than on academics. And if you adopted him at the age of seven, eight, or nine (this is especially true for boys), he's come to you when many kids are restless in the classroom; the instability in his life up to this time is not likely to improve that tendency.

You will probably have to serve as your child's advocate at school. It's a little like having a relative in the hospital. The doctors and nurses always seem to be a bit more attentive to patients when relatives visit frequently and speak to the attending medical personnel. If possible, make sure the child's adoptive father makes his presence known, since schools often seem to respond more readily to a father who takes an active interest in his child's education. Mike Harper did that with his son, Rod, who had been acting up at school. Mike dropped in on Rod's class once in a while unannounced—with the teacher's permission—and sat in the back of the room to observe. Rod actually enjoyed the extra attention; and the teacher viewed it positively too, seeing it as a sign that Rod's parents cared and that the youngster's chances of doing better were therefore enhanced. In turn, that made her pay more attention to the boy.

The educators in your town may not have much experience in dealing with children with your youngster's needs. Also remember that their responsibility is to all the kids in the system and they are not likely to appreciate a child who makes their job harder. If your child is disruptive in any way, school personnel will not view your child's interests as paramount. So you'll have to become the expert in the field and help the school find alternatives if your child doesn't respond well to standard pedagogical and disciplinary methods.

When you meet his teachers and guidance personnel at the school, make it clear that you think he may need some *temporary* help while he adapts to your family as well as the role of pupil. Doing this should enable your child to take advantage of any extra services the school may have, such as resource rooms, individual counseling, and tutoring, while avoiding his placement in a special class and possibly having him permanently labelled as a troublemaker or poor student. Ideally, what he needs are small classes, clear rules, and appropriate reading material to ultimately bring him up to his age level academically.

Unfortunately, our public schools have a good deal of trouble dealing with a child who is undereducated. In fact, such a classification does not formally exist. Instead, school personnel are often all too comfortable calling kids "neurologically impaired" or "emotionally disturbed." So you will have to be vigilant and resourceful to keep these labels from adhering to your child.

If your child is disruptive, the school may have him evaluated by a psychiatrist. They may even insist that he be medicated with a drug such as Ritalin, commonly prescribed for hyperactivity. This should only be a last resort and even then its use should be strictly limited. Ritalin occasionally has side effects that are serious and irreversible. Even when it works the way it's supposed to, it may leave a child somewhat "stoned." A friend of ours gave it to her adopted son for a brief time and got this response the first time she administered the medication: "Mommy, I feel very tired; is this the way you feel all the time and is that why you behave?" Try everything else possible before you resort to this.

Family therapy that uses a structural model is especially useful with children who are overactive and disruptive. The Philadelphia Child Guidance Clinic, 34th Street and Civic Center Boulevard, Philadelphia, Pennsylvania, 19104 (215) 243-2773, have pioneered this model of working with families and children. They should be able to recommend a therapist or clinic near you with expertise in this approach.

If your youngster develops academic or behavioral problems that seem intractable, consider placing him in a school with a higher teacher-student ratio where he can get the special attention he needs. You might use your adoption subsidy monies to help you to finance this special schooling if your local school district will not pay for it.

For a cheaper but effective alternative to private school, consider sending him to one of the private after-school learning centers you can find in storefronts in many cities these days. These organizations provide children with high teacher-to-student ratios and give the kids frequent tests to measure their progress. If you don't know where to find one, your child's school guidance counselor should be able to help.

ACKNOWLEDGING THE PAST

Helen Weiner felt relief. The foster parents of Jackie, the ten-year-old she had adopted three years ago, were moving halfway across the country. Helen really didn't care for them. She didn't like their manners, the way they kept their house, or their failure to set academic standards for their own children. But she put up with having a relationship with them because Jackie loved them and they still meant a great deal to her.

Sensitive adoptive parents will recognize that an older child arrives with emotional baggage. He's had time to develop relationships with other parental figures; unlike other adoptees he may have known his birth parents—perhaps all too well. And you may have to develop a relationship with some of these people. It's a different experience from adopting an infant, of course, unless you got your child through an open adoption process. If you never gave it too much thought before the adoption, it would be well to consider its importance now, because in adopting your child, you took in with him all the relationships that are central to his life. So while you welcome him to your home, leave some room in your family for the family ties he's already developed.

Agencies often encourage adoptive parents to meet their child's current and about-to-be-former foster family to help the child make the transition from one family to another. For one child we saw in our practice, who had been shuttled around to many homes, we brought her foster mother into the therapy to act as a sort of grandmother, giving her blessings to the child's adoptive family. You need not establish a relationship with your child's former foster family as a matter of course, but it could be helpful if your child has obvious enduring emotional ties to these people.

There is no hard-and-fast rule about how to handle your child's relationship with a former foster family. You could take him for an occasional Sunday afternoon visit to his former home, or have a child from that family stay overnight with you if your child remains close to him. But short visits, telephone calls, and letters are probably preferable to over-night stays, since you want to do everything you can to encourage your child to shift his loyalties to your family. However, you might want to remain especially flexible if your youngster shares an ethnic or racial background with the foster family that you and he do not have in common. In that case, this tie may be even more important.

Negotiate the terms of any continuing relationship with the foster family at the very beginning of the adoption. For example, if a relationship does continue, you will have to come to an agreement about how to handle the possibility that your adopted child may bring up important matters about himself with the foster family that he is not yet comfortable discussing with you. That could range from the type of food he is used to eating or anxiety about competing in team sports at school to doubts about whether he's liked enough by his adoptive family to remain with them.

THE PARENTAL CHILD

The Andersons adopted two children: nine-year-old Patricia and her thirteen-year-old brother, Ronnie. The boy liked his new family, and wanted to stay. He especially liked his new adoptive father. But Patricia was having a hard time. She had developed a close attachment to the mother in the foster family they had been staying with and under the stress of separating from her, the girl's asthma began acting up. Realizing that his sister was profoundly unhappy, Ronnie, against his own self-interest, began to systematically misbehave in a way and to an extent that forced the Andersons, an experienced adoptive family of special-needs children, to begin family treatment.

Siblings placed together come with their own behavioral patterns. On one hand, brothers and sisters have a model for a close emotional relationship: their ties to each other. That bodes well for their developing a similar relationship with you. On one hand, some interactions between siblings can cause adoptive parents a considerable amount of trouble. This is particularly true of the parental child phenomenon. Here the oldest child sees himself as a caretaker for his siblings.

When the therapist engaged by the agency to see Ronnie spoke with him, he revealed the essence of his problem. "Don't you ever just feel like having fun and being a kid?" the therapist asked him. "Lady," he replied in a flat tone of voice, "are you joking? I've never been a kid. I was born old."

Ronnie and Patricia each eventually got what they wanted. After they were returned to the foster family from which they had come to the Andersons, Ronnie misbehaved again. This time he was acting for himself. The brother and sister were separated, Patricia staying with the foster family she had liked and Ronnie getting a second chance, alone, with the Andersons.

The parental child is not neurotic. His sense of duty is likely to be a response to an objective situation. But that doesn't mean that such a child is necessarily stuck in that role forever. Louis, for example, took on this heavy responsibility at an early age when his mother, a prostitute and drug addict, locked him and his four brothers and two sisters in their apartment when she went out. Louis would break out of the apartment so he could steal food for his siblings and himself. When he was later adopted with his two sisters, Rose and Anna, he understandably did not quickly surrender his position of guardian. Fran and Howard Jensen, Louis's adoptive parents, had to find a way to transfer his authority over Rose and Anna to themselves, since the boy needed to live the life of a child as much as his sisters, and the Jensens needed to have their authority as parents accepted by all three children so they could protect and nurture them. They made the transition gradually, telling Louis, "You've known your sisters longer than we have, so we hope you'll help us to discover what kind of care they need. You've done a good job of watching after them, but there are many things they need now that you can't provide. Besides, you need some time off, too, from all the responsibilities you've had to take care of. We would like to convince you that you can begin to trust us to take care of the girls."

Succeeding with a parental child means working with him and not just trying to move in and usurp his authority, since he's not likely to give it up under those circumstances. You have to validate his perceptions and compliment him on the job he's been doing. It may even be necessary to treat him as if he were considerably older than his years, since he's been acting the part—at least in one segment of his life.

When we have worked with these children in family therapy, we've found that the younger children are often in a bind regarding loyalty. We've often had to work, over a period of time, to get the older child to give the parents permission to assert authority with the younger siblings.

Parents should openly acknowledge the sibling pattern to each of the kids and be explicit about the new relationship. Make it clear to the parental child that there is now someone else to care for the younger brother or sister. Give him credit for watching over his sibling, but tell him that you will shoulder much of that responsibility now. Let the parental child know that there may still be times when his sibling will come to him for help; at other times the younger child can go to their parents. And remind him that he is now free to act his age and enjoy his childhood.

If you're in this situation, remember that you have to earn the trust of all the children. The relationship they have forged has worked for them under very difficult conditions. They won't give it up until you prove to them that you are trustworthy and consistent, and that will take time.

SOME UNPLEASANT FACTS

There's a good possibility that the older child you adopted was physically or sexually abused. Or your child may come from a family in which antisocial behavior was the family norm. Perhaps his birth parents expected him to steal or to sell drugs. Or he may have had a parent who was mentally ill.

It's not uncommon for a special-needs child, two or three years after her placement, when she feels safe, to act out symbolically to show what happened to her. For instance, she may dance in a manner that suggests she has had sexual experiences inappropriate to her age. Or a child may tell her adoptive parents directly about the sordid details. Naturally, adoptive parents feel outraged when learning what their child had to endure, especially when they hear it directly from the victim. Adoptive parents often respond to such horror stories with bitter characterizations of the birth parents, particularly of the birth mother, thinking that their empathy will comfort the child. But that's a big mistake.

Nothing good ever comes from denouncing your child's birth family, no matter how upsetting their behavior may have been. Your child will resent it. If you're truly enraged, after comforting her, go out for a walk and burn off the anger with physical exertion. When you're feeling calmer, sympathize with your youngster and tell her how sad you feel that she had to go through such an ordeal, and promise her that in your family it would be inconceivable that any child would ever be beaten, made to go without food, forced to do terrible things. Even though she may already have lived with you for several years and you've gained her trust, continue to reassure her anyway; she'll appreciate hearing it again.

As awful as your child's early life experiences may have been, it might be useful for you to at least try to see her birth parents' behavior in perspective, since she probably retains some kind of loyalty to them and it could help you to empathize with her. Her birth mother and father may not have been fortunate enough to have parents as loving and caring as you; their economic and social circumstances may have been dire. Try to imagine them as victims like the child you adopted, because that's what they were.

Further, if the adoption agency's description of the birth parents influences your view of them, remember that social workers had to build a good case in court so they could have your child removed from her original home; they were not trying to paint an objective portrait of troubled human beings. So their files may contain a description of the birth parents at their absolute worst. Yet your child's appealing characteristics must have come from somewhere; in the midst of the terrible troubles in her family there must have been at least a glimmer of warmth.

DISCIPLINE

Kids who have been shunted around from foster families to institutions and back again have a harder time dealing with complexity and ambivalence than do other children. More than other adopted kids, they need clear rules of conduct consistently enforced. It's important that they come to see you as an adult who can take care of them and that you can tell them the right thing to do in most situations. Besides kindness, they need predictable, fair, and equal treatment from you. So don't waste time agonizing over the hard life they've led. Give them their share of household chores as you would any other child. And tell them what sort of behavior you expect from them.

All parents have to correct their child's conduct, but discipline is a delicate subject with these children. If your child was abused by a birth parent or other adult, avoid all physical punishment. Find other ways to control his behavior, such as sending him to his room (but not if isolation was a theme in his upbringing) or taking away some of his privileges.

You would think that Renee and Peter Thompson, a teacher and CPA living in New York City, would have had no trouble devising an effective way of getting their eleven-year-old adopted daughter, Susan, to comply with their standards of behavior. They already had two grown birth children and they knew something about parental discipline. But Susan was running rings around them.

Susan had entered foster care because her mother was a chronic alcoholic whose boyfriends subjected her daughter to frequent beatings. Six months after she was placed with the Thompsons, the preadolescent was still teasing her hair, using eye shadow and lipstick, and dressing to kill. What's more, she was complaining to her social worker in the northern, rural part of the state where she came from that she missed the country and wanted to return to the foster-care system in that area. The worker was getting jumpy and the Thompsons knew it. That pushed her adoptive parents to enter therapy.

After some conversation it turned out that the Thompsons, feeling sorry for Susan because she had been through so much, had been letting her stay out as late as she pleased, buy whatever clothes she wanted, and generally make up her own rules of conduct. When they had the temerity to decide that she needed at least some limits and that her freedom had gone far enough, the girl all but laughed in their faces. When they tried to take away her TV and other privileges to get her to change her behavior, she told them that she didn't care, a response that demoralized her parents and caused them to quickly back off.

It was pointed out to the Thompsons that they knew how to raise kids and should be able to set limits on their adoptive daughter. They replied that no punishment they tried worked. They had also attempted to reason with Susan, bringing her into their discussions of what constituted acceptable behavior, but that hadn't produced anything positive either.

Susan was quite up-front about where she thought she stood. "They can't make me do anything," she proclaimed defiantly. Further conversation clarified the nature of the problem in the Thompson family. The parents were allowing their child to blur the boundaries between her and themselves when they let her into their discussions of what to do about her actions, and they simply were not standing firmly enough when they made attempts to change her behavior.

The essence of effective discipline is not the specific punishment or how long it lasted but rather the conveying of a tone of seriousness to their daughter. Brief but sure punishment is almost always the best kind. Susan had to understand that her parents meant it, that if they said something would happen, it would. Threatening without following through was worse than no punishment at all, because it encouraged Susan to hold her parents in contempt. They had to see their threats of punishment as a promise that they would keep. By acting consistently, with no ambiguity, they would also be teaching their daughter that she could always trust them to do what they thought was best for her.

The Thompsons got the point. The next time Susan went against their wishes, they discussed it among themselves, excluding their daughter, as suggested. They concluded that a week without her bike might change Susan's attitude, and they informed their daughter of her punishment. At first, she was indifferent; but this time her parents were adamant. After a week without the bike, when it became clear that now her parents would not back down, Susan actually displayed some contriteness. Not that she turned on a dime. Two weeks later the Thompsons told us that Susan had called them, well past her curfew, from Times Square. We told them to call the police the next time she did that, and to let Susan know that that's what they planned to do.

An interesting thing happened after that. Over the course of several sessions—it took about nine or ten in all—a gradual transformation occurred not only in Susan's behavior but also in her appearance. Bit by bit the heavy makeup and other marks of pseudosophistication disappeared to reveal the eleven-year-old underneath. Given the strain of her childhood, innocence was perhaps something she would never know, but at least she was now both acting and looking like a child, to her parents' enormous relief.

Another family in treatment felt they needed to use corporal punishment on their adopted child to get him to mind them. These parents had tried all of the normal types of discipline and they were willing to use these methods at first. They were concerned that if, when these other methods didn't work, they couldn't use corporal punishment that they would not have a last-resort threat. As they raised their other children they had resorted to occasional spankings. They themselves had been spanked as children. They didn't like changing what had always worked for them. Because we were unsure of the child's experiences in former homes and couldn't absolutely rule out that he had been abused, we were reluctant to allow them to use corporal punishment, but we also didn't want them to feel incompetent as parents of this difficult child with special needs.

To create a strategy that would enable them to handle the child's misbehavior without doing anything inappropriate, we agreed with them that it was the scariness of the noise of a slap, not just the hitting itself, that is effective in getting a response from a child. We suggested that they clap their hand against a book not too near their child's ear to produce the desired result. It made the parents feel less helpless, and it got the child's attention without hurting him.

There is also a legacy of physical and sexual abuse that might present a serious impediment to the smooth integration of an older child into your family beyond limiting the kinds of sanctions you can use to impose discipline. It involves a survival mechanism that the child may have once legitimately used but that is now grossly inappropriate. Many kids know that if they're unhappy and want to lash out at you, they can charge you with child abuse.

If that happened a whole investigation might ensue. The people who investigated you would not be obliged to return to tell your neighbors and others who were interviewed that the accusations proved unfounded. By comparison, this experience would make your adoption home study seem like a lark.

Kids usually threaten to turn you in before they actually try it. If your child should make such a threat, take it seriously. Even if your child is already adopted, call your agency worker right away and tell her that you want this threat included in your child's record. Send a follow-up letter to the agency with details of the incident, such as what the youngster did, what you did, and the precise threat. Such a record can help you in the event your child makes a complaint against you. Ask your agency worker to help you and your child develop an alternative way for your child to get help if he is angry with you. Remember that it has been his experience that parenting figures are untrustworthy and sometimes brutal. He may feel the need, for a while, of having someone outside the family available to him when he is angry at you or scared while he learns to trust you. Something you said or did may have triggered a memory for him of a time when somebody did, in fact, abuse him. A family therapist who works with the whole family, but agrees to see just your child from time to time, should be helpful to both you and your child as you work to build a trusting relationship. Try also discussing his grievances with him, aiming to come up with other ways he could express, and you could deal with, his unhappiness. And tell him that if he did carry out the threat other people would interfere with your home life, preventing you and him from becoming a family.

Fathers of girls who were sexually abused should be particularly aware of their child's past when they act affectionately toward their daughter. A confused adolescent girl with a history of abuse may not know how to differentiate affection from abuse. Try to gauge her limits by first making small gestures, such as placing your hand on her shoulder. If she's comfortable with that, then you might hug her. In other words, let her give you clues as to how you should act.

SERIOUS MISBEHAVIOR

You will need patience, persistence, and the willingness to act firmly if your child has major behavioral problems, such as stealing or inappropriate sexual conduct. We are not saying that you should expect the older child you adopted to do these things, but in our experience such conduct is not unheard of for these children.

Dealing with a child who has serious behavioral problems can wear down even the best parents. Should you encounter misbehavior on this level, family therapy should probably be the first order of business. Also, for your sake and the child's, take advantage of any institutional assistance you can get, such as the local Big Brother program. Get together with other parents who have adopted older children and take in each other's kids for a brief time, allowing one set of parents time off from their responsibilities. Perhaps a member of your family would be willing to take her for a few days, a week, or a month to give you a respite.

If you can afford it, consider sending your child to boarding school if it will help.

If her conduct is troublesome enough you might have to consider placing your child for a time in a residential treatment center, as a last resort, where she can receive close supervision. This might have echoes of abandonment for her, but remember that you will be visiting her regularly, calling her, writing to her, and bringing her home for weekends and it's still better than letting her push you beyond your limits, possibly resulting in the abrogation of the adoption. We have had the experience of two children who spent time in residential treatment and they returned home greatly improved. Be certain that the residential treatment facility that you choose isn't one that believes adopted children have to be "rescued" from their adoptive parents. As unbelievable as it sounds, some of them actually believe that their institutions are better for children than living with their own families. Residential treatment center staff have often only had experience with children who have problems related to brutal treatment by their parents. They may have difficulty understanding that your child came to you with certain difficulties that had nothing to do with you.

If your child steals, it may be because he has not had things of his own and needs to learn the difference between his property and others'. It could be behavior necessary for survival in the environment he came from. Or he may be testing you. If nobody has ever loved him or treated him well, he might be telling you through his behavior: "You may think I'm cute, but other people haven't trusted me and why should you?"

Should you encounter this conduct, make it absolutely clear to the child what is and is not acceptable in your family; you may have to do this over a period of time until he realizes that stealing will keep him from becoming a full member of the family. Meanwhile, take precautions to secure your valuable possessions and those of any other kids in the family. Put locks on doors and desks, even though it's unpleasant.

If you have other children, you will need to pay special attention to their feelings in the matter. After all, to the normal emotions associated with sibling rivalry you have just added a very complicated element. Besides not trusting the new child, his brothers and sisters may be embarrassed by his behavior at school and with their friends in the neighborhood. Reassure them that you will protect their property, that their new sibling is passing through a difficult period of adjustment, and that he will settle down. Also tell them, in your adoptive child's presence, that he is acting this way because he is not yet able to control his temptation to steal, but that you are helping him to learn how. Make it sound like a problem rather than some inherent evil lodged in the child.

If you have entered family therapy, sessions need to be focused on your children's concerns as well, perhaps in sessions which, from time to time, include only the children in the family.

If your other kids panic and simply want to get rid of the newcomer because of his outrageous activities, tell them you know that they're going through a hard time but be sure they understand that their new sister or brother is here to stay.

We realize that having a child who steals can be an emotional drain on adoptive parents. But we emphasize that if you're firm in asserting the wrongfulness (both morally and personally) of such behavior and stand your ground, he's likely to abandon the habit. Since this is the sort of thing that's useful to talk over with parents who have had similar experiences, seek out other people who have adopted older children and had to deal with this behavior. If you can't find them in your local adoptive parents' group, check with the North American Council on Adoptable Children for your local chapter.

Bear in mind that your family's attitude toward this kind of problem is as important as your child's behavior. Few children are inherently bad; most problems have solutions, and there are ways out of virtually every seemingly dead end.

Liz Trent and her husband, Paul, for example, thought they were really up against it and were ready to throw in the towel. Their fourteen-year-old adopted son, Jack, was stealing from their three birth children, and he was showing no remorse when caught. The Trents could put up with a lot from Jack, but they found his apparent lack of a conscience in this matter chilling.

When Jack and his family came into therapy the focus was not on thievery, at least initially. First the therapist established that in other ways he was an integral and contributing member of the family. His parents, for example, proudly talked about the way he helped his younger sisters with their homework. It was only after taking a session to lay this groundwork that the therapist asked him why he stole. "I don't know," he replied. "I see something that I want and a little voice in my head says don't do it, but I don't always listen." You mean it's like hearing a transistor radio? he was asked. He agreed. So maybe he had to turn the volume up. Yes, he nodded, with a smile.

At that point the therapist knew that Jack would soon realize that if he tried a little harder, he could hear his conscience on a regular basis. But just as important, his parents now understood that his conscience was there all along. Their child was not hopeless, and they were capable of giving him the help he needed to get on the right track, to hear and heed his already existing conscience more often, and to stop stealing.

The same difficulties early in life that might lead a child to steal could, paradoxically, also cause her to do something just the opposite. Sometimes older adopted kids will hoard food when they first join a new family. If this happens, don't let it offend you. It's not a comment on your caring and generosity but rather a reaction to a life of uncertainty and deprivation. She'll get over it, but in the meanwhile you might respond to this behavior by leaving a basket with some special treats in her room each night, telling her "this is yours." After a while, she'll realize that the food supply won't run out.

Over the years we've discovered that many children not described in the adoption agency's records as having been sexually molested were in fact abused in this especially terrible way. This type of violation sometimes confuses a child about the nature of his sexuality to the point where he behaves sexually in ways improper for his age. He may even act as a sexual victimizer himself.

How might you know if your child was sexually abused? Some of the signs include acting frightened when near a male (true of boys as well as girls), premature sexual activity, and a heightened interest in sex. However, such behavior is not a definite indication of abuse. Perhaps your child came upon a couple having intercourse and his knowledge and interest stems from that incident.

If your child acts out sexually, you will need to first set up sleeping arrangements that discourage this practice. For example, you could have the child sleep in a bedroom next to yours so you can see anyone going by, institute an "open door" policy in the house, with kids using the bathroom to change, and have two boys or two girls share a room, so one might know if the other had left the bedroom during the night.

Then, over time, you should teach the child how to be a brother or sister, something he may never have had the opportunity to learn. He may also never have learned how to express affection to family members in an appropriate way. He can learn to read to younger ones, for instance, teach them a game they don't know about or a skill they don't have, bake some cookies for them, or comfort them when they feel down. Since acting like a sibling may seem so obvious as to make it difficult for you to break it down into learning tasks, you'll probably come up with many more specific things for him to do if you think for a while about how you and people you know interact with a brother or sister.

Parents are naturally very concerned for the emotional health of a child who has been sexually molested. But often, we believe, they choose methods of treatment that may be of questionable good and could even be harmful. For example, we doubt that anything helpful can come from having a six-year-old sit on a Saturday morning with a group of kids of varied ages who have also experienced sexual trauma and try to relive her experiences by talking them out. Catharsis does not produce a cure, and it could reignite uncontrollable feelings related to the incident, bringing back into the present something better left in the past. Unless that abuse affects her current functioning, it might be best to put off any therapy she may need until she is older.

However, always be willing to talk to her about it if she brings it up. You may want some counseling yourself in handling her concerns and fears when she brings them up. Should she express some fearfulness that stops well short of incapacitating her, you could respond to it by pointing out how different her present circumstances are from those prevailing when she was abused. Say to her, "You were little when it happened. Now you are bigger and stronger. You can run fast now and get away. You can scream louder and fight harder. You have a mommy and daddy to tell now." Contrast her powerlessness then with her increased size and strength as well as the protection and support she gets from your family.

If early abuse left her feeling powerless, what she needs now are activities that empower her. Anything that bolsters her self-confidence, such as sports, would be in order. One interesting idea we've encountered is to give such children self-defense training in the martial arts.

THERAPY—A TOOL YOU MAY NEED

Kids adopted at an older age are considerably more likely to see a therapist at some point in their lives than children who join their adoptive family while infants. We have provided information about such services in the appendix, and we urge you to keep the information handy just in case. If you live near one of the increasing number of family therapy centers in major cities, you might even want to get in touch with them now to find out what kind of services they offer should you ever need them.

If the youngster you adopted as an older child requires therapy—and it's by no means certain that he will—it's not a negative judgment on you. In one family, the mother taught a large class in an inner-city elementary school and had just been promoted to the rank of assistant principal. But that didn't enable her to stop her adopted son from disrupting first his public school class and then his class in the strict parochial school she had sent him to thinking they would certainly be able to control him. She was a skilled professional in working with children, but she knew when she needed outside help.

How do you know if your family needs therapy? If your child is destructive or if you're feeling frustrated and you've tried everything after receiving advice from all quarters and nothing has worked, you should consider the therapy option. Complaints from neighbors or the child's school would also point to a serious enough situation to warrant at least a session or two with a therapist.

When therapy becomes necessary, we urge you, particularly if you adopted an older child, to use a family therapist. Too often the adults in their lives have singled out these kids for negative attention. Family therapy takes the burden off the child and spreads it around, making the job of getting better a family project; and it involves the child in a process that emphasizes her place in the family. When choosing the therapist, ask him if he's worked with child-parent problems like yours and how successful he's been— you'll probably get an honest answer.

At the Center for Adoptive Families about 150 families who have adopted older children have been treated over the

Special-Needs Adoptions

past five years. The kids' average age at adoptive placement was older than nine years and they were, on average, twelve years old when they came for treatment. They usually had been in the family for two or three years. Many had been misbehaving over a long period of time, and their offenses were often major. For example, they may have been stealing from the neighbors or expelled from school for serious offenses. About 30 percent of the families had already tried other kinds of therapy, and many of these parents were one step away from reversing the adoption. Yet of these 150 families, only one went through with returning their child to foster care. This child had discovered his birth mother, destitute in a run-down neighborhood, and felt it his duty to go back and care for her.

It should offer you some comfort that even under the worst scenario, violent behavior by your adopted child, a brief course of therapy may be enough to restore her conduct to a level that makes her acceptable to her family, her school, and her community. That did not seem evident to Jane Alsop, however, when she brought her nine-year-old daughter, Marian, in for treatment. Marian had pushed another nine-year-old down a flight of stairs at school. Fortunately, the victim was doing much better than Marian's mother, whose nerves were frayed to the point of snapping. She was even having thoughts of returning Marian to foster care, though she loved her daughter very much.

This was a hard nut to crack; mother and daughter were reluctant to talk much. Finally, to break the ice, a music therapist was brought in. She began strumming a guitar, and soon the girl began singing. Marian improvised lyrics that were to the point: "Mommy, when you took me home you were so happy, but I wasn't. You didn't know how sad I felt about leaving the other family. Because you were so happy, I couldn't tell you how much it hurt."

Marian sang out about the pain of separation from her foster family. Instinctively, her mother picked up the theme and sang: "I never knew you felt that way. I'm really sorry.

I should have listened to you then, but I will now." This operatic interchange wasn't the end of the therapy, but it allowed a more typical outpouring of feelings to proceed and in a few sessions it was clear that the crisis would pass.

Quick therapeutic reversals in conduct can also occur in situations that are nowhere near as dangerous, but extremely demoralizing for families who adopted older children. Most parents, like the Crawfords, would feel that way about a fifteen-year-old girl with a long history of bed-wetting. It was bad enough that Connie had that problem when the Crawfords adopted her at age twelve, but since it is not uncommon among children with special needs they felt that they could live with it for a while. But its continuance was beginning to undermine their faith that their daughter would make a successful transition from adolescence to adulthood. It didn't help that Connie was starting to get into fights at school, losing her temper as well as control of her bladder.

Psychiatrists had told Connie's parents that her bed-wetting—sometimes twice a night—was probably the consequence of her having been sexually abused as a young child. That may have been true, but it didn't end the problem. Nor had the drugs prescribed by other doctors. Mrs. Crawford tried the old standby cures for bed-wetting. She saw to it that Connie had nothing to drink for hours before bedtime. And she and her husband woke the girl up just before they went to bed so that she could go to the bathroom at the last possible moment before everyone went to sleep. But they got no results.

Playing up successes often works well under a variety of circumstances. For Connie this meant asking her to think of the nights when she had not wet her bed. There were none. Finally, Connie was asked if she ever lost control of her bladder during the day. "No," she said. "I'm shy about going to the bathroom at school, so I use the bathroom at home in the morning and then I don't go again until late afternoon, when I get home."

This proved to be the opportunity that led to results. Connie needed to extract herself from the debilitating and seemingly endless habit of bed-wetting, and she wouldn't be able to do it without stepping back and focusing on the times when she did have control. She was enlisted in a "scientific study" of other kids who had this problem and told that she could help because of her amazing bladder control during the day. She was asked to keep a record of how she managed to maintain that control. Keeping that record gave her the perspective she needed and helped her to concentrate on her successes. Within two weeks she was having dry nights, and after a few more sessions of talk her control problem—temper as well as bladder—was in the past tense.

By focusing on the times when they are successful, people can learn to recognize their own latent abilities to deal with their problems. You don't always have to bring emotional conflicts and long-buried anxieties into conscious awareness to resolve the problems they're currently causing, you just have to deal with what they are currently doing when the problem is not occurring and have them do more of it.

Ed Peterson also had a problem. For Ed, a teacher, his seeming inability to get through to Mickey, the nine-year-old he and his wife, Margaret, a public administrator, had adopted, was driving him to distraction. True, Mickey loved to ask his adoptive father to cook the dishes the boy liked best. And he also asked Mr. Peterson to join him working on projects. But then Mickey wouldn't eat the food his father so lovingly and laboriously prepared; and as soon as his dad began helping him with a project, Mickey lost interest and simply walked away. Ed Peterson was not just saddened by Mickey's behavior; he had come to think that his son altogether lacked the ability to establish a relationship, that perhaps he was a defective human being.

In therapy it was explained to Mr. Peterson that it was hardly that serious. He just had to realize that it was not realistic to assume that Mickey would start acting the son to his adoptive father without first learning what the role meant. And, being a teacher, Ed Peterson was in a good position to teach his child how to be the son he wanted.

To break his son's cycle of asking-getting-rejecting and to replace it with one of sharing and respect, Mr. Peterson and Mickey were given an assignment. He and his son were to plan a project together two times each week, but it would not be something they would do right away. They were to wait till the next day, after Mickey came home from school, to work on it. Further, they were to spend only half an hour on the project, and it had to be something that produced a product, like a drawing or a kite.

The point was that instead of asking his father for something, Mickey had to negotiate with him and come to joint decisions on the details, thus giving the son a direct interest in the activity. It also taught Mickey delayed gratification, based on having to wait a day and build up his anticipation of the activity. It was important that they make something tangible both to create a ritual of father-son interaction and to produce a permanent physical embodiment of that cooperation. Every time Mickey looked at that kite it would remind him of the pleasurable experience of building it with his dad.

The plan worked. Ed Peterson felt a renewed confidence in his ability to teach his son what the boy needed to know, and Mickey got an inkling of how much satisfaction he could get by working with his father until they had completed what they started. When last heard from, father and son were planning a fishing trip together.

Of course it's not always this easy; but things are rarely as hopeless as they may seem. We are not suggesting that you rush your child into therapy simply because you adopted him at an age beyond infancy. It's appropriate only if specific serious problems arise at school and in the community and threaten your ability to parent him.

CHILDREN
WITH DISABILITIES

Some of the most satisfied adoptive parents are those who have adopted a special-needs child identified as having a disability. Some of these parents already have a child with the same condition and therefore know about his or her special needs and may already have altered their house to accommodate them. The most important problems their child has are usually clearly visible and may even have a name—such as Down syndrome. Nobody blames these parents if their child continues to have limitations, and whatever progress the child can make offers immense satisfaction to the parents and reflects well on them.

Disabilities, however, are often present when they're not so obvious or clearly labeled. These may be a little harder to accept and deal with. Children born to mothers who had little or no prenatal care, or who were alcoholics or drug addicts, for instance, are at high risk for intellectual disabilities. Parents who adopt any special-needs child should be aware that school difficulties could result from such conditions. For example, an I.Q. of 75 or less recorded in your child's case record *may* indicate some mental retardation with which hyperactivity is often associated, although it is by no means a sure thing; and the intellectually stimulating environment that you supply in your home could raise his I.Q.

I.Q.s as low as 50, although pointing to the presence of mild retardation, do not mean that your child will not be able to learn; indeed, one label often applied to these kids is *educable*. Children with this level of impairment can usually learn up to about a sixth-grade level. They can develop sufficient social and vocational competence to make their way in the world, although they sometimes need a little help in dealing with stressful or complicated situations.

Children with I.Q.s ranging from 35 to 49 are moderately retarded and considered "trainable," capable of learning up to a second-grade level and holding down a semiskilled job. They are likely to need guidance to deal with social or job-related pressure.

Severely mentally retarded children, with I.Q.s of 20 to 34, may or may not learn to talk and are likely to have problems with motor coordination. At most they will be able to do very simple work, and even that will have to be supervised. Below an I.Q. of 20, a child is profoundly mentally retarded and will always need help in caring for himself, although even some of these kids have the potential for learning some self-care skills.

If you have adopted a child with a physical or intellectual disability—or both, since the two may be present together—the nature and extent of the disability will have a lot to do with the style of parenting you use and the particular strategies you devise to deal with any difficulties that occur. The nearest group of parents of children with similar disabilities would be one place to go for advice and support in dealing with those complications. Major groups include United Cerebral Palsy, 66 East 34th Street, New York, New York 10016, (212) 481-6300; the March of Dimes, 303 S. Broadway, Tarrytown, New York 10605, (914) 428-7100; the Association for the Help of Retarded Children, 200 Park Avenue South, New York, New York 10003, (212) 254-8203; the Juvenile Diabetes Foundation, 432 Park Avenue South, New York, New York 10016, (212) 889-7575; the American Foundation for the Blind, 15 West 16th Street, New York, New York 10011, (212) 620-2000; and the American Society for Deaf Children, 814 Thayer Avenue, Silver Spring, Maryland 20910. In addition, consult your adoptive parents' group or adoption agency–sponsored support group. *Exceptional Parent* is a magazine for parents of children with disabilities that could also be useful. Your agency and the National Resource Center for Special Needs Adoption are good places to go for further resources.

A parent looking for a pediatrician for a disabled adoptee should keep one important point in mind besides the criteria we offered earlier in this book for choosing a doctor. The doctor you select will have to accept the fact that your child will have limitations. That's not as obvious as it may sound. Many doctors have trouble dealing with a child they can't "cure" and always view that child's health in terms of what further steps they might take to improve his functioning— even if it means the child must endure gruelling tests and painful medical procedures. Of course, if something as direct as surgery or a medication would make a difference, it may be appropriate. But for most disabled kids, their condition will probably require management, and little more.

Many parents—adoptive and birth—sometimes forget that a disabled child is, first of all, a child. He is likely to have more in common with other kids than he does differences, especially in the case of a physical disability. Much of what we've discussed so far in this book is still relevant to your child's upbringing. For a mild disability, it may all apply.

Some points that we have made about nondisabled adopted kids relate even more strongly to adoptees with disabilities. You will have to expend a good deal of energy serving as an advocate for your child in the outside world. For example, in her school you'll need to be aggressive to see that she not only gets whatever special attention she needs, but also that she doesn't get too much of it. If she can benefit from being "mainstreamed" and school personnel automatically want to put her in a special class or program, you will have to see to it that your child's best interests are served.

Talk openly with your child about his disability, just as you do about his adoption. Provide him with opportunities— within the family and with other people who have disabilities—to talk about how people react to this way he differs from them. He needs this just as he needs to express any feelings he has about not growing up in the family into which he was born. But as in bringing up the subject of adoption when he hasn't for quite a while, don't dwell on it obsessively.

If you have other children, try to be sensitive to their

feelings about the special attention your disabled adoptee may require. Encourage them to share with you any thoughts or feelings the subject evokes. Your adoptive parents' group may have a program for siblings of disabled adoptees. Some special schools such as the Eagle Hill Schools for disabled kids in Connecticut and on Long Island also have such programs. One teenager, who had always felt embarrassed by her younger, hyperactive, brain-damaged brother, who she thought of as "dumb," came away from one of these programs with a new appreciation of him. "I never realized how much work it is for him to do things," she remarked after the teacher described dramatically how difficult it was for him to do all the little things she took for granted.

Another way you can make your other kids more comfortable with the idea of having a disabled adopted sibling is to involve them in any special care your adoptee needs.

Although you have demonstrated empathy and caring by adopting a child with a disability, you can't possibly know what it actually feels like to grow up disabled in a world where most people don't have an obvious disability—unless, of course, you have one yourself. So like any adopted child who can benefit from knowing an older person who was also adopted and has thus "been through it," your adoptee can gain much from a similar relationship with a disabled grown-up. The parents' support group concerned with your child's disability should be able to help you with this.

Adolescence can be a very rough time for adoptees who also have a disability. They become very sensitive to the way they differ from their peers. Sometimes their friends of earlier years pull away, shutting them out of their crowd. At a time when sexuality takes center stage for all kids, your disabled adoptee may have a particularly hard time of it, since for some strange reason it's a common attitude that disabled people are asexual. You might want to stay especially alert to conflicts your child has over this issue. Should your youngster appear to be having great difficulty with it, a session or two with a sympathetic counselor or therapist could help.

This may not, however, be the appropriate step to take for an intellectually impaired child. This child needs most to be with others like him- or herself in order to have something approaching a rich social life. To fill this need, inquire at the organizations we've listed for referrals to special camps, schools, and after-school programs. If you live in or near Boston you might also want to write to Project Impact, 25 West Street, Boston, Massachusetts 02111, for further information on this subject.

Although there may not be a lot you can do to ameliorate the specific painful occurrences of the teenage years, you can support your child by reminding her that this too shall pass. Point out that it gets easier once she emerges into adulthood—that's the truth!—and that no slight she endures as a teenager reflects on her personality or character. In other words, be her ally.

Finally, much not terribly useful material has been published about the inevitability of low self-esteem among disabled kids, just as similar theories have been formulated about adoptees in general. Your positive attitude about your child will go a long way toward counteracting any negative influences from the outside world. If you convey to her your optimistic feeling about the nature of her possibilities, she'll believe it.

ADOPTING CHILDREN WITH PSYCHOLOGICAL PROBLEMS

We have often pointed out that children who have been removed from their birth families under conditions of abuse or neglect may have also experienced continued abuse and neglect in foster care. These children have been subjected to inordinate stress during their lifetime and have had to develop ways of coping with this stress. It is not possible to predict how severe individual reactions to certain kinds of stress will be. There are just too many factors involved, including the child's inborn temperament, the age of the child when the traumatic experience occurred, the nature of the child's relationships with others at the time, her later experiences, and a range of other issues. It is important to remember, however, that the loss of a parent is an especially severe stressor. In order to survive the kinds of experiences that are usual for foster children, your child has had to develop certain behaviors. It is obvious that a child raised in a loving and secure home, who receives positive attention from family, neighbors, peers, and teachers, will have certain expectations about the world and where she fits in. A child who has been abused, neglected, lived with different families, and moved from school to school will have different expectations for herself and for others.

It is common for children who have experienced disruption of parenting and/or abuse to have developed certain behavior patterns that are labeled *adjustment disorders* by the American Psychiatric Association. These ways of reacting are just that—reactions. They do not say anything intrinsic about the nature of the child. They reflect his or her reactions to experiences. They can therefore sometimes change over time as a result of a changed, new family environment that is supportive and relatively stress free. The range of symptoms associated with adjustment disorders can change when stressors are removed from the child's life, but it will take time. Some of the symptoms your child may express are sadness, tearfulness, nervousness, worry, jitteriness, truancy, vandalism, fighting, poor academic functioning, and social withdrawal.

If the traumas which your child experienced prior to adoption are grave, such as rape, abuse, serious physical injury, especially head injury, and malnutrition, and were caused by others, especially parents, the child may exhibit symptoms of *posttraumatic stress disorder*. The symptoms of this include vivid memories, dreams and nightmares about the event(s), feeling as if the experience is occurring again when something reminds the child of it, less interest in activities which used to be important, feeling detached from other people, limited expressions of feelings, sleep disturbances, guilt, memory impairment, difficulty concentrating, and avoidance of activities related to the experience. In the chronic stage of this disorder, the child may do quite well for a period and then, from time to time, when something triggers the old memories, she may be flooded with feelings and thoughts related to the trauma. Such a disorder generally takes a very long time to heal. It is important to remember that as the child experiences positive interactions in your family, she will grow to feel protected and stronger and therefore less vulnerable to victimization by others. When she reexperiences the traumas, you should gently remind her of just how different things are now. After all, she is bigger, stronger, and smarter. She now has parents who will protect her against others. She will gradually learn, through her experience in your home, that she has parents who do not hurt children in terrible ways. It is difficult to see your child suffer so much, but it is also necessary to remember that through the constant experience of the difference between what her life is like now and what it was during the times of trauma, your daughter (or son) will be able to develop the strength and resources to balance the earlier experiences.

To our way of thinking, it is unlikely that psychotherapy can completely exorcise her early experiences. They are part of her life. Her more dramatic reactions to these memories will fade with time. What psychotherapy can do is reinforce your efforts to show your child just how different things are now and how unlikely it is that she will ever have to suffer in that way again.

Many adopted children are also diagnosed as having an *attention deficit disorder with hyperactivity.* The symptoms of this syndrome include:

- he fails to finish things
- he often doesn't seem to listen

- he is easily distracted
- he has difficulty concentrating on tasks requiring sustained attention
- he acts before thinking
- he has difficulty organizing work
- he needs lots of supervision
- he can't wait his turn
- he runs about excessively
- he has difficulty sitting still
- he always is on the go

We again suggest you view your child's behavior as a reflection of his early experiences. He may have come from a chaotic family, moved from foster home to foster home and from school to school. It will take time for him to learn that he can depend on things to happen because there is consistency in his new family. You can work with him on activities that will symbolically help him to learn to trust in the predictability of certain outcomes. For a while it will be good to have clear rules, times for doing things, and clear consequences, so that he can grow to trust in the predictability of his new home and family.

Separation anxiety disorder includes a group of symptoms that are also quite reflective of the experiences of many former foster children. A child with this diagnosis is afraid of being separated from those to whom she is attached. She worries that harm will befall loved ones or that they may leave and not return. She may worry that they will be lost, kidnapped, killed, or the victim of an accident. She may fear going to school. She may be afraid to go to sleep and have nightmares. She may also suffer from a number of physical symptoms including headaches and stomachaches to avoid leaving home. She may also be sad, have difficulty concentrating, and have temper tantrums. This disorder is not uncommon among all children and usually follows a life stress such as loss of a relative, illness, a school change, or moving to a new neighborhood. For a former foster child, it is fairly common, especially as she grows to love and trust you and then becomes afraid she will lose you. Again, the predictability of her experience in your family and with you will help her give up these symptoms.

Children may come to you with developmental disorders which range from specific delays in reading, writing, arithmetic, language, and articulation to a combination of any of the above. In many cases these delays are reflective of the child's past experiences which have often included chaotic family life and inner-city schools with far too many pupils for him to receive the individual attention he needs. Although it is more likely that your attention, help, and encouragement will have a greater impact on many of these delays if the child is younger than six when he comes to you, even older children have made remarkable gains following adoption. An excellent school with small classes will further reinforce your work with your child. Please remember that school performance depends on your child's motivation and willingness to learn. If her experiences in schools have been unrewarding, it will take a while to help her establish new expectations about school and schoolwork and about her own skill and competence.

QUESTIONS AND ANSWERS

I just found out that my child was sexually abused by an adult in one of the foster homes in which she lived. I'm wondering if I'm up to the task of parenting a child with that history. How can I tell if I can do the job?

We've seen many families in this situation. After the shock of hearing about it wears off, you'll realize that you've been a good parent and there's no reason why you can't handle even this. In fact, that she feels safe confiding in you demonstrates the trust you have built between you and her. You and your husband may want to have some counseling to help you feel more competent to effectively parent her. Remember that most studies that describe the treatment needs of children who have been sexually abused may not be applicable to your child, since she is no longer living in the family in which the abuse took place. The cues that might remind her of the abuse aren't there. It will probably be easier for her to put this experience in the past and get on with her life than it would be for a child who continues to live in the same environment in which the event took place.

☐

My nine-year-old is very sweet and has fit into our family remarkably well. However, she often acts quite immaturely and I'm beginning to worry about this. Am I doing anything wrong?

You are not likely to have done anything to cause this behavior. Children who have been moved from family to family in foster care, or have been physically or sexually abused, as many special-needs kids have been, are often delayed in their maturation. They develop strengths where they need them, sometimes making them seem sophisticated in some circumstances and babyish five minutes later. It will probably take time for your daughter's behavior to even out, perhaps even a few years. In the meanwhile, let her behavior at any particular time suggest whether she needs you to take charge and treat her as a dependent little girl or give her the increased opportunities for self-responsibility of a more mature child.

☐

I've read about life books, but the agency from which we got our child did not put one together for him and the social worker did not have the time to do the job once our son was placed with us. Is there anything we can do about this now?

You can get information about putting together a life book from the National Adoption Resource Center (address in appendix). They may even be able to recommend a worker who will contract independently with you to develop a life book with your child based on the information you have and his memories.

□

My seven-year-old has started to wet her bed. Do you think she needs a therapist?

We doubt it. It's not uncommon for children her age to respond to major changes in their lives and the anxiety that often accompanies them with bed-wetting. Have your doctor make sure that this problem does not reflect a medical condition. If it doesn't, it will almost certainly go away with time. Reassure your child that you love her. Adoptive parents in similar circumstances have told us that they have been able to get their child to stop bed-wetting by going into the child's room after she falls asleep and telling her that they love her and that she will always be with them. We're not sure why this works—maybe the child partially awakens and hears it—but it *does* seem to work for some people.

□

It's been more than six months since our child was placed with us and we don't seem to be any closer to getting his adoption finalized. Every week now he asks, "When am I going to be adopted?" Our lawyer says it's because the papers are just "sitting there" at the court, which has a backlog of cases. Is there anything we can do about this?

Perhaps you could call the adoption clerk at the court and try to find out what is holding things up. If you explain how this delay is affecting your family the clerk may be willing to speed things up. If this doesn't work, ask your lawyer if it would be worth trying a different court. In the meanwhile, you might create your own adoption ceremony with your family, or perhaps arrange for an adoption celebration through your church or synagogue.

□

Our child's foster family was distraught at having to give him up. They were sobbing and crying when the time came for him to leave them, and they implored us to keep them in our child's life. Is that really a good idea?

There's nothing wrong with continuing some contact between them and your child as long as the arrangement you devise is in everyone's best interest. First, make sure your child wants to continue the relationship. Talk to the foster parents to see if they fully understand the importance of strengthening the child's new and permanent ties to you and your spouse. If you don't have an extended family nearby, and if you and your foster parents share certain common interests and beliefs, you may grow into a relationship similar to that of an extended family.

□

We were our son's foster parents prior to adopting him. We therefore know his birth mother and she says she wants to remain in at least occasional contact with us and him. Our son seems a little uncomfortable at this prospect. What do you recommend?

There isn't any one correct course of action for such a delicate situation, since the right thing to do would vary with the particular situation such as the circumstances surrounding the child's entry into foster care and the mother's current functioning. We suggest that you consult your agency about this matter. They should be able to direct you to a foster family who could advise you about how they handled such a situation.

□

In the foster homes in which he lived, our child received corporal punishment when he misbehaved. He seems to have gotten used to it. I sometimes have the feeling that when he acts up he is trying to provoke me into hitting him. Sorry to say, he's come close to succeeding a few times. But we just don't treat kids that way in our house. How can I get him to listen to me without using force?

You needn't feel guilty for having felt pushed to the verge of slapping him. But you don't have to give in to the impulse and you probably will be able to substitute a nonphysical correction and punishment system for what he has known in the past. When you're feeling provoked, remind yourself consciously that that's what's happening. Such awareness usually reduces the pressure to act on the provocation. Make it clear that his misconduct will consistently earn for him a different kind of punishment, say confinement to his room for a specific time period. Let him know that this is in place of the way his misconduct was dealt with elsewhere. Tell him that you are confident that he will soon learn the rules of your family and will get used to the ways that you are different from other families.

□

The special-needs child we adopted has been in individual therapy for some time, starting before he was placed with us. Will it damage him to end his treatment?

Ask your child if he wants to continue treatment. If he does and it seems like he's developed a close attachment to the therapist, discuss with the therapist how you can begin to cut back, over a period of time, the frequency of his sessions with the ultimate goal of termination. One way to ease your child out of treatment is for you to start sitting in on some of the sessions if the therapist agrees to this, so that they take on a family orientation. If your child still feels an attachment to the therapist after ending treatment, you might arrange for the two to occasionally get together for a social visit, maybe going for a Coke at McDonald's if the therapist is willing to do this. You will have to pay for the therapist's time, though. This will give your child the experience of having a relationship with an adult he cares for end in a gradual, nontraumatic way.

9

Single Parents

—Jennie, a thirty-eight-year-old woman who works in the field of child welfare, has broken off a ten-year relationship with a man. She's dated some, but met nobody in whom she is particularly interested. Increasingly, she realizes, she wants to be a parent. Although her career demands much of her time and energy, she has reached a point where she can afford to hire someone to help with child care. But she's wondering if it's fair to bring a child into a single-parent family.

An increasing number of women and men in this country have decided to (or been forced to) have and raise children without any intention of ever getting married or living with another adult. These "unmarried parents," as the newest euphemism less negatively puts it, constitute a new kind of family. Unfortunately, single parents can often still anticipate prejudice, such as when their child's teacher ascribes their youngster's misbehavior in school to the lack of two parents in the home. Only recently, because of their numbers, and mostly in urban areas, have these parents begun to make a dent in the stigma on such households.

Single adoptive parents, both men and women, are creating one of the newest of these family groups. Adoption agencies started placing children with single parents about fifteen years ago. Most of the placements have been with women. If we still must cope with a stigma on adoptions, an even greater one on older-child adoptions, and a still larger stigma on single-parent adoptions, you can imagine how hard it is for a single male to negotiate this process. Often there is the unspoken suspicion that this adoptive parent is a potential child molester. Men willing to cope with this must be strong and self-confident. Most men who adopt are social workers, teachers, therapists, or former police officers.

Some speculate that most people find single-parent adoptions more acceptable than single women giving birth. In any case, it's still adoption, with all the prejudice that goes with that process. "Why don't you wait for a man and have a real child," single adoptive mothers still occasionally hear. "How will a man accept this child—you may never get married," goes another of these judgments. For much of the public, adopting without a mate may still suggest a doubly "unreal" family: only one parent and no biological connection to the child.

Reliable studies that tell us how successful some female-headed families have been in raising their children have not yet appeared. The inclusion of teenage mothers has skewed available statistics about this group. Many investigators still assume they are dealing with "broken homes" in most single-parent families. Further, any inquiry into the experience of single adoptive parents has to take into account the large number of special-needs kids raised by these mothers and fathers. Many agencies, viewing the one-parent household as the least desirable kind of home for a child, have been willing to give such parents only those children they could not place with more traditional families.

We have a feeling that when studies come out that separate single parents by choice from the single-parent family in general and single-parent adoptions in particular, they will report a success story. The people now undertaking this parenting are better prepared for it. Because they are often doing it by choice, they tend to have a realistic notion of what's involved. They are conscious of their numbers and often help each other out, and they can draw on the experience of numerous others who came before them. These are active mothers and fathers who know that to make it work they have to do a great deal more than their peers in two-parent families.

We wouldn't want to minimize the work involved. Raising an adopted child as a single parent is difficult even without having to contend with prejudice. The lack of another person with whom to share some of the burdens of child-rearing can seem, at times, like one long struggle. To surmount the logistics of getting the child from one place to another, caring for her when she's sick, providing her with companionship and emotional nurturing—all the while trying to lead your own life as an adult and make a living—can be overwhelming at times.

Single-parent adoption also complicates the already difficult job of adoptive parenthood. As an adoptee, your child may require more parental attention from time to time to ensure that some of her unique needs are met. But you will have less time and energy to devote to fulfilling them than would two parents together. You will also lack the perspective couples can give one another simply by having a second adult in the family. For example, has your child brought up the subject of adoption lately? Perhaps, with all of your responsibilities, you've been so busy that you haven't had time to notice the silence. Yet, as with everything else, ultimately it is your job to keep an eye on that aspect of his development. There's no one else around, at least not full-time, to pick it up.

YOUR SUPPORT NETWORK

Whether a single adoptive parent by choice or life circumstances, you will need outside help in raising your child. Some of that assistance can be institutional. Summer camp is one useful resource—an opportunity for both you and your child to have time away from each other. You might explore an organization like Big Brothers or Cub Scouts which could provide a male role model for your young adopted son if you are a single woman. Other service groups like the Girl Scouts might provide a sense of belonging for your daughter. However, as a single parent you have to be alert to complications that might arise from such participation. How will your daughter handle a father-daughter night if you are a single adoptive mother? It might be wise to decide on a strategy for such occasions before they arise. One way to handle this is to have a male friend or relative fill in for your child's father. Fortunately, many schools and groups, particularly in urban areas, are becoming more sensitive to this situation and are making these occasions "parent night" or "family night."

A single adoptive parent must do whatever she can to avoid long periods of isolation from other adults. If it is only her and her adopted child, a single mother can begin to feel imprisoned. Louise Hogan didn't realize the full significance of coping with an adopted baby by herself until the experience was on her and like a flood it almost swept her away.

In order to spend the first few months of parenthood caring for her child, Louise had taken a leave of absence from her company. The corporation she worked for, like a small number (IBM and Johnson & Johnson, to name two), had granted her the adoption equivalent of maternity leave. Her child arrived in the winter. The bitter cold never relented, making it months before she could even take the baby for a stroll in her carriage. To make matters much worse, her baby was colicky. After three weeks of being cooped up in a small apartment with the incessantly crying infant, it didn't look like Louise would make it to spring with her nerves intact. Finally, on a Saturday morning at 8 A.M., near hysteria, she called her only close friend with a desperate plea for respite. She just had to get away from her child for a while. Fortunately for Louise, her friend managed to create some free hours for the besieged mother by organizing an ad hoc "relief team" of sympathetic women.

Another woman we know who had adopted as a single parent told us how she was also caught unprepared, but nevertheless, although shy, was able to marshal her resources to lift herself out of the isolation trap. For Tracy Brodrick, the experience seemed to come upon her suddenly, even though she had been intellectually ready for adoptive parenthood. There she was with a baby, a small house to take care of, and few phone numbers to call when she needed help. She had taken a leave of absence from work for the first few months she had the child, intending to hire a baby-sitter to take over during the daytime when she returned to her job. But as her adoption leave from work drew to a close, she knew she would be coming home at the end of the work day to a second, and probably harder job: parenting her child. Now finally aware of what she was in for, she felt overwhelmed.

"Looking back on what happened then, I guess it was an example of necessity being the mother of invention," Tracy recalls. Instead of letting her circumstances immobilize her, Tracy got organized. She started a play group for mothers and children in the neighborhood, herself creating an institution she needed, since it didn't already exist. She thought up ideas for kids' parties and similar occasions that would bring her into contact with other young mothers, striking up friendships with several of them. By the time her daughter was in her second year, Tracy had organized a bunch of mothers willing to exchange baby-sitting chores on Saturdays, freeing each to squeeze in some recreation, shopping, cleaning, and decompressing from their week's work.

Shortly before her daughter's second birthday, Tracy joined a nearby adoptive parents' group in which a single-parents' branch had recently been formed. Many couples join adoptive parents' groups to hear how others have dealt with adoption-related difficulties; but single parents, we have found, are even more interested in the social interaction the organizations provide. It's the pot-luck suppers, picnics, and museum days that draw single parents toward such groups. With these new friends, single parents have an opportunity to share their child's milestones—the first sip from a cup, for example—that always call for some kind of public notice and celebration.

Support networks are clearly crucial to single parents, adoptive or nonadoptive. So if, like Tracy, you do not have one in place, you might want to pull people into your life to help out. If you are temperamentally shy, try to approach this network-building task as something necessary for your child's welfare. Just as you would do whatever you had to do to protect her health and safety, no matter how uncomfortable the particular task might make you, you must provide for her and yourself in this way, too.

Some single adoptive parents have even joined with others like themselves to institute a new kind of family. Typically, in this new version of the family, a single woman with an adopted child will join forces with another single woman or a single man who has adopted to provide each other with the kind of help and emotional support that married couples might assume will be forthcoming from each other. For single parents with only one child, this arrangement also permits their children to experience some of the benefits of having a sibling. This family system may get together whenever an occasion seems to call for it—on a holiday, for example—or they may meet regularly for joint activities, such as Sunday afternoon in the park.

Relatives might also constitute an important part of your support network. In fact, a supportive family can make an enormous difference in the day-to-day life of a single parent. It's not always easy, though. In a situation which includes death or divorce, you no longer have a mate to act as a buffer between you and your parents. Sometimes, parents go so far as to treat adult children as children once again. If you adopted as a single parent, this new development might aggravate whatever tensions already existed between you and your parents, possibly reducing the amount of useful assistance you can expect or may want from them.

Ordinary parent-adult child interaction can sometimes add a minor annoyance to the experience of the single adoptive parent. For instance, ask yourself, would it upset you if you leave your child with your mother while you attend to other chores and hear from her when you return: "He never cried for me the whole time *I* took care of him"? Many people feel this is worth no more than a benign grin in response. But if it bothers you, you might want to negotiate with your parent. Tell him or her how much you appreciate their help, but make it clear that the remark just happens to rub you a bit the wrong way and would he or she just not say that, for your sake?

JUST THE TWO OF YOU?

Who says growing up with just one parent doesn't have its advantages? For one thing, your child doesn't have to share you with another adult. For another, children with a single parent, especially an only child, have an opportunity to develop their independence at an earlier age.

Melissa, an only child of a single parent, at the age of twelve planned a vacation for herself and her mother, the kind of thing most of us don't do until we're adults. Her mother was just too busy to work out the details, so she told her daughter to go to the travel agent and make the arrangements herself. At first the agent didn't take the girl seriously, but a call to her mother made it clear that Melissa was authorized to deal with him. Melissa even delivered the check—over a thousand dollars—to pay for the tickets and accommodations. Now a successful professional in her thirties, she still fondly remembers the experience and the self-reliance it taught her. And her mother appreciates how Melissa's independence made life easier for her.

On the other hand, children growing up with one parent and no siblings spend much more time in the company of adults than do other kids, which sometimes causes complications. These children grow up faster than do their peers. By the time your child is about ten years old, she may respond to you in conversation almost as an adult would, thus further encouraging you to treat her as if she were older than her years. The result may be confusing to both you and your child.

As your chief confidant, your youngster may feel a loyalty and protectiveness toward you that could cause difficulties. For instance, she might not come to you with her feelings about an adoption-related difficulty such as bad dreams or a remark somebody made to her about her adoption for fear she will be overburdening you.

How much of your personal life and frustrations do you want to share with your child? How much should you? Will you feel "left out" when your child reaches adolescence and becomes more peer centered? Two children can complain to and confide in each other, and neither will feel pressured to be the most important person in your life. Each is freer to act her age. But even if it's just the two of you, you can still create an atmosphere in your home that will take the pressure off you and your child. First, as we have pointed out, go out of your way to bring other people into your life, and get involved with groups that will provide social outlets for your child as well. Second, make sure you and your child create a sufficient degree of silliness in your house. For example, have a pillow fight once in a while; you'll both enjoy it.

Humor can even work as an effective disciplinary tool. One single adoptive mother we saw had a seven-year-old daughter who bit her when angry. The mother had not yet discovered a way to stop this unacceptable behavior, and none of the advice she had received from friends and neighbors worked. She had tried talking to her daughter as well as administering all kinds of conventional punishments. We suggested that she entirely change the framework in which she was interacting with her child. The mother was to buy a Halloween mask and have it ready to put on the next time the child tried to bite her. If that didn't work, she could try banging on a pot with a spoon. The woman, who was very serious by nature, was somewhat taken aback, but agreed to try it.

The mask worked. Her daughter laughed hysterically— so did the mother—the first time she got this treatment. The shock and surprise took the youngster totally out of the mood that had led to the biting. After two or three similar incidents, the child got the message: the Halloween mask was ridiculous, and so was her biting, which she stopped.

If the responsibilities involved in raising an adopted child by yourself sometimes blunt your sense of humor, you can reactivate it by getting some perspective between yourself and your daily cares. In the middle of a day in which most things are going wrong, you have to be able to step back for a moment and look at what's happening without feeling threatened, worried, annoyed, or defensive. In other words, you need to put some emotional distance between yourself and the hardships of single parenthood.

Jogging, shopping, a glass of wine after work, a long-distance call to an old friend can often do the trick. Pamper yourself; you deserve it.

Distance and perspective are not only prerequisites for maintaining a sense of humor, they are also necessary for effective parenting in general. In two-parent families, the complementary personalities of husband and wife can provide built-in alternative ways of seeing and varying approaches to a child's problem behavior. On a bad day, when one parent has had more than enough, he or she can be spelled by the other.

Bringing two viewpoints and styles to parenting also makes it more likely that at least one parent will be a good match for the way a child acts at a specific age. For example, when Scott Roberts was going through his "terrible twos," his mother Janice, a bookish person, couldn't cope. But her husband Dick, who is more active and impulsive, had just the right response to Scott's shenanigans. He took the youngster's behavior in stride, and his son responded positively.

With an adopted child especially, sometimes you need to see things dispassionately in order to stay alert to the extra complications raised by adoption issues. Since you don't have a mate to check your own perceptions of what's going on in your family, we suggest that you try the following technique to give yourself a more objective point of view of how your relationship with your child is working. It's something to use when nothing, from reasoning with your child to punishing him to yelling and screaming, has worked.

Try stepping back from the immediate, from the emotions of the moment that throw everything out of proportion, overwhelm, and immobilize you. The key to creating the distance you need to put things in perspective is cultivating your powers of observation.

There are parents who come to us with seemingly insurmountable problems. They're tried everything reasonable one could think of, and still can't get their child to behave. We ask these parents to visualize themselves wearing a white lab coat and carrying a clipboard. We ask them to think of themselves as scientists, objective observers paying attention to facts and behavior in their families, not to how they feel at the moment.

We emphasize that this exercise is an experiment and it will last for perhaps a week. And we remind parents that these observations are not designed to cause everything to fall neatly and immediately into place. Family interaction will not be changed instantly for the better because of it. We just want them to look, to observe, as a first step toward a solution of the problem.

The idea is to figure out what works and what doesn't work in your relationship with your child. By taking a step back you can sometimes see the difficulty as a sequence of events: how it begins, what you typically do, what she does, and so forth. Then you can systematically alter the one variable you can control completely: how you respond. Eventually, you will find the response that gets the best results.

Social workers, teachers, ministers, doctors, probation workers, psychologists, and others in the helping professions who have become single adoptive parents sometimes fall into the trap of "therapeutic parenting," substituting professional skills for basic parent-child interaction. For example, when a child misbehaves, it might be more appropriate after you and he have talked it out and that hasn't worked just to send him to his room rather than to engage in a marathon conversation about his feelings. Talking it out at this point might do no more than distract from the issues at hand and give you a false sense that you had dealt with a difficulty.

A therapist friend of ours, a single adoptive parent, has a child who has a good cure for therapeutic parenting. This adolescent knows it when she hears it, and immediately responds: "Mommy, *stop* shrinking!"

Still another way of getting a handle on your difficulties with your child is to realize that there are always alternative explanations for why he is behaving in a certain way. For example, it might be tempting to describe as depressed a youngster who has been walking around with his head down, talking little, and staring out the window. But thinking of it as "depression" might suggest doctors and medication and a problem that could quickly get out of hand, demoralizing any parent. Depression usually involves symptoms such as disturbed sleep (too much or insomnia), lack of appetite, agitation, hopelessness, and helplessness. If that does not resemble what your child is experiencing, it might be more reasonable to describe his behavior in less threatening and paralyzing terms. For instance, he might be feeling blue, sad, or overwhelmed, something that the two of you or your child alone might deal with objectively or will run a natural, brief course and then improve.

In fact, adopted children are often confronting issues which sometimes cause them to be quiet, thoughtful, and sad. They need to be allowed to experience and master these feelings themselves. Redefining behavior may help to put things in perspective and get you back on the track of taking control of your life and acting effectively.

A lack of knowledge can also lead a parent to mistakenly interpret her child's behavior in ways that leave the parent feeling helpless. The executive who came to us not long ago with two adopted children who fought constantly "knew" that the incessant conflict resulted from her having adopted them from different birth families. The way she saw it, such adoption-based behavior was obviously out of control. But this mother happened to have been an only child, we pointed out, and didn't have experience with the usual battling of siblings. No longer viewing her children's behavior as pathological, she could ignore it or contend with it, as she chose. And when the children realized that their mother was not reacting to their fighting as she did before, they did less of it.

Don't automatically trust your first reactions to give you an accurate explanation for what you're experiencing or think you're experiencing when encountering a troublesome incident or pattern of behavior. That's particularly true if you think you've spotted pathological conduct. Check in a child-development book to see if you simply have missed a type of behavior found in many kids of your child's age. Ask friends and relatives to take a look and confirm or correct your perceptions. Consult with your child's teachers and guidance counselor. Only if these steps produce no satisfactory solution do you then need to turn to therapy for help.

HALF FULL OR HALF EMPTY?

Single adoptive parents may have more stress than other mothers and fathers resulting from responsibilities in their lives. That's why so many of them have developed the ability to see burdens, pressures, mishaps, and mistakes in the best light possible. For example, change is always stressful, and when that change involves the impending loss of a job, it can be absolutely terrifying. That's especially true for single adoptive parents like Mary Roberts, who did not have a second income in the family to see her and her child through a period of unemployment.

When we met Mary she was stunned by the prospect of being laid off and could hardly think straight. But after several conversations, another picture began to emerge— one of a woman who had been unhappy in her job for years, and who often found that her job frustrations affected the way she interacted with her daughter. We gradually helped Mary to focus less on the coming loss of her job and more on the opportunity that now presented itself: starting a new career. With the assistance of a loan she is now going to school to pursue an occupation that has her very excited: paralegal work.

Cathy Washington is another single adoptive parent we saw who turned something she regarded with dread into an opportunity. Cathy had an all-too-familiar dilemma: she had never told her now adolescent son that she had adopted him. Guilt at never feeling up to the task of telling him the truth, and the thought that he might no longer trust anything she said if she did tell him, was even now keeping her from breaking the news to him. Our task was to help her understand that she would feel enormous relief once she told him. This, indeed, could be seen as an opportunity to recast her relationship with her son based on frankness and honesty.

It wasn't easy, but eventually she decided to take that step. Now she can't believe she didn't do it sooner. Her son's reaction to his mother's revelation was typical of what many adoptees say when confronted with such information: "Big deal, I've known that for years."

It isn't always that easy. Some children do have a negative reaction for a while. For example, it would not be unusual for a child's grades at school to drop for a term or two while he comes to terms with his parent's disclosure. The disruptive effect of this new knowledge, though, can be eased by a mother or father who then works hard to rebuild the child's trust in his parent. In any case, enduring this temporarily difficult time is still preferable to keeping his adoption a secret.

Approaching life in a way that allows one to recognize small successes has allowed many adoptive parents to cope with serious complications more effectively and energetically. Sharon Jones raised an adopted child by herself that way. She adopted an older child who the agency had not been able to place. Although physically disabled, Billy, her adopted son, was so emotionally troubled that he was still capable of wrecking the house when upset. Sometimes, when things got that out of hand, she would even have to call a man in her adoptive parents' group who had volunteered to come over and hold Billy until he could get his feelings under control.

But Sharon could more often than not focus on the little signs of progress and Billy's accomplishments through all the troubles, such as his learning how to read and how to ride a bike. And she knew that it was only because of her caring that Billy was able to spend most of his time outside of institutions.

Sharon succeeded because she had realistic expectations; she knew Billy's limits and looked for small signs of progress. She knew what was possible for her son. By the time he was fifteen, Billy had calmed down enough for her to feel secure in adopting an infant. Besides giving her the satisfaction of raising a child from infancy who had no serious problems, the baby also brought out her older son's sense of responsibility, furthering his progress. Serving as an assistant caretaker, under Sharon's close supervision, did wonders for his self-esteem, enabling Billy to see himself as much more than just a kid with overwhelming problems.

Sharon is an unusual person; few people could or would take on the task of raising a child like Billy. But her approach to life can benefit any parent who has to cope with more than her share of burdens, particularly a single adoptive parent.

WHEN YOU DID NOT CHOOSE SINGLE PARENTHOOD

If you've become a single parent of an adopted child through death or divorce, adoption complications may demand much from you just when enormous stress may drain you of your customary energy and emotional resiliency. If your mate has died, you will need to comfort and reassure your child, while coping with your own feelings of loss. Every child finds this period difficult, but for your youngster this may be especially true. She has already lost one set of parents, and this most recent catastrophe may invoke fears and fantasies of separation.

However, you should realize that all parents have trouble comforting a child under these circumstances. Nor does the ache of such a loss ever absolutely disappear. One important thing you can do to minimize the trauma, though, is to make sure your child feels free to talk about his loss. Some kids think that they don't have the right to grieve as much as their surviving parent because they perceive their mother or father as having suffered a greater loss than theirs. Under the age of five or six, your child might even think that he had in some way caused the loss of his parent—perhaps by wishing him or her dead in a moment of anger. Younger children may also be excessively fearful of losing their surviving parent—not entirely irrational, since now they know it can happen. You might want to check *Books to Help Children with Separation and Loss* by Joanne Bernstein (R.R. Bowker) in the library for summaries of books for youngsters three to sixteen with a special category devoted to death of a parent.

It's hard to protect children from the tension in a marriage that is failing. Kids are very good at picking up the strains in a relationship, and the weakened marital bond is likely to make them feel anxious. But adoptive parents who finally realize that they do not wish to continue in their marriage need not feel guilty about the temporary disruption and emotional upheaval their children have already experienced. It will pass and their children will regain their equilibrium. Besides, once parents have decided to separate, they can make it a point to cooperate in anything involving their youngsters—no matter how much they disagree about everything else—thus minimizing the strain on their children.

Adoptive parents who divorce should do their utmost to separate with a minimum of strife. If possible, before you separate, try to plan how you and your spouse will handle matters concerning your children. Create a structure in which hostility related to other issues does not spill over into the area of child care. For example, you could agree in advance that when you speak on the phone about the children, that is the *only* legitimate subject of discussion. No matter what your feelings about each other may be, you should stay in contact, if only so your child can't play one of you off against the other. If you're having trouble with any of this, a counselor might be able to help. Remember that the first year following separation is usually the most difficult and things will get progressively easier as time progresses.

Cooperating with your former spouse in anything involving child rearing is crucial, though perhaps difficult, in minimizing the emotional toll the parting takes on your child. Still assimilating the information you have given him about his adoption, your child now has to come to terms with yet another missing parent. He will need to talk about this new state of affairs. How he discusses it and how you should respond will depend on his age and emotional development when you and your spouse parted.

Discuss your divorce with your child as you would his adoption, sympathizing with his sadness and giving him only as much information and explanation as he can absorb. Like adoption, it's a subject that you and he will be coming back to for more clarification as time goes by. Make it clear that he has done nothing to bring about the separation. Whenever he brings up the topic, be honest with him. Avoid giving him the impression that there's even the slightest chance you and your former spouse will reconcile, unless you have reason to think it will happen. Tell your child that both of his parents still love him, but that he will not be living with mommy and daddy together anymore because they just have too many differences. Don't withhold information he obviously wants, since that would compound the effect of his lack of knowledge about his birth, creating still less clarity and more secrets in his life.

You might want to point out other kids he knows, adopted or not, whose parents have divorced. Remind him that they were able to adapt to their new situation and that they are still loved by each parent. Reading together Jill Krementz's book *How It Feels When Parents Divorce* (Knopf) might be helpful. During the separation process, you can go far toward calming his fears by telling him how you and your spouse have arranged for him to see each of you, where he will live and when, where his toys will be, and which school he will attend.

Besides competently raising your child, you have an additional task as a single adoptive parent: leading your life as an adult—in whatever time you can grab from your daily responsibilities. But that, too, will affect your child. Perhaps you will once again become romantically involved with another adult. Your child may also form an emotional attachment to this person. If you are a single woman with an adopted child, this especially presents some potential problems. Your child's birth father is probably a peripheral, hazy figure to her. Other men moving in and out of your (and therefore her) life may cause her to relive fears of abandonment. You may appreciate the possibly temporary nature of these relationships, but she may not be able to absorb and deal with the emotional consequences of still more partings. As she grows older she may assume that men never stay in relationships.

It's not your fault that the facts of your new life could have this effect, but you do have to keep your child's perceptions in mind. While it's understandable that you might want your child to like the current man or woman in your life and that you would find it tempting to integrate that person into your family activities, we feel it's better to avoid it until the relationship has gotten to be both steady and reliable. Unfortunately, that may mean depriving yourself of that person's overnight company.

This is a particularly difficult situation for mothers of adolescent daughters. If she sees you having several relationships, she may ask why it's okay for you and off-limits for her. If she is an only child she may experience a blurring of the lines between herself and you and think herself more sophisticated than she actually is. A professional acquaintance of ours, a single adoptive parent through divorce, recently asked her sixteen-year-old how she would feel if her mother got involved with a man again. The teenager, a girl with a good sense of herself, said that she would probably not be ready for it and hoped it didn't happen until she was away at college.

If you're having any problems with divorce and custodial issues, we suggest that you contact your local branch of N.O.W., the National Organization for Women, or Parents Without Partners, for some practical advice about your particular situation.

Divorced fathers might also want to exercise similar discretion about having their children get to know the new women in their lives. Fathers who do not have custody of their children and see them only on weekends could confine their sleepover dates to weekday nights.

When death or divorce produces a single adoptive

parent, the pressure on the remaining or custodial care-giver to be a superparent can be overwhelming. If that parent is a male, he may suddenly have to learn "mothering" traits his parents never encouraged him to develop. But, male or female, if you have become a single adoptive parent in this way, you may occasionally think that you never would have adopted had you known you would have to do the job alone. Remember that birth parents, too, have such thoughts. There's no law that says you have to make up to your child for the absence of his other adoptive parent. Don't be too hard on yourself, and acknowledge that for at least quite a while it will be complicated for you and your child.

QUESTIONS AND ANSWERS

I'm a single adoptive parent and an attorney with the possibility of becoming a partner in my law firm. I didn't feel guilty when I left my infant in the care of my house-keeper, but now that my child is in his second year I feel like I'm missing some precious time with him when I come home late at night. How can I do justice to both my career and my child?

Instruct your housekeeper to encourage your child to nap early in the evening. Then wake him up at ten so you can spend some time together. Weekends should be split between time spent just enjoying him and time spent just for you with someone to take care of him. When your child gets older, try to coordinate your time off with his school vacations. People on the fast track often have a great deal of energy, so take advantage of this quality.

☐

I have a feeling that my four-year-old is in a very unstim-ulating environment. She spends a lot of time watching soap operas with my housekeeper. What can I do to enrich my child's day?

You could put her in full-day day care or nursery school. Schools of nursing often have student nurses who babysit and enjoy playing with children. Or you could hire a college student to come in for a few hours a week to actively play with your child and to supplement your housekeeper's baby-sitting duties.

☐

Since I became a single adoptive parent I rarely go out at night and I hardly get to see my friends anymore. It looks like I'm getting stuck in the isolation you warn about. How can I restore some of my social life without slighting my child's needs?

You do need adult company. It's necessary for your emotional health; if that suffers you'll surely be a less effective parent. Try meeting your friends for weekday lunches or breakfasts. These days, many people do much of their socializing at work. Perhaps you could make an effort to cultivate more friendships where you work. That would make it easier for you to squeeze a social life into your busy day.

☐

In the Parents Without Partners group that I joined, I'm the only one whose child does not have a father. At the group's social gatherings, my child is uncomfortable when the other kids talk about their daddies. Is there anything I can do about this?

School-age kids have a need to see themselves as similar to other children. We have a feeling that if you look a little harder into the membership of your group you might turn up either a single adoptive parent or another single parent where there isn't a father around. Perhaps they are members but haven't been to the group's social functions lately. Your single adoptive parents' group is an excellent resource here as well. If there aren't any in your group, at least make sure that you get together with such parents and their kids outside the group so your child does have playmates who also have never known their fathers.

☐

I'm a single adoptive parent. I was teasing my nine-year-old son the other day and my mother told me that she thought I was being too sarcastic, possibly hurting his feelings. I like to joke with him; it's an important part of our relationship. Now that I think about it, there are times when I'm not sure if he fully understands my jokes. How can I tell if my humor is going above my child's head?

First, take care that you don't let a little leftover anger from a quarrel slip into your humor. Sarcasm often cloaks such feelings. When you kid around with your child, remember that he's nowhere near as sophisticated as you are. Young children like humor that is broad, obvious, to the point. They also love word-play. This is their level: Why were one, two, three, four, five, and six afraid? Because seven ate nine.

☐

I always wanted to have my own child, and it was exciting to find out that I could adopt as a single parent. But I'm a teacher and I have to deal with kids all day. I'm tired when I get home, and I have less patience for "kid stuff" than I would like to have. Is there any way out of this dilemma?

It sounds like you need an hour's break to decompress between the time you finish work and the time you start interacting with your child. Try hiring a baby-sitter for that hour so you can separate your work day from the evening.

☐

I'm an adoptive father. I just don't seem to be able to handle work and child-rearing too since my wife died. How can I get some help with this enormous burden?

Single parents' organizations are always especially appreciative of new male members. These groups are good sources of support and advice for people in your position. You might also want to read *Who Will Raise the Children?* by James Levine. It's out of print, but your library may have a copy.

10
The Multiracial Family

When Ken and Sherie Barkley went to the airport to pick up Kim, the Korean baby they had worked so hard to adopt, they made sure that Ken's cousin and his wife, who would be the child's godparents, were right by their side with a video camera. To this day the Barkleys need little encouragement to haul out the two-hour tape and slip it into their VCR for a guest's edification.

Even without the recorded story, they would never forget a detail of that incredible afternoon—their arrival at the airport well before the plane was due, the seemingly interminable wait in the midst of other adoptive parents about to get their babies, and then, as the plane touched down, the woman from the agency commanding them: "Now you stop crying, every one of you, the children will be here in a minute!" And that heart-stopping moment when the door opened and eleven men and women paraded in, single-file, each carrying an infant to new parents and a new life. "Stop crying"? She might as well have ordered Niagara to stop flowing.

Of course, what seemed like a culmination was really a beginning—of a lot of work as well as of pleasure and fulfillment. Raising a child from another culture or race requires adoptive parents to be knowledgeable about and sensitive to the particular issues involved in such adoptions.

Particularly since the civil rights struggles of the 1960s, many Americans have become accustomed to taking pride in their ethnic and racial heritage. At our best we have come to celebrate our differences. But when those differences occur within a family, as they do in many adoptive families where there are children from other races or foreign countries, things get a bit complicated. Although some black and Asian families adopt children of other racial and ethnic backgrounds than their own, much of the transracial adoption that we know about concerns white families adopting children of color from either the U.S. or abroad. A number of interracial couples have adopted interracial children as well.

About 70 percent of the foreign children adopted by U.S. families are non-Caucasian, so there's a good chance that your family is likely to be multiracial if you have adopted at least one child from another country. Even if you don't bother to think of yourselves in that way any longer, others will.

If you have an adopted child of color in your family, whether she was born here or abroad, her road to adulthood will probably have a few more curves in it than the one traveled by other adoptees. Most obviously, she (and you and your other children) will have to deal with prejudice, racial as well as that concerned with adoption. That you can count on.

Prejudice that denigrates her background and geographical separation from her roots will add to your parental tasks. You will have to do what you can to make sure she grows up knowing *who* she is, culturally and racially, as well as confirming her identity as a member of your family.

YOUR MULTIRACIAL FAMILY

Multiracial families have one clear advantage over adoptive families in which parents and kids come from the same general background. In the family of mixed background, there can never be any doubts about whether to tell the child about his adoption. Indeed, the timing of the first discussion is built into the child's development. As soon as he's old enough to notice that he's different from you, or one of his playmates prompts him to notice that difference, you have to talk about it.

But multiracial families have to be prepared to be more than honest with their child; they also have to be ready, as much as possible, to stand in solidarity with him. You will have to be conscious about how society will treat him—and you, since you will encounter some discrimination as a result of being his parent. If you've never experienced discrimination before, this can be especially difficult.

The worst thing you could do in the face of this reality is to deny it, to fall back on platitudes about how we're all the same and therefore think that you have only to treat your nonwhite child as you would a white child and all will be well. Society will not let you do this and your child would suffer as a consequence if you tried. To a great extent, the success of your adoption depends on your absolute willingness to acknowledge the way your family differs from other families and how willing you are to accommodate yourselves to those differences.

A nonwhite child, understandably, will find it hard growing up in an all-white family in an all-white neighborhood going to an all-white school. Before you consider such an adoption you should live in an integrated area and have friends and a lifestyle which includes adults and children from your child's race or culture. Plan to be involved in an adoptive parents' group where your child can associate with other children and adults who look like her. Your adoption agency and adoptive parents' group would be good places to go for suggestions. OURS, 3307 Highway 100 North, Minneapolis, Minnesota 55422, is a good resource for parents of children from foreign countries. If you've adopted an American black child, the North American Council on Adoptable

Children, 1821 University Avenue, Suite S-275, St. Paul, Minnesota 55104, will recommend an adoptive parent group for you. Your local NAACP or Urban League have a number of appropriate activities. You might also want to read black-interest newspapers and magazines to find out about upcoming events that would appeal to your family.

If your family is multiracial, some tensions may arise within your family over the issue of color, and you might have to make an occasional diplomatic intervention. In one multiracial family the nonwhite son, developing a strong pride in his racial heritage, announced that he liked having dark-skinned biological parents because he thought that nonwhite people were better looking than white people. When his white sister objected, their mother tactfully interceded to suggest that her brother was entitled to his opinion and the matter was left at that. In fact, they were also pleased that he had developed a positive sense of himself.

The attitude of strangers will play an important role in your life. As part of a multiracial family, you've lost your anonymity. You'll know that the first time someone comes up to you at the supermarket and says of your child something like, "She's a little tan, isn't she?" Or you may hear what a woman we know heard when shopping with her whole family: "Your kid black? Is that your husband? He's not black." Strangers actually feel free to say things like that!

What's the best reply to such comments? Like responding to boorish remarks about adoption itself, it depends on your mood, temperament, and energy level. Again, humor can help, as long as the comments to which you're responding aren't consciously malicious. When Fred Wilkins brought his adopted black baby to work with him, strapped into the carrier on his back, a fellow worker walked over and asked, "Is that your son?" Fred said "Yes," and looked pleasantly at the other man, who was waiting for the next sentence of explanation that never came. For Fred it was pure pleasure—his sense of humor had an edge to it on this occasion—as the man stood there awkwardly for half a minute at a loss for words and finally turned and walked away.

One young interracial girl we know, adopted by a white family, developed a clever way to answer annoying questions about who was what in her family. If she's walking with her father, she says that her mother is black; when with her mother, she replies that her father is black; and if she's with her grandmother, she says that the other side of the family is black.

As a parent in a multiracial family, you will have to accept that the most innocent of your youngsters' adolescent activities could cause complications in your community. What if, for example, he asks a girl from another race to the senior prom? Should you try to protect him from what might result in a painful experience for him? Your best course of action would probably be no action, unless there were unpleasant consequences. Your child is old enough to make that decision for himself. Back off and let it happen. The possibility of complications in the community is why it is essential that you live in an area that is integrated with people who share your child's racial identity. The experience of being black in this country is largely one of unrelenting racial discrimination. A black youngster cannot grow up with a firm sense of his identity and pride in it without appropriate role models and without acceptance by his peers, an acceptance that is unlikely unless he lives in a neighborhood and attends a school with others of his racial background.

FOREIGN ADOPTIONS

Foreign adoptions began in earnest only in the 1950s with the war orphans from Korea. Children fathered by American soldiers with Korean women had a hard time of it in Korea. Religious groups and public figures such as the writer Pearl Buck, who founded Welcome House to bring war orphans to this country, encouraged Americans to adopt these children. Similar efforts resulted in the adoption of some offspring of GIs and Vietnamese women in the 1960s and 1970s. Today Americans adopt about eight thousand foreign children annually from countries like Korea, El Salvador, the Philippines, India, Sri Lanka, Honduras, Guatemala, Mexico, and Colombia.

If you adopt a foreign child, be alert to any health problems your child might have brought with him that a pediatrician accustomed to treating only U.S.-born children might miss—tuberculosis, parasites, hepatitis, the effects of malnutrition, even leprosy, for example. For an excellent, detailed rundown of everything you should know about this subject, see Lois Melina's *Raising Adopted Children: A Manual for Adoptive Parents* (Harper & Row).

While your doctor will ultimately deal with any medical problems your child may have, ensuring that he grows up with a healthy sense of who he is culturally will be your job. We do not have a long tradition of American parents raising children from other cultures, so it is only in the past twenty years that books and articles on this kind of child rearing have begun to appear in substantial numbers.

Balance is an important factor in providing the right amount of connection between your child and the culture from which he comes. By all means expose him to his heritage even before he's old enough to express his own desires in the matter. Take him to museums which have exhibits on his birth culture, give him children's books that feature the customs of the country from which he came, attend religious services organized by people from the place where he was born or largely attended by them. Then, when he gets older, take your cues from him. Let him decide when enough is enough, but certainly make it possible for him to have friends who share his cultural background in your neighborhood and at his school.

If you push things too far, it will not encourage your son

or daughter to delve further into his or her roots. We have heard many comments from Korean-American adopted kids about being sick of having to go once again to a Korean restaurant instead of McDonald's, which they preferred. "Here go Mommy and Daddy again, being ethnic," is a typical reaction. Still, it's better to overdo it a bit than to not do it at all.

Sometimes parents who have adopted foreign children are so conscientious about maintaining their child's link to the culture she came from that they worry when the youngster seems to be losing touch with it. One mother of a five-year-old Korean child worried that after one year with her adoptive parents the girl had completely lost her ability to speak Korean. But this is common, probably the result of the child not having any opportunity to use her native tongue. She could relearn it in the future, if it became important to her.

Nor should parents worry if a younger child doesn't even realize that there is an important difference between herself and them. For example, a three-year-old may not appreciate that difference. She might need another year or two before she reaches the stage in her development where visible differences take on that much significance for her.

On the other hand, try not to overreact to comments your child makes comparing the way she looks to your appearance. One child we saw told her parents that she wished they were the same color as she was. Initially they were concerned that their child was unhappy in their multiracial family. But when they listened more carefully to what their child was saying, they realized that she was referring to the annoyance of always having to explain that she was adopted. She had no problem with her racial identity; indeed, her comment showed that she had a healthy racial pride. It was an adoption, not a racial complication they were dealing with.

Association with adults who are of his background is important for the child adopted from a foreign country. So make an effort to provide him with opportunities to make such connections. Buddhist temples, Korean churches, benevolent associations, and other cultural and fraternal groups bringing together people from your child's culture are good places for you to ask about activities in which you could meet people from the relevant country.

Prejudice, while perhaps not as large an element to contend with as in the raising of a black child, is always in the background in the lives of these kids. Realistically and painfully, it could begin at home. Did you adopt your child as an infant? Perhaps you didn't think much about what your youngster would look like once he got older. His darker skin tone and deepening ethnic features may really make him look foreign now. Adoptions that don't work are those in which white parents adopted mixed-race children when they really only wanted to adopt white children but couldn't because white children were in short supply. If the only part of your child that you like is the white part, it is unlikely that you will be able to provide a healthy environment for that child to grow in. In a society such as ours, where racism is basic to the experience of people of color, returning to a family in which you are accepted and loved is essential if one is to survive the cruelty of the outside world. Is this possible if a child's parents do not love the most descriptive and visible part of her? It is essential that you work to resolve this issue for your child's mental health and stability through every single method available to you.

None of us is totally without prejudice. If you're raising a child from another culture you have to work diligently to be conscious of any such feelings, especially if you're a white person raising a black child. That doesn't mean you should allow yourself to become paralyzed with guilt if you have a stray thought along these lines. But anything more than that would suggest that you need to work on this immediately, to talk it over with a mate, friend, or therapist.

Sometimes a cultural misunderstanding can get blown up all out of proportion—still another reason you should make a major effort to learn about and understand the customs prevalent in the country from which you got your child. The Albertsons, for example, were in a quandary about what to do about their Korean son, adopted at the age of ten, who insisted on harshly bossing around his younger sister, who was born to the Albertsons after they adopted their son. Understandably, the girl was furious at this practice and relations between the siblings were becoming increasingly strained.

Fortunately, their mother and father had the good sense to ask a Korean adult they knew about what might be causing this clash. He explained that in Korea parents expect the eldest son to act as a parental child, and his siblings to defer to him. The boy is not a true authority figure, so he has to impose his will. Since that would not work in an American family, the parents now knew what they had to do: negotiate with their son to provide him with a role that made both him and his sister comfortable. They pointed out that in their family he didn't have to have the responsibility of parenting his sister. They told him that his sister would respect and look up to her older brother. He could be protective of her, but he also had to respect her rights.

To encounter images that might make her feel uncomfortable about her background, your foreign-born child may not have to do anything more than turn on the television. An eight-year-old from Colombia was watching a program with her adoptive parents when they noticed that she had grown increasingly silent. Finally, obviously holding back tears, she got up, went to her room, and slammed the door shut.

The program they had been watching was a special about the smuggling of cocaine from Latin America into this country. It showed people resembling their daughter being arrested for participating in a drug ring that netted millions of dollars. Later, when she was in a mood to talk, her parents explained to her that only a small percentage of people from her country were involved in the activity. They also pointed out that cocaine was a cash crop in Colombia— that only source of income and survival for many poor people.

Your adoptee could face a difficult time at school, depending on where you live, possibly requiring your intervention. When Harriet Carson's Native American adopted son had to listen to his teacher describe Custer's Last Stand as simply a massacre of American soldiers by "savages," she went to his school and had a long talk with the teacher, citing books—two of which she brought along— that portrayed the incident in a considerably more objective and complex way.

For a child adopted from abroad, searching for a birth parent is problematic at best. Enrique, born in the Philippines, is a teenager who talks of wanting to find his birth mother and speak to her at least once before she dies. He came to this country as an adoptee at the age of three. He knows the general area of the Philippines from which he came, but can't narrow it down any more than that. He does not understand or speak the language spoken there, so he would need an interpreter if he went through with a search.

The chances are slim that he would find what he was looking for, and the search would be much more expensive than that carried out by a native-born adoptee in this country. But nothing is impossible. For example, there's always the chance that somebody in the orphanage that took him in might remember which village he came from.

TRANSRACIAL ADOPTION OF BLACK AMERICAN CHILDREN

Much of what we have said so far about transracial adoption applies to the adoption of all nonwhite children. But the history of oppression and discrimination that black Americans have had to endure requires that white parents adopting a black American child must make sustained efforts to understand what their child may come up against outside the home.

For example, your child will develop a sixth sense about prejudice that you may have to be consciously attentive to in order to pick up. Among things she is likely to notice: disparaging looks from whites when your family walks by, slow and begrudging service from waiters and store clerks, and comments from teachers in which racism lies between the lines. Other people of color may have similar experiences—but these things are likely to happen more often and in a more mean-spirited manner to black Americans.

Black and interracial families adopt at a higher rate than any other groups in our population. These days, all other things being equal, agencies try to place black children with black families. But there are now about thirty-eight thousand black adoptable children—more than minority families can adopt. If they are not to grow up in institutions, many of these children will have to be adopted by white families.

Some people fear that children of one race raised by parents of another race will be psychologically damaged. However, effective parenting of nonwhite kids by white mothers and fathers who realize that they are now a nonwhite family has been shown by several studies to produce psychologically healthy children.

In a study of three hundred Midwestern multiracial families in which white parents had adopted black children, Rita Simon and Howard Alstein reported that the kids, most of them now teenagers or adults already living on their own, felt close ties to their families. Race was often a complication in their upbringing, but usually concerning the outside world, not within their families. Their parents were equally pleased with their experience, and 84 percent of them recommended transracial adoptions.

The children in the study fared as well as other adopted kids. They loved their families, felt loved, and were normal, happy youngsters by any objective measure used by the researchers. They had little problem with racial identification, although the youngsters who appeared white were more likely to identify themselves as white. The parents of these adoptees had raised their children to feel positive and comfortable about themselves.

However, we would not want to underplay the complications involved. Early on your family will have to work out strategies with which you are all comfortable for dealing with prejudice. For instance, even as a young child, as soon as she steps out of the house, your black adoptee could encounter a prejudicial remark from a neighbor's kid. What should you do about this? What if someone pejoratively refers to her as an "oreo"?

We suggest that in such incidents you avoid immediately launching into a lecture to your child about "the way things should be," which many well-meaning people are prone to do. Nor is it a good idea to let your anger eclipse hers. Rather, listen to her and tell her you understand how sad and angry racism makes her feel.

This same low-key approach might also prove useful any time you have to deal directly with possible insensitivity by other kids. For example, Joanne Carter found it helpful one Halloween when she noticed a neighbor's child leaving his house wearing a trick-or-treat costume that included blackface. Not wanting her four-year-old black adopted daughter to have to see her appearance mocked, Joanne took the neighbor's child aside and told him that such a costume would make her feel very sad and would hurt her daughter's feelings. However, she made it clear that she knew that the boy did not mean to do any harm. He took her reaction in the spirit in which she offered it. When he later rang the bell asking for a treat, he was dressed as a goblin.

As he gets older, discrimination directed against your son may take different forms. For example, your child may discover that storekeepers keep a special watch on him when he shops. Some proprietors may refuse to permit a black male to enter their stores, especially at Christmastime. If this happens, he will probably want to talk to you about it. If you want his love and respect, you must be there with empathy and a knowledge of what he faces.

Because of this phenomenon, Mark and Laura Walker put their black adopted son through a regimen whenever he wanted to go downtown to shop for clothes with his white friends. "Do you think you're dressed neatly enough?" his mother would remind him, trying to anticipate the reaction of the storekeepers and department store security people. "Is your hair combed?" she challenged him before he could get out the door. "Aw, Ma, I look just like the other guys!" "No you don't," his mother replied with a trace of a wry grin. He hated the routine; she knew it was unjust and she hated it too. But it was for his own protection, so they went through it.

As with a nonwhite child adopted from a foreign country, your child needs to take pride in her blackness, so you will have to take steps to help her connect with her heritage. Take an interest in black affairs, and discuss them with her when she's old enough to talk about them herself. Also make sure that your youngster has regular contact with children like herself and adult role models of her own race. Make an effort to find black physicians and dentists. If you send your child to camp, be sure it's an integrated one— your black friends and black church groups can probably advise you where to find one.

School could be a series of traps for your child. Overt prejudice aside, you and your youngster may have to contend with the distorted expectations of some teachers and administrators about your child's potential and the significance of any problems he happens to have in his school career. When Nan Miller's black adopted son was a little slow to read, his teacher called in his mother to voice some strong fears about his ability to do the rest of the work coming up in that grade. Nan could hear the unspoken words between the lines: "He is a black child, you know." As a practical strategy, to head off debilitating labels like *slow learner* that the school might be applying to her son before long, Nan took matters into her own hands. She taught her son to read herself. Almost overnight, his teachers' expectations for him shot up.

Even when other students, teachers, and administrators consciously make an effort to be fair to your youngster, they may give her a hard time. For example, if you have the only nonwhite student in town, your child may be made to feel like the school's official person of color. She could be constantly called on to tell what it's like to come from a different racial background and talk about discrimination and tolerance. The office of class president might even be thrust upon her as a matter of course by her well-meaning classmates.

The process of applying for college could turn up some stumbling blocks. Sandy Drummond, a teacher in a large Midwestern city, paid a visit to the guidance counselor at the Quaker school her adopted son attended to see why she had been discouraging the youngster from applying to black colleges. The guidance counselor told her that only one of their students from the previous year had opted for a black school. Then this "professional," naming the student, told Sandy that the girl just dated and partied—implying that this is what black colleges were about.

Private schools and colleges may want your child not so much for her particular talents as for her ability to help them meet quotas. A nonwhite student with middle-class sensibilities may be a hot commodity for them. But will it be an equal bargain? Will they provide her with nonwhite personnel sensitive to her own and other such students' needs? How many members of the faculty are nonwhite? That's something you'll have to investigate carefully if she applies to one of these schools.

QUESTIONS AND ANSWERS

It seems that nobody is talking anymore about white parents adopting black children. I also can find virtually nothing written on the subject. What's going on? I'm beginning to feel as if I don't exist, and our black daughter has also asked about this silence.

What you have noticed is a result of political differences among people who work in this field. Organizations such as the Association of Black Social Workers have taken positions against transracial adoption. Many child-welfare agencies have supported them, although they continue to place black kids in white homes. Despite the large percentage of black families who have adopted, there aren't enough of them to take in all adoptable black children. Tell your child about this; and tell her about the results of the study by Simon and Alstein, discussed in this chapter. Also tell her that you feel that you did the right thing, but that you'll always be willing to discuss the subject with her. Try to reconnect with your old adoptive parents' group to plan a reunion.

☐

We don't live in an integrated neighborhood. The other day my neighbor, who has been acting very unfriendly since we adopted our black son, called him a "nigger." What should we do?

Tell your neighbor just how unacceptable you find that kind of language, but don't expect to change the mind of somebody who would talk to a child like that. You can also use this ugly incident as an opportunity to work with your child on ways that he and you can confront the prejudice that your family is likely to encounter. As we have made clear, we believe that it is essential to live in an integrated community so that your youngster has an opportunity to have friends of his background and so there will be adults who are black, as well. It is less likely that your neighbor would have used such language against your child if you lived in a racially mixed neighborhood. A move to a more integrated neighborhood is worth considering, not so much as a response to this one incident, but as a means of providing a more comfortable environment for your whole family. Think of the message you are giving to your child if you choose not to live with people of his racial background.

□

We know that our adopted son's birth father was black and his birth mother was white and Irish-American. Should we be telling our child about his Irish heritage?

Definitely—it's part of who he is. However, the reason you should give greater emphasis to his black heritage is that society will respond to him as a visibly black person and he needs to take particular pride in that identity.

□

We are a white couple who have adopted a black child and we want to move into an integrated neighborhood. What's the best way of finding a house in such an area?

Your local chapter of the Urban League should be able to put you in touch with a black real estate broker who can help you out.

□

I was supposed to meet my son at the toy department of our city's largest department store for a little Christmas shopping. When he was more than half an hour late I went outside the store to look for him and discovered that they did not let black children in unescorted to shop at this time of the year. They claim that black children have a very high theft rate. I was furious at the store's management, but I didn't know what to do about it.

Black people must constantly deal with such slights. We suggest that you talk to a black friend who has a child your son's age to see how he or she would handle this situation. If you don't have black friends, we strongly suggest that you cultivate some. Studies show that black youngsters adopted by whites form the most secure and healthy racial identities when their family's network of friends is integrated.

□

My nine-year-old Korean daughter is an average student but her teacher expects more from her because all of the other Asian-American kids in her class do so well. However, my husband and I are satisfied with our child's progress and we don't want to burden her with unnecessary pressure. What's the best way to handle this?

The best way is the direct way. Tell the teacher that you're pleased with your child's work. As long as she seems to be doing her best you would not want her pushed to achieve levels that might simply be beyond her reach.

□

We have adopted a child who saw horrible events in her native Cambodia, including the murder of her parents. She's wonderful and I'm amazed at how she has progressed at school. But the depth of her tragedy is so obviously with her. I would like to lighten her emotional burden, but I just don't know how. Can you help?

She's not likely to ever completely get over such a trauma. However, because of the nurturing environment you give her she can be a stronger person when something reminds her of those terrible times. As it becomes more a part of her past, it will not have quite as powerful a grip on her as it has now. But, sadly, it will never disappear.

□

My husband has been offered an excellent job in a part of the country where we think our adopted Indian daughter might encounter prejudice. Do you have any suggestions?

NACAC and OURS (see appendix for addresses) can put you in touch with people in that state who can identify the best areas—if they exist—where your family could live.

□

The kids in my Korean son's class have just learned about World War II and they have started to call him a "dirty Jap." What's the best way to put a quick stop to this?

If you child's teacher hasn't picked this up and adjusted her teaching to deal with it, you should speak to her or her superiors about doing it. These kids need not only a lesson about ethnic stereotypes, but also one about differentiating between the various peoples of Asia.

□

We live in a white town. Our dark-skinned Colombian daughter was not asked to her high school prom and she is just devastated. How can we console her?

Tell her you understand how hard it is for her not to be included. Help her to understand how racial prejudice is involved in this issue and that it does not reflect on her personality. If she lived with more people who were similar to her she may not have had this experience. Although it won't make up for it, do something special with her— perhaps a dinner in a nice restaurant—as at least a partial compensation. To minimize the chance of this sort of thing happening as she gets older, start thinking now about helping her to choose a college that has a sizable number of minority students on campus. Many college guidebooks now give for each school the percentage of students who are nonwhite or from foreign countries.

11
Emerging Trends

How much is the family bending under the pressures of the outside world? Where is this venerable institution heading now? *Time* and *Newsweek* seem to ask these questions every few months. Their editors know that we never seem to tire of reading accounts and analyses of the changing relationships between mother, father, and child.

As adoptive parents, you know, perhaps better than your nonadoptive peers, how much the family has borne the weight of change in our society. Originally, you may have adopted because it was the only way you could become parents, giving little thought to the social significance of such a decision. But in doing so society's evolving attitude toward unwed parenthood has become part of your and your child's lives. If you have adopted a special-needs child, you must have been struck by the realities of dealing with one of the possible consequences of poverty—a family's inability to care for their child. Adopting a child who is a member of a racial minority in this country would have brought home to you the meaning of prejudice. And single adoptive parents have pioneered in our shifting notion of what constitutes a family in the first place.

Today, within the community of adoptive parents, there are mothers and fathers who have gone even farther out on the frontiers of expanding family possibilities. Some are creating new family forms and traditions through open adoption. Others are offering a more traditional family setting for children with devastating, even terminal, conditions and diseases. Few would have even considered these children adoptable until very recently. These pioneering adoptive parents have little to guide them; as a result some may need considerable amounts of support. They have succeeded in providing love and nurturance, if only briefly, in a human and personal way, with no expectations.

While our evaluation of these trends and suggestions to participants in them must still be tentative, it's worth noting that there is little happening now in adoption that is entirely new. These trends are variations on and extensions of the kinds of adoptive parenthood we have already discussed—with a few extra complications.

OPEN ADOPTION: A REEMERGING TREND

The couple who had arranged to adopt Patty's baby through a private placement had promised to have their lawyer help the young pregnant woman get counseling before the birth. When Patty came to us, she was near term. During a session, she asked that we meet the people who would bring up her baby. While we had not planned to do this, it seemed to be a reasonable request, and we agreed.

Our conversation with the prospective adoptive mother was particularly poignant. Since she had met the woman whose baby she and her husband would raise, she felt sadness as well as joy at the prospects of becoming a parent. She realized fully that someone was losing something precious in order for her to get a child.

There is much to be said for giving information about birth parents to adoptive parents—or even having the two meet—when a child is placed. Besides providing adoptive parents with important medical information about their child's birth family, and reassuring birth parents that their baby is going to a good home, it may also be more psychologically satisfying for all concerned. The birth parents have a better chance of working through their feelings about having to place their child with other people. The adoptive parents, because they know the identity of the birth mother, will not have to deal with fantasies that someday a stranger will knock on their door demanding the return of her child.

Over the past ten or fifteen years, many professionals in the adoption field have made the point that secrecy is harmful. They urge not a new way of handling adoptions, but rather a return to an old one. Only since 1940 have states kept adoption records closed to protect the privacy of birth parents. Since both birth and adoptive parents have been increasingly urging the opening of these records—not to mention adoptees wishing to search for their birth parents—closed records appears to be an experiment that has not succeeded.

In several ways we appear to be moving away from closed-records adoptions. In most agency adoptions foster parents know about their child's biological family. Evolving state laws regulate private adoptions. This is done to prevent lawyers and others from running a black market in babies. These laws require that babies be placed from birth parents to adoptive parents, with the lawyer serving only to facilitate the process. The adoptive parents receive biographical information from the birth parents, who in turn get to choose who will adopt their baby—sometimes from among several couples. In some private adoptions, birth and adoptive families meet.

One of the oldest adoption agencies in the United States, Spence-Chapin in New York City, has recently begun a program in which birth mothers may choose their baby's adoptive parents. Agencies placing children from foreign countries sometimes stipulate that adoptive parents must agree to continually send photographs and updated information about their child back to their youngster's biological family.

On the broad and developing continuum of open adoption, one of the most open varieties has developed in California. In that state, some birth mothers wanted to remain in contact with the children they surrendered for adoption. Enough adoptive parents seem to have either liked the idea, too, or at least felt they could handle it. Subsequently, they were willing to allow the birth mothers something even more wide-ranging than visitation rights when they negotiated the terms of the adoption. Neither state bureaucracies nor private agencies handed down any of this. It developed to meet a need on the part of the people involved.

When Californians first began working out open adoptions a few years ago, they ran into a few problems. How could an adoptive family guarantee a birth mother access to the child when they could not anticipate what the future would bring? For example, what if they wanted to move out of state? Or how could they justify acknowledgement of the birth mother's interest in staying in touch with the adoptive family in the light of the family's need for privacy? What if the two parties to the agreement later differed on how to interpret their agreement? What if the adoptive family felt that the birth mother was trying to set herself up as a coparent?

Sharon Kaplan often hears these questions. A social worker for almost thirty years, and herself an adoptive parent, she has been at the forefront of the open-adoption movement through the private California adoption services group she founded, Parenting Resources for Growth and Development. Her organization counsels people involved in all types of adoptions, but has gained a reputation for particular expertise in open adoptions. In fact, they have trademarked their term for this process, *Cooperative Adoption*,℠ which Sharon Kaplan defines as giving the child access to both families over time. The emphasis, she says, is on cutting children's losses whenever possible and shifting the emphasis from adult needs such as infertility problems to the child's needs and rights.

Kaplan says that those interested in participating in open

adoptions are most likely to succeed if they are trusting by nature, have faith in themselves and a good sense of humor. They should also be self-confident. The ability to negotiate relationships, communicate, and problem-solve are other crucial skills for these parents. These are all teachable.

Adoptees, many feel, gain much from open adoption. Secrecy is difficult for any child to cope with, but especially for an adoptee. Open adoption, by its very nature, banishes the most basic of adoptive family secrets. There are no skeletons in the closet; indeed, there is no closet. These children know who they are and where they came from.

Some speculate that kids raised through this process will have less sense of rejection than do other adopted children. Since they are brought up in this arrangement, it appears to be the most natural thing in the world to them. They might even be less vulnerable to teasing or malicious remarks about their lineage than are other adopted kids. Yes, they have more than one set of parents, but they seem to be comfortable with the notion, which has always been in the open. Besides, given the incidence of divorce in our society, having multiple sets of parents is no longer enough to make them unique.

What kind of relationship develops between the birth mother and the child she places for adoption? While it varies in each case, typically, it seems to resemble one between a child and an aunt or uncle or friend of the family. The adoptee is likely to call his birth mother by her first name and eventually refer to her as "the woman who gave birth to me." There's a good chance that he will not be confused about his relationship to any of the adults on his family tree and will be able to describe each relationship, even when asked to do so at an early age.

The birth mother also seems to gain through open adoption. Some birth fathers also have been more involved in this practice than in traditional adoptions and seem satisfied too. The birth mother often establishes a close relationship with the adoptive parents before she gives birth, which gives her an in-depth look at the people who will raise her child. At the hospital, soon after the baby is born, but not before she has had a chance to spend some time alone with the infant, she gives the child to his new parents in a "handing over" ceremony. This ritual is often recorded on film or videotape. Then, according to observers, for the next few weeks or months, she goes through a grieving process, not for the loss of her baby, but for the mothering role she will never have with the child. Counseling, at this point, is very important.

The birth mother stays in touch with the adoptive parents, receiving photographs of her birth child as the youngster grows. She may visit the child regularly, call, or write. The first year and a half or so usually marks the closest period of this relationship. Then, often, the birth mother works through her feelings about her decision and is likely to pull away to some degree from the adoptive family. Now, she is able to proceed with her life, "not feeling like a victim and much more assertive and able to plan her future," as Sharon Kaplan has observed. Four or five years later she may reconnect with the adoptive family, seeing them at holidays or on the child's birthday.

For adoptive parents, open adoption offers the absence of the tension that others sometimes experience when there is a veil of secrecy over the identity of their child's birth parents. There are no worries about what an older child might find if she decided to search for her birth parents. We've even heard stories of adoptive parents who are comfortable with the arrangement and get some unanticipated baby-sitters in the bargain: the birth grandparents.

There are some potential drawbacks to open adoption. For example, parents, birth and adoptive, who have participated in open adoption may experience powerful, turbulent emotions surrounding the issue, feelings that call for some counseling or brief therapy to handle adequately. In one therapy group for birth and adoptive mothers, Mother's Day brought out some of these feelings. Adoptive mothers openly spoke of their jealous feelings toward the birth mothers who were able to give birth to the child; birth mothers also freely admitted their envy of the adoptive mothers who could raise them.

Some professionals in the field suggest that open adoption could interfere with adoptive parents' "claiming" their child as their own. Anyone who enters into an open adoption should be very conscious to avoid the notion that this is some kind of coparenting. One needs to remember always who is the child's legal guardian, who is the only one to make final decisions on how to raise her.

The obligation to uphold the agreement with the birth parent under open adoption is ethical rather than legal, so adoptive parents must carefully consider how far they are willing and able to go to accommodate a birth mother's wishes before agreeing to this arrangement. Of course, you are most likely to stick to an agreement that you take great pains to plan, and living up to such an agreement will ultimately be in the best interests of everyone involved.

LEGAL-RISK ADOPTION

The desire to adopt young children has lately been causing many adoptive parents to take extra risks. For children, placement in a foster home rather than in an institution has traditionally been a tradeoff: never knowing how long it will last, whether this is the final stop or if there will be yet further moves. Now some prospective adoptive parents are choosing to have children placed in their homes before the birth parents have relinquished their parental rights to the child. Agencies placing these kids do so in the belief that the birth parents will eventually surrender these rights or have them taken away by the courts, but it's not a sure thing. These adoptive parents are willing to take the risk that they could lose the child if parental rights are not terminated. Though it's a risky business, many satisfied adoptive parents have adopted in this way and are glad they did.

If you have a child enter your home under these circumstances, you are technically classified as a foster parent. Should you plan to do this, carefully consider whether you can live for perhaps as long as four years with the knowledge that you might have to surrender your child to the birth parent. It does happen, as witnessed by the occasional heart-rending stories on the evening news of preadoptive parents kissing their child goodbye for the last time.

Parents who take this route should look for an agency that seems to have their interests in mind as well as the child's. While the agency will provide an attorney to handle the termination of parental rights, it's a good idea, in addition, to have your own lawyer, to protect your rights to the utmost.

Your lawyer should make sure that the agency makes a diligent effort to provide the birth mother with opportunities to seek rehabilitation and thus become eligible to regain custody of her child. If the agency does not do this, the birth parent might later sue to regain custody on the basis of not having been given a sufficient chance to rehabilitate herself. If you can't afford a lawyer, consult your local Legal Aid Society to see what constitutes a diligent effort. For more information on this subject, inquire at your adoptive parent group or at the Legal Aid Society.

FRAGILE BABIES

Adoptive parents are some of the most highly motivated and dedicated mothers and fathers we have met. Some of them take kids whose birth mother's substance abuse makes their children's prospects for leading a normal life questionable; others adopt and give a loving home to children with terminal illnesses.

In America today, there are an increasing number of

babies who are paying a tragic price for their birth parents' use of crack, speed, angel dust, heroin, and methadone. These children have low birth weights, suffer damage to their central nervous systems, and may not respond well to physical affection. It's often hard to know how to comfort them, which can be confusing and frustrating. Kids afflicted with fetal alcohol syndrome, as a result of their mother's alcohol abuse during pregnancy, are likely to have some serious physical and intellectual disabilities. If you adopt one of these children, you will have to devote much time to her medical care and to intellectually stimulating her. Many hospitals have programs to help you with this task.

You can probably assume that your child has sustained some neurological damage, although he or she might eventually function quite well. The bottom line is that you can't depend on it. However, be cautious about interpreting any studies you see regarding these children. The conclusions of such research generally do not take into account the effects of a warm, nurturing environment on the child's capacities. Such studies are surely needed and will, we hope, eventually be available.

Parents who adopt babies with AIDS or infants who test positive for the AIDS virus may face even more prejudice than they had counted on. Our lack of hard facts about exactly how and under what conditions this disease may be spread has contributed to public fears, and some families have been ostracized. Try to be as honest with yourself as you can be if you are contemplating such an adoption. Can you stand up to the stress to which other people may subject you?

A baby who tests positive for AIDS at birth will not necessarily get the disease. It could be as much as eighteen months before you will know. So adopting such a baby means living with a terrible uncertainty about the infant's prospects. If he does get AIDS, your child will need almost twenty-four-hour attention; he could be killed by common infections that would make other children sick for just a few days, and you will have to stand by while he's subjected to frequent and painful medical tests. And he will die while still very young.

To help you cope with your emotions surrounding death and dying and with the medical procedures necessary for managing the disease, you will probably need counseling. A hospice could be a good source of referrals for this kind of help.

GAY ADOPTIVE PARENTS

Gay men and women have been in the forefront of those offering to adopt children with AIDS, but as far as we can tell society is making it no easier for them to do this than to adopt healthy children. Prejudice against gays is just as pervasive among people empowered to place children for adoption as among the rest of the population. They express fears about the child's sexual development and the possibility that he might be sexually abused by a parent. Studies showing these fears to be unfounded—that gay parents are no more child abusers than are heterosexual mothers and fathers—have done little to change attitudes.

If you are gay and wish to become an adoptive parent, you will have to decide if it's more important to you to make a political statement, doing everything openly, or to take the steps needed to fulfill your practical need to become a parent. Some agencies are less prying than others. To identify them, ask within the gay community. We understand, however, that gay adoptive parents have had the most success going through private adoption. We also hear that they find gay parents' groups and single adoptive parents' groups good sources of support.

QUESTIONS AND ANSWERS

I'm an adoptive mother who knew the birth mother of my child for the last two months of her pregnancy. No matter how much I try not to feel this way, I still think of my baby as belonging to her birth mother, not me. Am I likely ever to feel differently?

The emotional transition from a prospective adoptive parent to the mother of a child takes time. You didn't have the experience of pregnancy and childbirth to help you adjust to the change in your identity. However, we can reassure you that caring for your child over time, while not the same thing as carrying her in your womb, will ultimately serve the same function: establishing close emotional ties between you and your infant.

☐

I've heard that some adoptees view themselves as "the chosen baby" and therefore feel compelled to excel. My agency gives birth mothers biographies of prospective parents, from which we were picked by the birth mother of our child. I think I feel something like a "chosen parent," with similar pressure to achieve perfection. Does this make sense to you?

Not only do some adoptees feel this way, first children or grandchildren often feel it too. You may well be experiencing the same phenomenon. Assuming that it hasn't restricted your ability to parent—in which case you might want to discuss it with a family therapist—we would just suggest that you try to remain aware of your feelings. Acknowledging these feelings, perhaps out loud to your spouse or a friend, should keep them from becoming disruptive.

☐

Our adopted son is two years old. We have a specific agreement with his birth mother that she can call monthly; but she's been calling more frequently, seemingly whenever she feels like it. We experience this as an invasion of our privacy and we fear it will increasingly get out of hand as time goes on. What should we do?

It's important to remember that you are the legal guardians of your child. If it came down to it, you could unilaterally break off contact with his birth mother, although it's preferable to resolve this problem short of that step. First talk to the birth mother and try to settle what may just be a misunderstanding or differences in your sense of time. If that doesn't work, try having the agency mediate your dispute, or go together for counseling.

☐

The birth mother of our child, with whom we have stayed in touch, has gotten pregnant again. We feel that it's important for our child to remain close to his birth sibling, but we're just not ready to adopt again. How does one deal with this?

You shouldn't feel compelled to take yet another of her children. But perhaps you can arrange to establish some kind of ties to the family who does adopt this child, thus keeping your child close to his sibling.

☐

We are adopting privately and we've already had some contact with the birth mother. However, we do not want to continue any kind of relationship with her after the child is placed with us. We're a little concerned because she knows what we look like and she will be going to school on a campus near where we live. What should we do if she happens to come across us and wishes to stay in touch?

The encounter you fear is not likely to happen, and there's no point letting the thought of it occurring frighten you. If it ever happens, you'll handle it then. If you find yourself continuing to think about it, remind yourself that you're the legal guardian of your child, with ultimate control over who has access to your youngster.

☐

Our six-month-old baby's birth mother was a cocaine addict. We are, indeed, frequently unable to comfort the child. Nevertheless we love him and we want to do absolutely everything we can for him. We've gone from doctor to doctor but none of them has helped much. Is there anything we're overlooking?

We still don't know as much as we need to know about babies with this condition. We suggest that you build a relationship with a major medical center affiliated with a university—travelling to it periodically if it isn't nearby—so that they can track your child's progress. This will enable your child to benefit from the latest research findings and treatments. Current studies of these babies underway now appear to indicate neurological difficulties and perhaps even visual problems requiring sophisticated medical diagnosis.

Epilogue: Therapy

Throughout this book we have periodically dealt with the use of therapy as a resource to help with some of the complications of family life, whether they are directly related to adoption or not. We emphasize that we do not recommend therapy for any adopted child or adoptive parents as a matter of course, only when a situation presents difficulties that need working out. Adoptive families and their children have no inherent pathology that needs to be "cured." On the contrary, we have observed that adoptive parents are among the most involved and motivated parents we've seen. So, as the saying goes, "If it ain't broke, don't fix it."

Should difficulties arise in your family, first try changing the way you've been dealing with whatever is giving you trouble. See what happens when you do something different, and then use what you observe to alter your approach. For example, suppose your child has been cursing and your telling him why you find it offensive hasn't stopped the practice. Instead of appearing shocked, thus letting him get to you, you could try a variety of sanctions. Perhaps writing out the profanity one hundred times will stop him. Or you could fine him, as they do in professional sports for rules infractions—a boy would understand that idea. When you hit upon something that works, try using it for other problematic behavior.

If you can't find something that works, ask friends, relatives, and others close to you and knowledgeable about your family or the difficulty involved for their opinion. The members of adoptive parents' groups are also good sources of experience-based knowledge and counsel when things aren't working the way they should. Ideally, speak to parents with an adopted child temperamentally similar to yours but a few years older. That family may have recently dealt successfully with the very complication that now confronts you. Your child's school guidance counselor is another person to consult if you haven't found a solution yet. And if these steps have not led to a resolution you probably should consider therapy.

As we've pointed out, adoption takes place within a family system. The kind of therapy that makes sense to us in dealing with adoption complications, therefore, is one that acknowledges that adoption affects everyone in the family and problems with any family member affect everyone else in the family to a greater or lesser degree. Systemic, or family, therapy—a usually brief, problem-solving process—recognizes this. Interaction patterns between mothers, fathers, and children can be analyzed and seen as related to the difficulties that arise within the family. Family therapists reject the notion that something inside the adoptee—in his psyche—makes him inherently troubled and therefore the sole proper focus of healing efforts.

The American Association for Marriage and Family Therapists can refer you to a professional in your area who works with this view in mind. The agency from which you adopted your child may also provide some post-adoption services that could include therapy. Group therapy may be helpful for an adolescent, particularly if he or she has little contact with other adoptees.

Epilogue: Therapy

While we urge you to try to find a practitioner who specializes in treating adoptive families, most family therapists who at least know something about adoption should be able to deal adequately with problems that may arise. If you have any doubts about a therapist's knowledge of and competence to deal with adoption, ask him or her some of these questions: What do you know about adoption? Must adoption result in pathology? What do you think about adoptees and their parents? Do you think adoptive families are the same as other families? Do you think that adoptive families are capable of working out their own solutions to adoption complications? Use what you have read in this book as a guideline to evaluate the answers. If the therapist will not deal with the difficulties until he first analyzes your motives for adopting, or if he thinks that what has happened to your child through the adoption process has caused him irreparable harm, look elsewhere.

For the most part, a therapist should help you to devise your own solutions, not hand down decisions and directions from above. He or she should try to get you to specify what kinds of changes you would like to see in your family, and then help you to work out the small steps you can begin to take to effect those changes. Without specific goals, you can't develop specific solutions. That could leave you feeling helpless, confronting big, seemingly overwhelming problems.

Your therapist should help you to see behavior in your family you've possibly overlooked. As we've noted often, that could involve successes you haven't noticed—accomplishments on which you can build. The more accurate information you can piece together about the way your family works, the more likely you are to make changes for the better. As you create these changes, the therapist should be helping you to see your role in bringing them about. What good is success if you can't take credit for it, empowering you to produce further successes?

Don't be surprised if the heart of your difficulty turns

out to be a parent-child interaction that just happens to take place in an adoptive family, with no further adoption connection. It happens more often than not!

Finally, an occasion may arise in which an adopted child wants or needs individual therapy. Perhaps she just wants to express her feelings about adoption away from the family. Or maybe she has been depressed and needs medication and individual attention. If your special-needs adopted child requires individual treatment, try to delay it until you have established strong ties to her. Rushing a child into individual therapy early in a placement adds an extra adult with whom the child must form a relationship. That could impede the delicate process of building a bond between you and her.

If your child requires or wants therapy, however, there is good news. We have found in our clinical practice that adoptive families are remarkably strong and committed to one another for the most part. We and other researchers have discovered that they respond quickly to treatment, get better faster and stay better when compared to matched samples of other parents and children who seek family therapy.

Resources

American Adoption
Congress
401 East 74th Street
Suite 17D
New York, New York 10021
(212) 988-0110

American Association for
Marriage and Family
Therapy
1717 K Street N.W.
Suite 407
Washington, D.C. 20006

American Foundation for
the Blind
15 West 16th Street
New York, New York 10011
(212) 620-2000

The Association for
Children
with Learning Disabilities
4156 Library Road

Pittsburgh, Pennsylvania
15234
(412) 881-2253

The Association for the
Help of Retarded Children
200 Park Avenue South
New York, New York 10003
(212) 254-8203

The Churchill Center
22 East 95th Street
New York, New York 10130
(212) 722-0465

The Foundation for
Children with Learning
Disabilities
99 Park Avenue
New York, New York 10016
(212) 687-7211

International Soundex
Reunion Registry (ISRR)

c/o Emma May Vilardi
P.O. Box 2312
Carson City, Nevada 89702
No phone queries

Juvenile Diabetes
Foundation
432 Park Avenue South
New York, New York 10016
(212) 889-7575

The March of Dimes
303 S. Broadway
Tarrytown, New York
10591
(914) 428-7100

The Mayo Clinic
200 First Street S.W.
Rochester, Minnesota 55905
(507) 284-2511

National Association for
Perinatal Addiction and
Research Education
11 East Hubbard Street
Suite 200
Chicago, Illinois 60611
(312) 329-2512

The National Resource
Center for Special Needs
Adoption
P.O. Box 337
Chelsea, Michigan 48118
(313) 475-8693

North American Council on
Adoptable Children, Inc.
(NACAC)

1821 University Ave.
Suite S-275
St. Paul, Minnesota 55104
(612) 644-3036

OURS
3307 Highway 100 North
Suite 203
Minneapolis, Minnesota
55422
(612) 535-4829

Philadelphia Child
Guidance Clinic
34th Street and Civic
Center Boulevard
Philadelphia, Pennsylvania
19104
(215) 243-2773

Project Impact
25 West Street
Boston, Massachusetts
02111
(617) 451-1472

Resources for Children with
Special Needs, Inc.
200 Park Avenue South
Suite 816
New York, New York 10003
(212) 677-4650

United Cerebral Palsy
66 East 34th Street
New York, New York 10016
(212) 481-6300

Index

bonding, 14–15, 37–41
books:
    on adoption, 24, 67, 110, 183,
      276
    on death and divorce, 264, 266
    on sexual maturation, 72, 150
breast-feeding, 35
Brodzinsky, David M., 66

camping trips, 209
Chess, Stella, 41
childproofing, 58–59
child rearing, procedural rules
    for, 56–58
child-welfare agencies, 4–5
cocaine, newborns and, 77–78
cognitive development, 63, 65–66,
    99–101
college, 169–171
community service, 152
criminal behavior, adoption and,
    20–21, 26
curfews, 155–156, 165–166
cursing, 301

dating, 176–177, 189
death of parent, 264
depression, 203, 260
development, child, 31, 41–44
    sources on, 44, 58, 76, 118
disabilities, adoptees with, 5,
    237–241
discipline, 60–62, 82, 89–92,
    112–114, 123–124, 166–168,
    222–225
    for abused children, 221–225,
      248–249
    humor as tool for, 257–258
divorce, 28, 265–266
drug abuse, 147–148, 190
dyslexia, 101, 102

emotional overprotectiveness,
    59

families, adoptive:
    child-centeredness of, 58–60
    complications vs. problems in,
      10–12
    counseling for, 9, 231–236,
      302–304
    different interests in, 115–116
    multiracial, 27–28, 271–288
    negotiation transitions in, 12
family therapy, 231–236, 301–304
fathers, adoptive, 34–35
    single, 251, 267–268, 270

fathers, birth, 25, 103
fetal alcohol syndrome, 297
food, hoarding of, 229–230
foreign children, adoption of, 6, 8,
    271–272, 275, 276, 280
foster-care, 4, 5–6, 192–193, 194,
    200, 204, 206, 245–246, 295
foster-care parents:
    adoption by, 5, 191, 295–296
    adoptive parents' relationship
      with, 217–218

gay adoptive parents, 298
grandparents, 22, 45–47, 74–
    75

heredity, environment and, 14,
    27
high school:
    alternatives to, 169
    dropping out of, 168–169
household responsibilities,
    150–152
humor, as discipline tool,
    257–258
hyperactivity, 96–97, 203, 243

illegitimacy, stigma of, 7–8, 26
incest, 71, 87
infertility, 7, 15–16, 36, 50, 54,
    55, 121
intelligence, 13–14, 27

junior high school, 136–141

Kagan, Jerome, 38
Kaplan, Sharon, 292–293, 294
Kirk, David, 6, 7
Kral, Ron, 16, 20

laws, adoption, 3–6, 31, 291
lawyers, 4, 6, 29, 291, 296
learning disabilities, 101–102,
    105–106
    behavioral problems and,
      96–99, 104–105, 137, 139,
      213–216
life books, 200–201, 246–247
lying, 63, 104, 196

medical histories, 23, 37, 52–53,
    290
menstruation, 120–122, 125
multiracial families, adoptive,
    27–28
    cultural misunderstandings in,
      278–279

Index